Cantie

Tamesis flu:

Coringhu
Iord
Cooling
Cliff
Allhalowes
Sct: Maries
Greane
GRANE INSVL:
Hiechm
Frendesbury
East
Alcow
Soeke
Vpchurch
Gillinghm
Chathm
Rochester
Woldhm
Burghm
Haslip
Borden
Newington
Neuenton
Medleton
Halftowe
Knowsferre Fwnke
Bredgate
Bicknor
Stedmury
Bobbing
Tunstall
Sittingborne
Bapchild
Buelland
Siunt
Tong
Muscon
Tenchm
Ore
Milsted
Redmershm
Kingesdowne
Ospringe
Esiling
Newenhm
Luddenhm
Liuseed
Nerton
Bedhersx
Ashforde
Binburye
Freusted
Dodington
Bosler
Deringe
Thornhm
Hollingborne
Wytchling
Longbeche
wode
Otterinden
Cofile
Harfeed
Oterden als Othm
Lose
Ledes
Brumfeld
Lenchm
Staluesfeld
W. Well
Charinge
E. Well
Boughton
Feuershm
Boughton
Sellinge
Shelwiche
Harbaldowne
Charehm
Badlesmere
Leueland
Moloashe
Godmersm
Challock
Boughcon
Wye
Chilhm
Nether hardes
High hardes
Walchm
Crundale
Pechm
CATER
Nackington
Hernehill
Blean wood
Blean
Graueney
Quinboro Caf:
SHEPYE INSVL:
Minster
E. Churche
Warden
Leysdon
Elmesey
Hernes in
Hertie
Heyn
Smacley
Whistable
Sesalter
Scure
Maidfo
E: Ferligh
E: Malling
Thrythe
fdinge
Hunton
Langley
Boughton
Chart
Suiton
Vicum
Lenton
Reuton
Boughcon
Egerton
Flucklye
Snenden
Chare pua
Heefield
Chare magna
Kenningec
Ashford
E. Woll
Kingesnothe
Willyngesborowe
Seuingcon
Mershm
Sestinge
Snode
Scan
Brabarn
Herce
Stewing
Haseinghou
Broke
Marden
Stapleherst
Fretinden
Sisinghersf
Hedcorn
Bidenden
Dochersten
Shadderhersf
Bissingeon
Reesinge
Aldingcon
Aufse Lyzene
Bevormehersh
Dim
Goudhersf
Cranbrok
Bedgeburye
Hemfted
Mawhm
Benenden
Hawkesherst
Sandhm
cherst
Robertsbridge
Nordiam
Beckley
Vdimere
Rye
Camber
Highbalden
Smaller
Rolunden
Halden
Newenden
Tenterden
Woodchurch
Ebbene
OKNEY
Witrifm
Persienroh
Plan
Selm
Ridingstret
Aplcdowre
Warchorne
Keuerdisdon
Orlanston
Newghurch
Snart
Snargat
Brouge
Ferifed
Jnechurch
Maye
Brokland
Gifford
RUMNEY
MERSHE
Old Rumney
Mydlo
Lyd
Ruun
Sct: Maries

THE REVELS PLAYS

Founder Editor: Clifford Leech 1958–71

General Editor: F. David Hoeniger

THE TRAGEDY OF MASTER ARDEN OF FAVERSHAM

Arden's House today. (The stonework is all that remains of the original Outer Gateway to Faversham Abbey. Arden was murdered in the parlour, the room on the ground floor in the centre of the photograph.)
(*Courtesy of the* Faversham Times)

The Tragedy of Master Arden of Faversham.

EDITED BY

M. L. WINE

THE REVELS PLAYS

METHUEN & CO LTD
LONDON

PR
2854
A2
W5
1973

This edition first published 1973

Introduction, Apparatus Criticus, etc.
© 1973 M. L. Wine
Printed in Great Britain by
The Broadwater Press Ltd, Welwyn Garden City, Herts.
Distributed in the U.S.A. by
HARPER & ROW PUBLISHERS INC.
BARNES & NOBLE IMPORT DIVISION
SBN 416 77310 9

For

ALFRED HARBAGE

General Editor's Preface

The series known as the Revels Plays was conceived by Professor Clifford Leech. The idea emerged in his mind, as he tells us in the General Editor's Preface to the first of the Revels Plays, published in 1958, from the success of the New Arden Shakespeare. The aim of the series was, in his words, 'to apply to Shakespeare's predecessors, contemporaries, and successors the methods that are now used in Shakespeare editing'. We owe it to Clifford Leech that the idea has become reality. He planned the series, set the high standards for it, and for many years selected and supervised the editors. He aimed at editions of lasting merit and usefulness, that would appeal to scholars and students, but not to them alone; producers and actors were also much in his mind. 'The plays included should be such as to deserve and indeed demand performance.' And thus the texts should be presented in a form that is attractive and clear to the actor, with some space of the introduction devoted to records of productions, and some of the notes to comments on stage business.

Under his direction each editor of the series has of course been expected to apply certain basic principles to his editing and other aspects of method, and to follow as a model some of the best previous editions. But in many matters the guidelines have necessarily had to be flexible, for the series includes works from a period of two centuries, from *circa* 1500 to *circa* 1700, many with peculiar problems of text and interpretation. And it is best to allow the individual editor room to do justice to his peculiar gifts and interests, and to express his own convictions or hypotheses. It is indeed the editors themselves who in each instance deserve chief credit for any excellence that may be found in their editions, or who must be held responsible for certain weaknesses. Yet no one knows better than the past editors themselves how many suggestions they owe to

Clifford Leech, and how often he kindly alerted them to weaknesses or saved them from error. It is fitting that he will now be known as the Founding Editor of the Revels Plays. At the same time he will continue to supervise some of the volumes already well in progress.

The text of each Revels Play is edited afresh from the original text (in a few instances, texts) of best authority, but spelling and punctuation are modernized, and speech-headings silently normalized. The text is accompanied by collations and commentary, and in each volume the editor devotes one section of his introduction to a discussion of the provenance and trustworthiness of the 'copytext', the original on which he has based his edition, and to a brief description of particular aspects of his editorial method. Other sections of the introduction deal with the play's date and sources, its place in the work of the author, its significance as a dramatic work of literature in the context of its time and designed for a certain theatre, actors, and audience, its reputation, and its stage-history. In editions of a play by an author not previously represented in the series, it has been customary also to include a brief account of the author's life and career. Some emphasis is laid on providing available records of performances, early and modern.

Modernization has its problems, and has to be practised with care and some flexibility if the substance of the original is not to be distorted. The editor emends, as distinct from modernizing, the original text only in instances where error is patent or at least very probable, and correction persuasive. Archaic forms need sometimes to be retained when rhyme or metre demands them or when a modernized form would alter the required sense or obscure a play on words. The extent to which an editor feels free to adapt the punctuation will largely depend on the degree of authority he attributes to the punctuation of his copy. It is his task to follow the original closely in any dramatic or rhetorical pointing that can be trusted for good reason. Punctuation should do justice to a character's way of speaking, and to the interplay of dialogue.

In general, the manner of modernization is similar to that in the Arden Shakespeare. Yet in the volumes since 1968, the '-ed' form is used for non-syllabic terminations in past tenses and past participles ('-'d' in Arden and earlier Revels volumes), and '-èd' for syllabic ('-ed' earlier). Act divisions are given only if they appear in the original text or if the structure of the play clearly points to them. Those act and scene divisions not found in the original are provided unobtrusively in small type and in square brackets. Square brackets are also used for any other additions to or changes in the stage directions of the original. But in no instances are directions referring to locale added to scene headings; for the plays (at least those before the Restoration) were designed for stages whose acting area was most of the time neutral and where each scene flowed into the next without interruption; and producers in our time would probably be well advised to attempt to convey this characteristic fluidity of scene on whatever stage they may have at their disposal.

A mixture of principles and common sense also governs the collations accompanying the text. Revels plays do not provide a variorum collation; only those variants which require the critical attention of serious textual students. All departures of substance from 'copy-text' are listed, including any relineation and those changes in punctuation which involve to any degree a decision between alternative interpretations; but not such accidentals as turned letters, nor necessarily additions to stage directions whose editorial nature is already made clear by the use of brackets. Press corrections in the 'copy-text' are likewise included. Of later emendations of the text (or errors) found in seventeenth-century reprints of no authority or editions from the eighteenth century to modern times, in general only those are given which as alternative readings still deserve serious attention. Readings of a later text of special historical interest or influence are, in some instances, more fully collated.

One of the hallmarks of the Revels Plays is the thoroughness of their annotations. Besides explicating the meaning of difficult words and passages and alerting the reader to special implications, the editor provides comments on customs or usage, text or stage business—indeed on anything he judges pertinent and helpful. Glosses are not provided for words that are satisfactorily explained in simple dictionaries like the *Concise Oxford*. Each volume contains an Index to the Annotations, in which particular attention is drawn to meanings for words not listed in *O.E.D.*

By 1970, seventeen volumes had appeared in the series, and a fair number are well in progress. The series began with some of the best-known plays of the Elizabethan and Jacobean era. Some years ago it was decided to include also some early Tudor and some Restoration plays. But it is not our object to concentrate only on well-known plays. Some lesser-known plays of whose merit as literature and as drama we are convinced are being included in the hope that they will arouse the attention they deserve, both from students and in the theatre.

F. DAVID HOENIGER

Toronto, 1972

Contents

Illustrations

ACKNOWLEDGEMENTS

For generous permission to reproduce the foregoing items, I wish to thank the editor of the *Faversham Times* and Mr and Mrs Michael Quin (the photograph of Arden's House today), the Trustees of the Huntington Library (the title-page of the 1592 Quarto), and the Trustees of the British Museum (the frontispiece to the 1633 Quarto and the detail from Saxton's map).

I also wish to express my gratitude to the Trustees of the Folger Shakespeare Library for permission to transcribe the account of Arden's murder from its copy of the second edition (1587) of Holinshed's *Chronicles* in Appendix II; to Mr M. P. Jackson for providing his transcription of the official account of the murder from the Wardmote Book of Faversham and to Mr Robert Lawrie, town clerk of the Borough of Faversham, for permission to reprint it in Appendix III; and to the Trustees of the British Museum for permission to transcribe the ballad of Mistress Arden's 'Complaint and Lamentation' (1633) in Appendix IV.

Preface

Ever since in 1770 the first editor of *Arden of Faversham* raised the spectre of Shakespearian authorship, considerable scholarship has focused upon the play. The difficulties in tracking down this material and, above all, in treating it in a compact form suitable for this series have been greatly reduced, however, by the generosity of Professor Jill Levenson, who supplied the present editor with a manuscript copy of her forthcoming bibliography of *Arden* (soon to be published in *Recent Studies in English Renaissance Drama*, ed. T. Logan and D. Smith), and of Mr M. P. Jackson, who made available his extensively documented Oxford B.Litt. thesis, 'Material for an Edition of *Arden of Feversham*' (1963). My debt to Mr Jackson, in particular, is expressed on many of the following pages. Mrs Diane Davidson has been equally generous in putting at my disposal the material that she had gathered for her accurately researched novel *Feversham* (New York, 1969), including her microfilm of the Wardmote Book of Faversham and her transcription of Harley MSS. 542, ff. 34–37B. Professor Louis Marder also provided me with unlimited access to a rich library devoted to Shakespeare and Elizabethan drama. To previous editors of a 'bad quarto' like *Arden* the present editor must acknowledge a very special debt.

For permission to collate and use as the basic copy for this edition their copies of the first quarto of *Arden* (1592), I wish to thank the authorities of the Huntington Library, the Bodleian Library of Oxford University, and the Victoria and Albert Museum. I also wish to thank the authorities of the other libraries and institutions cited in the Introduction (p. xxi and n. 3) which generously supplied me with microfilms and prints of their copies of the second and third quartos of 1599 and 1633, respectively. To the Huntington Library I am also grateful for a Xerox copy of the

Southouse MS. (HM 1341) of the play. I began to collect material for this edition when I held a grant from the American Council of Learned Societies, and a research fellowship later from the Graduate College of the University of Illinois (Chicago) subsequently enabled me to prepare the final copy of the manuscript uninterrupted by other duties.

It is my pleasure to acknowledge the help of many individuals who answered queries, checked translations, discussed textual problems with me, and assisted in various other ways: Pauline van Aardenne, Irving Blum, T. W. Craik, Dierdre Ford and her co-workers in the inter-library loan department of the University of Illinois (Chicago), Levi Fox, Arthur Freeman, Mark Gardner of the *Faversham Times*, J. C. Johnson, Robert Kispert, Robert Lawrie, Erich Lenz, Vanessa Mitchell, Robert Ogle, Katherine F. Pantzer, Keith Sturgess, Dorothy L. Swerdlove (and the research staff of the Library of the Performing Arts Theatre Collection of the New York Public Library at Lincoln Center), Michael G. Vyner (and Schott Music Publishers), and the staff of the Harvard theatre collection. Professor Allan Casson read an untidy first draft of the introduction, and his incisive criticism saved me from many errors of judgement. Similarly, Kathryn Schoonover, by her careful reading of proofs, has put me in her debt. To the former general editor of this series, Professor Clifford Leech, I am especially grateful for his initial encouragement. And it is no exaggeration to say that my greatest debt is to the present general editor, Professor Hoeniger, for his enormously helpful comments and suggestions; working with him has been a genuinely rewarding experience.

In Faversham today the physical setting of the Arden story is still largely preserved; and for vividly recreating an earlier atmosphere for me, I owe a very special thanks to Mr F. G. Bishop, the former town clerk, as I do to Mr and Mrs Michael Quin and their house guests, Professor and Mrs John Ellis, for opening Arden's House to me. The laughter of children at dinner there convinced me that the vexed spirits whom I had expected to hear in the parlour, the counting-house, and the guest hall were at last laid to rest.

M. L. WINE

Chicago, 1972

Abbreviations

(excluding editions of *Arden*, for which see p. xciii)

Abbott	E. A. Abbott, *A Shakespearian Grammar* (2nd ed.), 1870. (References are to sections.)
Clark	E. T. Clark, *Shakespeare's Plays in Their Order of Writing*, 1930.
Crawford	C. Crawford, *Collectanea* (First Series), 1906.
D.N.B.	*Dictionary of National Biography.*
Hart, *S.S.C.*	A. Hart, *Stolne and Surreptitious Copies*, 1942.
Holinshed	R. Holinshed, *et al.*, *The Chronicles of England, Scotland, and Ireland*, 2nd ed., 3 vols. in 2, 1587.
Jackson	M. P. Jackson, 'Material for an Edition of *Arden of Feversham*', unpubl. B.Litt. thesis, Oxford, 1963.
Miksch	W. Miksch, *Die Verfasserschaft des 'Arden of Feversham'*, 1907.
n.	note in Commentary.
O.E.D.	*Oxford English Dictionary.*
Onions	C. T. Onions, *A Shakespeare Glossary*, 2nd ed., 1953 (1919).
Q^c	Quarto corrected.
Q^u	Quarto uncorrected.
Qq	The first three quartos, collectively, of *Arden of Feversham* (1592, 1599, 1633).
Rubow	P. V. Rubow, *Shakespeare og hans Samtidige*, 1948.
S.D.	Stage direction.
S.H.	Speech heading.

Smith   M. B. Smith, *Marlowe's Imagery and the Marlowe Canon*, 1940.

Sugden   E. H. Sugden, *A Topographical Dictionary to the Works of Shakespeare and His Fellow Dramatists*, 1925.

Sykes   H. D. Sykes, *Sidelights on Shakespeare*, 1919.

Taylor   R. Taylor, 'A Tentative Chronology of Marlowe's and Some Other Elizabethan Plays', *P.M.L.A.*, LI (1936), 643–88.

Tilley   M. P. Tilley, *A Dictionary of the Proverbs in England in the Sixteenth and Seventeenth Centuries*, 1950.

trans.   translated for this edition.

PERIODICALS

J.E.G.P.   *Journal of English and Germanic Philology.*

Libr.   *The Library.*

M.L.N.   *Modern Language Notes.*

M.L.R.   *Modern Language Review.*

M.P.   *Modern Philology.*

N. & Q.   *Notes and Queries.*

P.M.L.A.   *Publications of the Modern Language Association.*

P.Q.   *Philological Quarterly.*

R.E.S.   *Review of English Studies.*

S.E.L.   *Studies in English Literature.*

Sh. Jahrbuch   *Shakespeare-Jahrbuch* (formerly *Jahrbuch der Deutschen Shakespeare-Gesellschaft*).

Sh. Q.   *Shakespeare Quarterly.*

Sh. S.   *Shakespeare Survey.*

T.L.S.   *Times Literary Supplement.*

The titles of Shakespeare's plays and poems are abbreviated as in Onions, and all quotations and line-references are taken from the Cambridge edition (ed. W. A. Wright, 9 vols., 1891–3).

Marlowe's works are cited from *The Works of Christopher Marlowe*, ed. C. F. Tucker Brooke, 1910, in the following abbreviations:

1 Tamb.	*Tamburlaine, Part One.*
2 Tamb.	*Tamburlaine, Part Two.*
Faustus	*Doctor Faustus.*
E2	*Edward II.*
Mas.P.	*The Massacre at Paris.*
J.M.	*The Jew of Malta.*
Dido	*Dido Queen of Carthage.*

Kyd's works, acknowledged and doubtful, are cited from *The Works of Thomas Kyd*, ed. F. S. Boas, new ed., 1955 (1901), in the following abbreviations:

Sp.T.	*The Spanish Tragedie.*
Corn.	*Cornelia.*
S. & P.	*Soliman and Perseda.*
Hovsholders Philos.	*The Hovsholders Philosophie.*
Brewen	*The Mvrder of Iohn Brewen.*
Ieronimo	*The First Part of Ieronimo.*

The following works also are cited in abbreviation:

Con.	Anon., *The First Part of the Contention of the Two Famous Houses of York and Lancaster* (in Vol. IX of The Cambridge Shakespeare).
Tr.T.	Anon., *The True Tragedie of Richard Duke of Yorke* (in Vol. IX of The Cambridge Shakespeare).
TRKJ	Anon., *The Troublesome Raigne of King John*, Parts One and Two, ed. G. Bullough in *Narrative and Dramatic Sources of Shakespeare*, Vol. IV, 1962.
End.	Lyly's *Endimion, The Man in the Moone*, ed. R. W. Bond in *The Complete Works of John Lyly*, Vol. III (1902).

B

F.Q.   Spenser's *The Faerie Queene*, in *The Poetical
                 Works of Edmund Spenser*, ed. J. C. Smith and
                 E. de Selincourt, 1912.

Leir   Anon., *The History of King Leir 1605*, ed. H. Hart
                 for the Malone Society, 1907.

Woodstock   Anon., *Woodstock, A Moral History*, ed. A. P.
                 Rossiter, 1946.

Introduction

I. TEXT

Early Editions

'The tragedie of Arden of Feuersham & blackwill' was entered in the Register of the Stationers' Company on 3 April 1592 by the London bookseller Edward White; and a quarto edition appeared in the same year with the following highly descriptive title-page obviously intended for use as an advertising handbill:[1]

THE / LAMENTA- / *BLE AND TRVE TRA-* / GEDIE OF M. AR- / *DEN OF FEVERSHAM* / IN KENT. / *Who was most wickedlye murdered, by* / the meanes of his disloyall and wanton / *wyfe, who for the loue she bare to one* / Mosbie, hyred two desperat ruf- / fins Blackwill and Shakbag, / *to kill him.* / Wherin is shewed the great mal- / lice and discimulation of a wicked wo- / man, the vnsatiable desire of filthie lust / and the shamefull end of all murderers. / *Imprinted at London for Edward* / White, dwelling at the lyttle North / dore of Paules Church at / the signe of the / Gun. 1592. / ★

The text, which begins on A₂ is printed in black letter, with occasional use of italics and stage directions in roman type. The play is not divided into acts or scenes.[2] The printer, to judge from the ornament at the end of the text, seems to have been Edward Allde.[3]

---

[1] See p. 2 and note to iii. 50.

[2] Complete details of the collation of the first three editions are given in W. W. Greg, *A Bibliography of the English Printed Drama to the Restoration*, I (1939), 183–5.

[3] Greg originally identified the probable printer as Peter Short on the basis of the ornament which was used twenty years earlier by H. Denham, whom Short succeeded; but, under 'Corrections' in vol. IV of the *Bibliography* (1959, p. 1608), he later observed that the ornament 'appears, however, to have been used by Edward Allde (J. Crow)'. Miss K. F. Pantzer of Harvard's Houghton Library informs this editor that Crow's observation can be substantiated from F. S. Ferguson's notes at the Houghton in which he identified the ornament as the sill piece of compartment 53 in R. B.

Only three copies have survived: the Malone (at the Bodleian Library), the Dyce (at the Victoria and Albert Museum), and the Mostyn-Perry (at the Huntington Library).

On 18 December of the same year the Court of the Stationers' Company met and handed down the following edict:

> Edw white·   Whereas Edward white and Abell Ieffes haue eche
> Abell Ieffes· of them offendyd· Viž Edw White in havinge
>   printed the spanish tragedie belonging to [Edw.
> *deleted*] Abell Ieffes / and Abell Ieffes in having printed the tragedie
> of arden of kent belonginge to Edw white: yt is agreed that all the
> booke of eche ympression shalbe as confiscated and forfayted ac-
> cordinge to thordonnanc[es], [be *deleted*] disposed to thuse of the
> poore of the companye for that eche of them hath seu'ally trans-
> gressed the ordoñanc[es] in the seid impressions.[1]

Earlier, on 7 August, Jeffes had been committed to prison for resist-ing a search by officers of the Company and for refusing to sur-render the bar of his press after 'he contemptuously p[ro]ceded in printing a book wthout aucthority contrary to our m^r his cõmaun-dem^t'.[2] Thus Jeffes's illegal edition of *Arden* can be dated from some time between 3 April and the date of his arrest since, as W. W. Greg points out, it does not seem likely, even if he were at liberty before the Court met on 18 December, that he would have been permitted to use his press.[3] Although the edition was ordered to be

---

McKerrow and F. S. Ferguson's *Title-Page Borders Used in England and Scotland 1485–1640* (1932) and from W. A. Jackson's notations of addi-tional uses by Allde of the sill piece in *S.T.C.* 12556.3 (1588) and by Oulton, Allde's stepson who eventually inherited most of Allde's printing stock, in *Wing* E 1589 (1642). R. B. McKerrow, in 'Edward Allde as a Typical Trade Printer', *Libr.*, 4th ser., x (1929), 121–62, notes that between 1587 and 1621 Allde printed more than fifty books for Edward White, Sr and Jr, and that 'he appears to have had the bad habit of frequently omitting his name from his productions.'

[1] Greg, *Bibliography*, I, 9, and W. W. Greg and E. Boswell, *Records of the Court of the Stationers' Company, 1576 to 1602* (1930), p. 44. The signi-ficance of the edict is discussed in W. W. Greg, 'The Spanish Tragedy—a Leading Case', *Libr.*, 4th ser., vi (1925–6), 47–56; W. W. Greg and D. N. Smith, intro. to *The Spanish Tragedy 1592* (Malone Society Reprint, 1948–9); and L. Kirschbaum, 'Is *The Spanish Tragedy* a Leading Case?', *J.E.G.P.*, xxxvii (1938), 501–12.

[2] Greg and Boswell, *Records*, p. 42.

[3] '*The Spanish Tragedy*—a Leading Case', p. 50.

'confiscated and forfayted' and not actually destroyed, no copy survives, and it is not possible to surmise its nature; it may have been
a mere reprint of White's edition.[1]

In 1599 White brought out another edition of *Arden* (this time
printed by 'I. Roberts'[2]), also in black letter and with the same fully
informative title-page. Again, only three copies are extant: two at
the Huntington Library and one at the Folger Shakespeare Library.
Elizabeth Allde, whose husband, according to an entry in the
Stationers' Register of 29 June 1624, inherited the play from the
estate of Mrs White, printed, in roman type, the third and last of
the early editions in 1633. Numerous copies of this edition survive.[3]

The second quarto clearly is reprinted from the first; and, in
turn, the third quarto substantially follows the second.[4] Neither of
the two later quartos ever attempts to correct the few major cruxes
of Q1 (as *perisht*, iv. 13; *gentle stary gaile*, viii. 17; and *fence of
trouble*, viii. 133). Q2 corrects a fair number of minor misprints in
Q1—as upside down letters and mis-spellings in both text and stage
directions—and Q3 follows these corrections (it also corrects Q1-2's
frons, vii. 18, to *front*). Instances where the three quartos differ in
readings are few, and in general Q2 influences the new reading in
Q3 (as, for example, at ii. 80; viii. 24, 97; x. 1; xiii. 138; xiv. 18,
72). In the few cases where Q1 and Q3 are in agreement against
Q2, it would seem that Q3 is merely correcting the carelessness
with which Q2 was composed at times (as at iii. 165; xi. 11).

The clearest evidence that Q3 was printed from a copy of Q2 is
provided by passages where it adopts patently incorrect readings

[1] White's illegal edition of *The Spanish Tragedy* survives in one copy
now at the British Museum; Allde was its printer.
[2] James Roberts, bookseller and printer in London from 1569 to 1615;
the printer of several Shakespeare quartos.
[3] The three editions are referred to hereafter as Q1, Q2, and Q3. The
following copies of the third edition have been consulted: British Museum
(three, including the T. J. Wise copy), Victoria and Albert Museum (two,
in the Dyce collection), Bodleian, Worcester, London, Edinburgh, Eton,
Harvard (two), Folger (three), Pforzheimer, Newberry, Huntington, Wm.
A. Clark (the Bridgewater copy). Slight variants among them do not affect
substantive readings (but see textual note at xviii. 2).
[4] Since White published both Q1 and Q2, we may assume that for Q2
no use was made of Jeffes's pirated edition; at any rate no departures in
Q2 from Q1 suggest that White may have consulted it.

(as at i. 218, 473; iii. 98; viii. 107) and where Q3 incorporates
Q2's substantive changes and corrections (as at ii. 93; iii. 139; iv.
107; v. 62; viii. 99, 156.1; x. 59; xii. 28; xiii. 148; xiv. 15; xv. 8).
Q3 also carries further the process of modernization begun by Q2:
in spelling, punctuation, and grammar (as at i. 150, 501; ii. 1,
105, although sometimes it introduces an irregularity as at i. 105).
It also makes a very feeble attempt to regularize the versification;
often, however, it merely capitalizes lines that the first two quartos
left uncapitalized in apparent prose passages (see commentary to
xii. 4–6, and collation at xiv. 365. A notable feature of the third
quarto is the frequent omission of single words which occasionally
creates a better line of verse but usually is the result of compositorial
carelessness. In no instance where Q2 leaves out a word does Q3
resort to finding it in Q1. Q3 also makes a few necessary emendations, and its tendency to modernize helps at times to clarify meanings (for examples of both, see addition of speech heading at viii.
167; vii. 18; x. 94; xiii. 12; but see i. 363 for an incorrect speech
heading and xiv. 192 for a mistaken expansion of an abbreviation).
Considering the extent of its tendency to modernize, one must be
struck by Q3's apparent preferences for freely varying allomorphs
(*while* for *whilest*, *enow* for *enough*) that sometimes regularize the
versification, sometimes do not, and sometimes make no change at
all. Its most striking feature is the frontispiece, illustrating the
murder of Arden at the 'game of tables'; the first two quartos are
not illustrated.

The play was not reprinted again until 1770 when Edward
Jacob, a Faversham antiquary and the author of a history of the
town, brought out an edition, 'printed, *verbatim*' he wrote in his
Preface, from the original quarto of 1592, which, he thought, 'perhaps may be *only* in the hands of the Editor; so far is certain, no
notice is taken of this Edition by *Ames* in his History of Printing; or
by any Person that has published Accounts of our old dramatic
Authors'.[1] Jacob carried the process of modernization still further,

---

[1] The editors of the Malone Society Reprint of *Arden* argue convincingly
(p. vii) that the copy Jacob believed to be unique was very likely the Dyce
copy: 'There is strong evidence . . . that the writing in it is his, and that it
lacked the last three leaves [as it still does] when he used it; the text of the
missing leaves he appears to have supplied from the Quarto of 1633. . . . The

sometimes following the readings of Q3 (which, he noted, 'is very incorrect') and often emending for better versification. His text particularly influenced the next two editions in English, Tyrrell's and Delius's, which, in turn, influenced most subsequent editions in their readings, lineation, and act–scene divisions.[1]

Ludwig Tieck, in his German translation of 1823, was the first editor to divide the play into acts and scenes and to supply a list of characters. The first English editor to do so was Henry Tyrrell in 1851, and Nicolaus Delius redivided the play in his edition of 1855. F.-V. Hugo, on the other hand, in his French translation of 1867, divided the play into scenes only; and Baskervill, Heltzel, and Nethercot followed his lead in their anthology edition of 1934.

In his preface Jacob wryly observed that some of the Faversham inhabitants 'have till of late, at a few Years interval, doubly murdered [the play], by the excessive [sic] bad Manuscript copies they used, and their more injudicious acting; to the no small Discredit of this valuable tragedy, whoever was the Author of it'. One such manuscript, neatly compiled by the Kentish antiquary Thomas Southouse early in the eighteenth century, survives as part of an octavo volume now in the Huntington Library (MS. HM 1341). A specially written prologue, dated 1716, and epilogue make it evident that the text originally was transcribed for a provincial production. The manuscript has been the subject of meticulous scrutiny by J. M. Nosworthy, who has convincingly demonstrated that the date of the prologue represents the year in which Southouse transcribed it rather than the date of composition of the text.[2] Nosworthy has also dissociated the text 'from any immediate connexion with the printed texts' and has further shown its likely

---

earliest edition mentioned in the dramatic lists from Langbaine's to Erskine Baker's in *The Companion to the Play-House*, 1764, is the Quarto of 1599.'

[1] See p. xciii below for a complete list of editions and translations. The Oliphant editions are noteworthy mainly for their elaborate stage directions that make the text read more like a novel than a play; and the Hopkinson editions, privately printed, have to be read with great caution because of their excessive number of misprints.

[2] 'The Southouse Text of *Arden of Feversham*', *Libr.*, 5th ser., V (1950), 113–29.

dependence upon some earlier transcript (which he would date about 1650[1]), probably a prompt copy used by provincial or local players which, in turn, seems to have derived, he believes, from a copy of Q2 in an uncorrected state.[2] The text of the play is completely intact (although the ending of scene vii is botched), but the process of modernization is far along; a list of 'Persons Represent[e]d' is also supplied. As with the two later quartos, none of the important cruxes is resolved, but some passages have been rewritten apparently for clarification (see textual notes at viii. 17 and 49, and x. 58).

Without doubt, as Nosworthy points out, the Southouse text 'can have no possible claim to equal rank or authority' with the quartos since 'it is scarcely an exaggeration to say that whenever the MS. differs from the Qs it also degrades.' It is curious, however, that a number of the minor emendations made by Jacob in 1770 and accepted by nearly all subsequent editors are to be found in the Southouse text; and some of its readings surprisingly anticipate those by other editors, who may or may not have seen the manuscript but who, in any event, certainly do not refer to it.[3]

Nature of the Copy

Comparison of the three early quartos establishes the priority of the first as the basic copy for any subsequent edition. The traditional view is that the text of Q1 (1592) is, aside from metrical irregularity,

---

[1] Nosworthy conjectures that the manuscript of *Arden* which the antiquarian Oldys was reputed to have seen at Canterbury (see Bullen's edition, p. xix) was not the original but the postulated theatrical transcript behind the Southouse text.

[2] Interestingly, the manuscript follows Q3 in wrongly expanding Q1-2's abbreviation of *M.* [*Master*] to *mistres* at x. 38.

[3] A brief excerpt—a soliloquy spoken by a repentant Mistress Arden apparently right after her husband's murder—from a reputed manuscript play called *Arden of Feversham*, 'written in 1639 by Henry Burnell, author of *Landgartha*, 1641', is quoted by Hopkinson in his 1898 edition. The manuscript was discovered, he writes, by a Mr W. J. Harmon in 1894 'among the Digby MSS. bequeathed by Langbaine' (which, in fact, was not the case) to the Bodleian Library. An extensive search early in this century by R. B. McKerrow and more recently by M. P. Jackson has failed to turn up the manuscript, and the likelihood of the excerpt's having been forged is strong. See Jackson, pp. 271-7.

'remarkably good', 'unusually good', 'sound', and that it 'offers on
the whole no great difficulties'.[1] W. T. Jewkes concisely summarizes
the arguments for this position:

> The text presents us with a full-length play which seems in
> good condition, since no dramatic discrepancies can be noticed.
> The stage directions are frequent and descriptive, and display
> considerable consistency. Over half the entrances begin "Here
> enter…," and centered directions which do not concern entrances
> appear in the form "Then he …," "Then they…" These forms
> would seem to have been a characteristic of the author. There are
> no marginal directions, and no evidence of the copy having been
> prepared for performance. The author's copy suggests itself as the
> copy for this text.[2]

In fact, however, the text of *Arden* is, in the words of Alfred
Hart, 'very poor';[3] and only a few of its faults can be attributed to
the compositor. Hart has demonstrated effectively, mainly on the
basis of parallel passages, that the 1592 quarto must be considered
as one of the 'Pembroke group' of so-called 'bad quartos', published
plays whose texts have been filtered through a reporting agent
(actor and/or scribe), associated in some way with the Pembroke
players, and thus contaminated.[4] Such quartos are removed, in

[1] The judgements, respectively, of Brooke, *Apocrypha* (p. xiii), Bayne
(p. v), Greg and Smith, intro. to *The Spanish Tragedy 1592* (p. xii), and
Warnke and Proescholdt (p. vii).

[2] *Act Division in Elizabethan and Jacobean Plays 1583–1616* (1958),
p. 229. Stage directions in the 'Here enter …' form are not found in the
other 'Pembroke' plays with which *Arden* is associated (see n. 4 below).

[3] *S.S.C.*, p. 384.

[4] Hart associates *Arden* with the 'Pembroke group of plays'—which also
includes Kyd's *The Spanish Tragedy*, Marlowe's *Edward II* and *The
Massacre at Paris*, Peele's *Edward I* and *The Battle of Alcazar*, Shake-
speare's *Titus Andronicus*, the anonymous *Soliman and Perseda*, *The
Taming of a Shrew*, *The First Part of the Contention betwixt the Two Famous
Houses of York and Lancaster*, and *The True Tragedy of Richard Duke of
York* (see Hart's diagram, *S.S.C.*, p. 374). To this group should be added
Shakespeare's *Romeo and Juliet* (see *Arden*, viii. 1, n.). Not all of these plays
are literally quartos in their original form; the designation is used for convenience (*The Spanish Tragedy*, 1592, is actually an octavo). The designation of 'Pembroke's Men' is applied generically to imply the presence
behind these publications of actor-reporters who must have been associated at one time with a company known by that name; see p. xlvi, n. 1,
below. Hart's work remains, even with modification from subsequent
scholarship, the most comprehensive study of the 'bad quartos'.

varying degrees, from a direct authorial source and very probably even from an acting version. Whether actually 'stolne and surreptitious', as the editors of the Shakespeare First Folio of 1623 claimed in referring to such publications as *The First Part of the Contention betwixt the Two Famous Houses of York and Lancaster* (the 'bad quarto' of *2 Henry VI*) and *The True Tragedy of Richard Duke of York* (*3 Henry VI*), they are considerably debased versions of their 'true originall copies'.

With these memorially constructed quartos *Arden* shares common signs of corruption, such as parallelisms to other plays, awkward repetitions (including anticipations and recollections), poor versification, breakdowns between prose and verse, and inconsistencies in the story line. Hart claimed to have found thirty-two parallel passages—or 'inter-play borrowings', as he called them—in other printed dramatic texts of the period; and, although the exact count must remain indeterminate since we obviously can never know how many parallels *Arden* may contain to plays that have perished,[1] their importance as regards text, date, and authorship is undeniable. But once that recognition is granted, their nature and what to make of them are both difficult to assess. What many commentators regard as parallels are often no more than linguistic commonplaces of the period, and the status of other passages is open to serious questioning. Furthermore, the matter of priority—whether a given parallel in *Arden* is original with that play or borrowed from another (see, for example, viii. 1, n.)—almost defies solution. The commentary to this edition records genuine parallels (besides those passages from other contemporary plays for purely illustrative purposes), but a more detailed discussion is left to Appendix 1.

Parallels in *Arden*, then, may hint that something is askew with the text; but it remains far safer to look for signs of corruption elsewhere. Scene iii provides such signs. Much of the dialogue here moves slowly, repetitiously, awkwardly (see especially the note to lines 134–5), and wavers uncertainly between prose and verse. The repetition in lines 40 and 44 does not look like the work of even a

---

[1] 'It must be kept in mind that barely a seventh of the plays acted by the Admiral's men reached the press' (Hart, *S.S.C.*, p. 116).

third-rate dramatist. Lines 85 and 117 are almost identical, suspiciously so. The scene contains two inconsistencies (see note to lines 92–4, as well as to lines 119–23, and the conflict between line 35 and lines 130–1).

What occurs textually in scene iii is typical of large portions of the *Arden* text. To an extraordinary degree the play repeats itself; whole lines and phrases, sometimes with only the slightest variation, recur. Many of these repetitions are no more than conventional dramatic formulae for exits and entrances, such as 'And so farewell', 'Come, let's go', 'See, yonder comes . . .'. Any of these might be found in good texts; but their excessive use here is, as Hart notes, 'characteristic of corrupt texts; the pirates were always in trouble when it was necessary to get characters on or off the stage'.[1] Actors' 'fill-in' phrases, such as 'Let it [them] pass', 'I warrant you', and 'Ay, but' recur repeatedly; and the repetition of certain favourite words like *resolved* or *resolute* and *weary* (life, i. 9; body, i. 42; with his trugs, i. 498; time, iv. 36; limbs, iv. 52; bird, ix. 39; way, ix. 92) at times betrays a paucity of vocabulary also characteristic of reported texts (although, admittedly, of certain authors, too). Occasional repetitions are defensible, of course, on logical grounds, as when information heard earlier in the play must be imparted later to characters who were not originally present; but the formulaic nature of even these later instances renders them suspect, as the example of i. 522–3, 568–9, ii. 103–4, and xiv. 126–7 illustrates.

Repetitions contribute significantly to one of the most characteristic features of reported texts: the poor state of their versification. On almost every page of *Arden* the variant repetitions of actors' catch-phrases, formulaic constructions, and interpolations of one kind or another play havoc with the versification. One common formulaic construction is of the 'Stay, . . . , stay' (or 'Draw, . . . , draw' or 'Help, . . . , help') type. At i. 121 the second 'stay' deranges

---

[1] Hart, *S.S.C.*, p. 318; see also p. 409: 'In a surreptitious quarto such as *Contention* the actors reduced [Shakespeare's] diversity of formulas to two, viz., "and so farewell" and "come lets go", and variants of these. Wherever one of these two occurs in the last line of a scene, corruption may be suspected, because Shakespeare usually provided the actors with a different method of talking themselves off the stage on each occasion.'

the line, but at iii. 135 its omission does the same thing; at xiv. 326, however, the construction finally works. Simple contraction would make Greene's line at iii. 85 ('And let us [=let's] bethink us of some other place') metrically smooth, but its repetition just a little later at iii. 117 without the upsetting conjunctive ('Let us bethink us of some other place') makes the first instance suspect. The removal of 'Ay' from the catch-phrase 'Ay, but' at i. 235 and the simple re-arrangement of lines 235–7 (to 'But . . . thou / Or . . . coming / Into . . . die') would create, as M. P. Jackson points out, three decent lines of verse, thus making the recurrent catch-phrase also suspect here.[1] The examples are literally overwhelming, and recognition of them has tempted editors to tamper with the text to make it metrically smooth.

Hart describes *Arden*'s verse as follows:

> . . . [it] exhibits many of the defects characteristic of a report and over a hundred lines are harsh or unmetrical. There are 63 lines of nine syllables of which 28 are defective in the first foot and 31 others in the interior of the line. Perhaps the best evidence of a reporter's presence is the large number of twelve-syllable lines, some of which have an extra initial syllable and a final unstressed syllable to make cacophony complete. In addition there are thirty unscannable lines of eleven syllables; in many of these the extra syllable is a monosyllabic enclitic such as 'but,' 'and,' 'for,' 'why,' etc., prefixed to an ordinary decasyllabon. Most of these defects are undoubtedly the work of actors.[2]

Hart's statistics are certainly debatable, especially if we allow for normal extra-metrical lines involving direct address and exclamations and the vagaries of pronunciation permitted in Elizabethan poetry (-*ion* suffixes, for instance, may be pronounced either mono-syllabically or disyllabically; *Alice*, more often than not in the text, is a monosyllable—as reflected by Q2's spelling of *Alce*). But the point is incontrovertible and justifies Jackson's observation that the *Arden* quarto 'repeatedly offends the ear of the sensitive metrist'.[3] In fact, an editor is tempted to regard much of the verse as prose

---

[1] Jackson, p. 21. See also *Arden*, i. 247, n. Jackson has studied intensively the ramifications of Hart's conclusions about the 1592 *Arden* quarto (see particularly pp. 12–30 of his thesis), and the present discussion is much indebted to his work.

[2] *S.S.C.*, p. 384.   [3] P. 12.

since the boundaries between the two are often imperceptible. It is indeed arguable, in view of the Epilogue's disclaimer that 'no filèd points [of rhetoric] are foisted in' 'this naked tragedy', that the metrical irregularity of the quarto represents an attempt to create a colloquial effect in keeping with the domestic setting of the play; but the ultimate effect is of clumsiness in the handling of verse rather than of a deliberate and studied 'low style'.[1] Where the versification seems least corrupt (especially in the earlier and middle scenes), the *Arden* playwright seems to be writing the 'almost uniformly decasyllabic, prevailingly end-stopped' blank verse, 'with the stress customarily on the second syllable of each foot', characteristic of his contemporaries in this earlier phase of Elizabethan drama.[2]

Aside from verbal repetitions, the *Arden* quarto contains several instances of retelling of earlier episodes or conversations which, though sometimes logically defensible, seem to testify to a reporting agent's difficulty in filling out the text; as when Alice, in scene i, recounts to Mosby her immediately preceding interview with Greene and the circumstances leading to her employment of him; when Shakebag, in scene iii, narrates in detail how Black Will has just had his head 'broken' in full view of the audience; and when Black Will, in scene xiv, acts out in detail the fight of the preceding scene for the benefit of Mistress Arden, who had been a bystander.

The quarto contains a few inconsistencies, none of them seriously impairing the development of the plot but pointing to some confusion—notably, Bradshaw's bringing a letter back from London to which he has never gone (see viii. 157–9, n.) and the introduction

---

[1] On actors' 'indifference to blank verse' see E. K. Chambers, *William Shakespeare* (1930), I. 157. On p. 159 Chambers observes that 'a lapse of memory may have been remedied by sheer faking; and for this we need not call in a hack playwright, since many actors, as Henslowe's records show us, were capable of putting together a play at need.'

[2] Hart, *S.S.C.*, p. 222. Elizabethan metrics, however, are more permissive than is sometimes realized, allowing as they do for trimeters, tetrameters, and alexandrines in decasyllabic verse; feminine endings; initial truncation (see i. 115 and n.); and irregularity in the marked and unmarked caesura (see i. 79 and n.). A thorough discussion of these practices can be found in D. L. Sipe, *Shakespeare's Metrics* (1968); see pp. 32–3 for a summary.

and characterization of Clarke the painter, who comes upon the scene praising Mistress Arden for wanting to do away with the man she hates (i. 269–71), who later (i. 620) seems to have no knowledge of what she is about, and whose device of the poisoned crucifix is totally forgotten by the end of the play.[1] Seeming inconsistencies in characterization must be approached more cautiously. For example, from their introduction in the second scene it would appear that the two comic villains, Black Will and Shakebag, were intended to speak in a highly colloquial prose; but one of the play's most 'poetic' passages belongs to Shakebag (the beginning of scene v), and both characters speak at times in a somewhat exalted language that seems out of character. Similarly, Michael's impressive soliloquy in scene iv, one of the most praiseworthy moments in the whole play, belies his normal characterization as a bungling servant. Such inconsistencies, however, if they are such at all, are often encountered in Elizabethan drama.[2]

Finally, in common with a number of the 'bad' quartos, the *Arden* text shows signs of progressive degeneration: the climactic scene of the play—the murder of Arden in xiv—is one of the least satisfactory textually. Whereas exits and entrances had hitherto been carefully provided, the business centring around the murder —the placing of Black Will and Shakebag in the countinghouse and the subsequent removal of the body—needs editorial clarification; and the verse is singularly deficient. Black Will's recounting of the fight in the preceding scene may be an attempt at padding.

Alone among earlier editors, Warnke and Proescholdt judged that *Arden*, because of its irregular line divisions, 'was probably printed from a stage-copy, and not from the author's own manuscript';[3] but the nature of the textual corruption does not point to a prompt-copy source. Many stage directions, it is true, anticipate exits and entrances in a manner characteristic of a prompt copy. But the descriptive and literary nature of almost all the directions (e.g., '*Here enters* ADAM *of the Flower-de-Luce*' at i. 104.1, '*Then she*

---

[1] See notes to i. 447, xiv. 172, and xvi. 17, as well as to iii. 92–4, 119–23, and 130–1, already referred to.

[2] Cf. the famous example of the second murderer in *Macbeth*, III. iii. In *Arden*, note Black Will at iii. 100–3 and at vii. 20.

[3] P. vii.

throws down the broth on the ground' at i. 367.1, and '*Then they lay the body in the countinghouse*' at xiv. 248.1) seems authorial and would be sorely at odds with the imperative directions necessitated by an acting version (e.g. '*Enter* ADAM)', '*Spills broth*', '*Remove body*').[1] Variations in the naming of characters in stage directions— as 'Alice' or 'his wife' (x. o.1); 'Clarke' or 'the Painter' (x. 45.1)— also seem characteristic of an author's draft;[2] a prompt copy would have to be more consistent. Further, the quarto never indicates prompt markings for props (the broth, a chair, a prayerbook, glasses of wine) or sound effects (knocking on the door).

A text that so frequently betrays signs of memorial contamination and yet reveals none of the markings of a stage- or prompt-copy justifies Jackson's conclusion that 'a scribe who perpetuated the memorial mistakes of actors' would appear to be the reporting agent.[3] But the exact nature or method of transcription is impossible to determine. To judge from the metrical deficiency and the kinds of interpolation in the text, it seems probable that the copyist relied on transcripts of the actors' roles or on dictation by them or on both.[4]

But whatever the source of its transcription, the copy given to the printer in 1592 seems to have been prepared especially for publication. The care with which stage directions evidently were prepared points to a scribe who was concerned that the reader should have a sense of what the play was like in performance.[5] As 'bad'

---

[1] See quotation from Jewkes, p. xxv above.

[2] 'The use of the indefinite article for "a Prentise" [iii. 49.1] and "a Sailer" [xiii. 0.1], who have not previously been mentioned, should be contrasted with the use of the definite article for "the Painter" [x. 45.1] and "the Ferriman" [xi. 1.1], whom the dialogue has already introduced' (Jackson, p. 7).

[3] Jackson, pp. 31 ff.

[4] The roles of Elizabethan actors literally were transcribed, with cues, on long rolls; see W. W. Greg, *Dramatic Documents from the Elizabethan Playhouses* (1931), II. 177, and the document reproduced in the first volume. The least corrupt passages in *Arden* may derive from just such a transcript. Q1's care in distinguishing between *count'nance* (i. 31) and *countenance* (i. 201), or between *coistrel* (v. 41) and *coisterel* (v. 59), or *husband's* (xiv. 269) and *husband is* (xiv. 273) are rare examples where the author's concern for metre is transmitted with precision. See also notes to i. 247 and xiii. 1.

[5] Stage directions that are lifted directly from the dialogue—such as

quartos go, *Arden* has much to recommend it. We can never fully know the extent of its corruption, but the text is at least of average length and probably not greatly abridged, if at all. The movement of the plot is always easy to follow, and certain scenes come through with particular vividness—notably iv (Michael's soliloquy) and viii (the quarrel between Alice and Mosby and their reconciliation).

A close study of Q1's type, spelling, and punctuation points to no more than one compositor. A notable feature is that all recto pages, except G_3 and I_3, are provided with signatures. The type used is the same throughout, the spelling has the usual Elizabethan variation (e.g. *Mosbie* and *Mosby* could appear within a couple of lines of one another), and the punctuation is at least consistently erratic (commas are a frequent mark of an end-stopped line). It is not possible to discover clearly whether type was set by formes or *seriatim* (page by page). In a bad quarto, passages of verse printed as prose, as well as the reverse, do not provide reliable evidence. The unsystematic resetting of headlines points to *seriatim* printing as more likely, with the compositor probably setting along from copy, doing what he felt like doing with the line lengths.[1] That the play ends on signature κ also points to *seriatim* printing since printing by formes would not permit the wasting of the remainder of the sheet.

The three extant copies of the 1592 quarto—the Malone, the Dyce, and the Huntington—vary only slightly in their states of press correction, minor variants being recorded on the formes of inner A, inner D, outer F, outer H, inner I, and inner K. Only the Huntington copy corrects the faulty headline on signature A_2, and the

---

those at i. 104.1, xiv. 248.1, and 350.1–2—are also indicative of a scribe's hand. See W. W. Greg, *The Shakespeare First Folio* (1955), p. 227, on similar directions in the 'bad quarto' of *Romeo and Juliet*.

[1] Professor Arthur Freeman, who is now editing Kyd, notes in private correspondence that the same phenomenon occurs in *Soliman and Perseda*, printed in the same year as *Arden* and in Allde's shop. He writes about *Arden*: 'The headlines are sufficiently irregular to provide no concrete evidence for single or double skeletons, or indeed the use of skeletons at all.' See his article, 'The Printing of *The Spanish Tragedy*' (also by Allde for White in 1592), *Libr.*, 5th ser., XXIV (1969), 187–99. See also Jackson, p. 4.

Malone copy alone retains the faulty signature of E_4 on what should be D_4 (possibly another sign of *seriatim* printing). The Huntington copy is the most complete; the Malone lacks the blank K_2, but otherwise the text is complete; and the Dyce lacks I_4–K_2 and contains, as noted before, notes and alterations in ink by a later hand, probably Jacob's.

This Edition

The editor of a reported or 'bad' text for which no 'good' text exists as a control faces two alternatives: he can emend freely, hoping to restore the text, as much as possible, to what he believes comes closer to the author's original autograph manuscript;[1] or he can restrict himself to emending only compositorial or printing-house errors, thus recovering 'what is often the equal impurity of the underlying printer's copy'[2] in the belief that improvement on the latter is no guarantee of restoring an original reading. This edition, with some few exceptions noted later, follows the latter, more conservative practice. To be sure, an editor can often detect with confidence the source of a particular corruption (compositorial misreading or extra-metrical interpolation, such as an actor's tag phrase or unmetrical full forms ['let us' instead of 'let's'] and the reverse); but his way of remedying it may still turn out to be debatable.[3] In all such instances, therefore, the quarto text has been retained. Among the collations will be found samples of typical, as well as more noteworthy, emendations and conjectures by previous editors.

[1] Cf. W. W. Greg's definition of a critical edition: 'to present the text, so far as the available evidence permits, in the form in which we may suppose that it would have stood in a fair copy, made by the author himself, of the work as he finally intended it' (in *The Editorial Problem in Shakespeare* [1951], p. x, although Greg has in mind 'good' quartos).

[2] F. Bowers in *The Dramatic Works of Thomas Dekker*, I (1953), 402, referring, in this case, to the 'bad' quarto of *Sir Thomas Wyatt*.

[3] See Jackson, pp. 36–47, who favours a considerably 'less conservative treatment' than provided in the present edition. Cf., however, Bowers, p. 402: '. . . we can often be aware of corruption in the "bad" text (though not always), but we may have no concrete evidence at all about the autograph reading which has been memorially corrupted. To attempt, therefore, to reconstruct a purely hypothetical text by metrical smoothing and verbal emendation is sheer folly except in isolated special cases.'

C

However, the reader of *Arden of Faversham*[1] in a modernized text in this series expects to understand all its lines, at least with the help of the commentary. No matter how difficult a passage might at first appear, if a plausible elucidation could be offered (see viii. 51), the original was not emended. But emendations were introduced where to have kept the original reading would have resulted in unintelligibility or nonsense (see iv. 13 or viii. 133). The spelling has been strictly modernized throughout even though this practice has caused occasional difficulty.[2] For the most part the textual notes cite the modernized spellings of the present text, and only spelling changes that might result in different pronunciations or affect the meaning are noted.[3] In a collation such as

129–31.] *so Bayne; as verse in Qq, lines ending* ordinarye, / Wil, / bloody?

the old spelling is that of Q1, with variant spellings in Q2 and in Q3 not cited since they do not affect meaning. The collations do record, however, a number of instances where Q3's modernizations may be of some historical interest. Moreover, following widespread custom in these matters and in deference to students of the history of printing, many omissions of words and other changes in Q3 have been recorded even though this later quarto has no claim whatever to separate authority. Further, a liberal sample of variants from the Southouse MS. has been included for obvious reasons; but from all later printed texts only those variants that deserve serious con-

[1] The present edition follows the customary spelling of the town; the *Arden* quarto follows its source in Holinshed in the spelling *Feversham*. Edward Jacob, in *The History of the Town and Port of Faversham in the County of Kent* (1744), p. 2, n., traces twelve different spellings but observes that Faversham is the one 'by which the corporation, as far as I can trace, denominated itself'.

[2] *Jelyouse* is Q1's spelling (*Ielious* in Q2) throughout the text, both in lines where it appears to have a trisyllabic pronunciation and in those which call for the customary dissyllabic. One cannot be sure that this spelling normally was pronounced trisyllabically since, as the *O.E.D.* confirms, it was a customary variant in prose and in other verse of the period where two syllables were called for; similarly, *jealous* appears in other contemporary texts where a trisyllabic pronunciation is indicated. This edition follows Q3's modernization as *jealous* throughout.

[3] Modernization of 'murther' to 'murder', or 'murthred' to 'murdered' has not been collated.

sideration have been provided. In all quotations from old-spelling texts, long 's' appears in its present form; and obvious misprints usually are not recorded. Standard abbreviations, such as *M.* for both *Master* and *Mistress*, have been lengthened without comment.

With modern spelling nothing is gained in retaining Q1's erratic and non-authorial punctuation. Light modern pointing is introduced throughout the text. Again, the textual notes record only those instances where changes in punctuation affect meaning. The practice of earlier editors has been followed in emending the lineation of the *Arden* quarto only where there is good reason to believe that prose rather than verse originally was intended or where the compositor (probably) divided a line of verse into two half lines or created one line out of a line and a half; the collation records such changes. *So* before an editor's name indicates that he was the first (but not necessarily the only one) to divide the text in that manner. *Conj.* refers to readings conjectured but not adopted by an editor. This edition retains Q1's stage directions, adding to them (in square brackets) only where the action may be clarified thereby.

For ease of reference, the practice of supplying marginal scene divisions to Q1's undivided text has been adopted. The act and scene divisions and locale designations by earlier editors obscure the fluid nature of Elizabethan staging. Actors performed on an outdoor stage with the very minimum of properties, and the action from beginning to end was continuous. Dialogue itself established the locale: the 'mist' sequence of scenes xi and xii, for instance, would be unfeasible otherwise on an open stage. Scenes i and xiv do not move from interior to exterior and back; the scene is where the character establishes himself. Elizabethan drama focuses on man, not on his environment.

2. SOURCES

Thomas Ardern, as his name is spelled in official accounts, appears to have been one of the 'new men' of the Renaissance, one whom we should describe today as being very much on the make. Apparently of a good family from Wye, about twelve miles south of Faversham in Kent, he served Sir Edward North in the Court of Augmentations created by King Henry VIII to arrange for the dispersal of church property after the dissolution of the monasteries in 1538. In time Ardern married Sir Edward's step-daughter, Alice Mirfyn,[1] and was commissioned thereafter the King's Controller of the Customs of the Port of Faversham by his father-in-law. Since Faversham, which is built on a navigable arm of the Swale, was the first major link since Dover between the main London–Canterbury highway and the sea, the post was inevitably lucrative. Having settled there, he soon acquired from Sir Thomas Cheyne, one of the more favoured recipients of monastic property, a portion of the Abbey lands and a house near the Abbey gate.[2] By the time of his death in 1551 he had been a jurat (similar to an alderman) of the town several times and its mayor in 1548, and he had acquired considerably more of the Abbey property; it could be said, in fact, that he had a stranglehold on the town.[3] If one account

[1] Who was also, of course, the half-sister of Sir Thomas North, the translator of Plutarch. Sir Edward was Chancellor of the Court of Augmentations and later, in 1564, became Baron North of Kirtling, a title passed on to his eldest son Roger.

[2] The Abbey (originally Cluniac, later Benedictine) was founded by King Stephen in 1147; he, Queen Matilda, and their eldest son were buried there. For Sir Thomas Cheyne, see ix. 94.1, n. In *The History and Antiquities of the Abbey and Church of Favresham in Kent* (1727), p. 22, John Lewis records that the Abbey property was granted to Sir Thomas in the thirty-first year of King Henry VIII's reign and that 'it was not long after, not quite five years, that the said Sir *Thomas Cheyney* sold all the Premises to *Thomas Ardern* Gent. of *Faversham*, as appears by his License of alienation, dated 16 *Decemb.* 36 *Henry* VIII [1545].'

[3] The Faversham Wardmote Book (fol. 58) records that on 22 December 1550 Ardern was 'hensfoorth to be utterlye disfranchised for euer' and nevermore to be jurat because he had 'gone aboute and labored by dyuers wayes and meanes to the vttermost of his po[r] [power] to infryndge and undo the said Franchises liberties and freedoms' which he, as a jurat, had sworn to uphold and maintain. Shortly after, however, he is listed among the jurats as if nothing had happened. His will, dated 20 December 1550 (Wardmote Book, fol. 281), left almost everything to his wife, his daughter Margaret, and his sister, in that order, except for some houses and lands, valued at forty shillings a year, which he gave to the corporation to provide for 'a sermon to be preached every year in commemoration of the several benefactors, and for the encouragement of others to go and do likewise, the residue to be expended in bread to be distributed to the poor' (from Jacob's *The History of the Town and Port of Faversham*, p. 135; the historian comments: 'This charity produced . . . a law suit, which seems to have been comprised between Mr. Ardern's daughter and heir, and the corporation, and the estates sold; nevertheless the anniversary sermon is

can be trusted, Ardern was fifty-six years old when he settled in Faversham, his wife twenty-eight, 'and had had familiarities with *Mosbie* before she was married, which made her friends desirous of marrying her with *Arden*'.[1]

The *Breviat Chronicle* for the year 1551 records very shortly after it occurred an event which was to be remembered for many years:

> This yeare on .S. Valentines / daye at feuersham in Kent was co- / mytted a shamefull mourther for / one Arden a gentilman was by the / consente of hys wyfe mourthered / wherfor she was brent at Canter- / bury, and there was one hanged in / Chaynes for that mourther, and at / Feuersham was ii. hanged in chay / nes, and a woman brente, and in / smithfelde was hanged one Mos- / by and his syster for the same mu[r-] / ther also.[2]

In his private diary for 14 March 1551 Henry Machyn, a London merchant-taylor, recorded the execution of Mosby and his sister in Smithfield, as well as the sentences of the other accomplices in 'the death of a gentyll man of Feyversham, one M. Arden the custemer' (i.e., the controller of customs).[3] The 'horribleness' of that provincial domestic crime had compelling interest even for that great chronicler of the deeds of the high and mighty, Raphael Holinshed, who somewhat apologetically interrupted the survey of King Edward VI's reign in his *Chronicles of England, Scotland, and*

---

still continued to be preached upon Mid-lent Sunday, and the bread distributed to the poor, agreeable to his well intended charity, at the expense of the corporation'; by mid-nineteenth century both payments and sermons had stopped).

[1] From manuscript notes, apparently by a Mr Burton, found in a lumber-room at the Dolphin Inn in Faversham, and recorded in *The Monthly Journal of the Faversham Institute* (August, 1881). The writing seems to be in an eighteenth-century hand, and the writer claims to have travelled throughout Kent and the Isle of Sheppey to gather information from the 'a:ncientest people' about the principals involved in the Arden story. To what extent the oral tradition can be trusted it is not possible to determine; the play itself may have guided it.

[2] Quoted from a copy in the British Museum by G. H. Blayney, '*Arden of Feversham*—An Early Reference', *N. & Q.*, CC (1955), 336.

[3] *The Diary of Henry Machyn, Citizen and Merchant-Taylor of London from A.D. 1550 to A.D. 1563*, ed. J. G. Nichols for the Camden Society (1848), p. 4.

Ireland (London, 1577; second edition, 1587) to 'set . . . foorth somewhat at large' what 'otherwise . . . may seeme to be but a priuate matter, and therefore as it were impertinent to this historie'. John Stow devoted a paragraph to it in his *Annals of England* (London, 1592; 1631); Thomas Heywood, the poet-dramatist, made note of it in his *Troia Britanica* (London, 1609, p. 462); John Taylor, the water poet, observed in *The Unnaturall Father* (*Works* [London, 1630], p. 140) that people were still talking about it and would never forget it; and in 1633, the year that saw publication of the third quarto of the play, a ballad of Mistress Arden's 'complaint and lamentation' could be purchased and sung to the popular Elizabethan tune of *Fortune my Foe*.[1] One judges just from these extant references that the circumstances surrounding the murder of Faversham's wealthiest and most prominent citizen must have inspired numerous pamphlets, broadsides, and sermons now completely lost to us.

The Wardmote Book of Faversham contains the official account of what actually took place in the victim's parlour at about seven o'clock on the evening of Sunday, 15 February 1551, as well as the sentences meted out to the murderers and their accomplices afterwards.[2] Holinshed, whose long and detailed narrative clearly has furnished the playwright with his plot (and even, at times, some of his wording), seems not to have consulted or known about it; but he claims at the outset to 'hauing the instructions deliuered to me by them, that haue vsed some diligence to gather the true vnderstanding of the circumstances'. The chronicler's narrative covers, of course, a wider perspective than the town records; but where it differs in corresponding details the play always agrees with the former. Thus, in the small matter of names, both the chronicle and the play have *Arden* (instead of *Ardern*), *Mosby* (instead of *Morsby*), and *Shakebag* (instead of *Loosebag*); both provide no Christian names for Arden (Thomas), Mosby (Thomas), and Bradshaw (George), and no surname for Michael (Saunderson). Where the

---

[1] See Appendix IV, where the ballad is reprinted as a curiosity since, it is apparent, it is entirely dependent on one of the earlier editions of the play.

[2] See Appendix III for the complete account.

play differs in this respect from the chronicle, it also differs from the Wardmote Book: the latter refers to the painter as William Blackborne, who is simply 'the painter' in the chronicle and 'Clarke' in the play (although one stage direction reads: 'Enter the painter'); similarly, John Greene of the town records becomes simply Greene in the chronicle and Dick Greene in the play. The epilogue to *Arden* observes, as does Holinshed, that Black Will was burned on a 'stage' (or 'scaffold' in the chronicle) in Flushing whereas in the official account he disappears 'so that he could not iustly be herd of syns that tyme'; and, although both Holinshed and the Wardmote Book tell of the later capture of Greene, the play follows the former in observing that he was hanged at 'Osbridge' (Ospringe).[1] In the play, as in the chronicle, Greene and Bradshaw first encounter Black Will by chance on their way to Gravesend; the Wardmote Book records that he was sent for from Calais. Holinshed and the playwright also view Bradshaw as an innocent victim of circumstances whereas the Faversham records directly implicate him in the crime.

Following Holinshed, however, has not confined the playwright by any means; for he freely compresses and expands his source to meet the demands of dramatic presentation and otherwise changes it to fit the requirements of Elizabethan staging practice and the limitations of a typical acting company. Besides changing in a major and original way the characterization of the three leading figures,[2] he combines, for example, Mosby's sister and Alice's maid (Cicely Pounder and Elizabeth ['Elsabeth'] Stafford, respectively, in the Wardmote Book; they are not named in Holinshed) into the one character of Susan and makes her the centre of a sub-plot that roughly parodies the main plot at the same time that it brings into bolder relief the 'horribleness' of Alice's and Mosby's crime; he omits the characters of Arden's daughter, who plays no actual part in the murder,[3] and of the grocers Prune and Cole who, 'before the murder was committed, were bidden to supper', and replaces them

---

[1] See Epilogue, 1 ff., n.   [2] See below, pp. lxviii–lxxiii.

[3] But missing, possibly, a genuinely melodramatic effect; for Holinshed writes that, after Arden's murder, 'mistres Arden caused hir daughter to plaie on the virginals, and they dansed, and she with them, and so seemed to protract time as it were.'

with characters who already have been introduced.[1] On the other
hand, he enlarges considerably the role of Shakebag as a foil in
villainy to Black Will (who alone carries most of the burden for
executing the murder in both Holinshed and the Wardmote Book),
and creates on his own the significant role of Franklin as a kind of
moral spokesman for the play and as the one sympathetic friend to
whom Arden can confide his innermost feelings. He also creates the
characters of the apprentice and of the ferryman to relieve the
intensity of the main plot and to add by their presence realistic
local colouring. Scene xiii, in particular, reveals incisively how
from a hint in the chronicle the playwright creates theatre: Holinshed's mere statement that Arden's body lay buried in the same
plot of ground that he had wrested from the Widow Cook, now re-
married to Dick Reede the mariner, and for which she had cursed
him unsparingly turns into Arden's tense encounter with Reede at a
climactic moment in the play just before the murder scene.

The Arden narrative is precisely the same in both the first and
second editions of Holinshed except for the usual printing-house
sophistications in spelling and punctuation; but the possibility that
the later edition of 1587 might have inspired the playwright more
directly has been overlooked. What leads to this conjecture is the
appearance of marginal glosses not to be found in the earlier edition
of 1577 which are revealing for the moral stress that they place on
passages where Holinshed's tone is essentially dispassionate and
for the way that they highlight dramatic possibilities inherent in the
narrative.[2] For example, where Holinshed merely relates that
Alice, after a quarrel with Mosby, 'being desirous to be in fauour
with him againe, sent him a paire of siluer dice... After which he
resorted to hir againe', the glosses read: 'Loue and lust' and 'A
paire of siluer dice worke much mischiefe'. Before their sentencing

---

[1] The presence of the innocent Bradshaw among the dinner guests in
scene xiv serves to reintroduce him just before his sentencing as an accom-
plice and thus to heighten the sense of his victimization.

[2] For this reason Appendix II transcribes the account of Arden's murder
from the second edition. Except for one reference to Mistress Arden as a
'wicked woman' and another to Black Will as 'a terrible cruell ruffian' and
for a couple of allusions to the 'horribleness' of the murder at the beginning
and the end of his narrative, the chronicler's tone is basically neutral or
objective.

in scene xviii of the play, Mosby calls Alice a 'strumpet'; there is
no dialogue at this point in the chronicle (Holinshed simply lists the
sentences), but an earlier gloss reads: 'O importunate & bloodie
minded strumpet!' A gloss describes Bradshaw as 'Simplicitie
abused', and another later characterizes his unjust sentence: 'Innocencie no barre against execution'. The chronicle describes Black
Will as a 'terrible cruell ruffian', but the marginal comment more
clearly describes the Black Will of the play: 'Blacke Will maketh no
conscience of bloudshed and murther'. Greene and Bradshaw's
chance encounter with the two murderers (scene ii of the play)
evokes a strong commentary: 'Marke how the diuell will not let his
organs or instruments let slip either occasio[n] or opportunitie to
commit most heinous wickednesse'; and Arden's imprint on the
same ground that he had wrested from the widow Reede and where
he was buried becomes, to the glossarist, an 'example' that 'God
heareth the teares of the oppressed and taketh vengeance'. The
most telling gloss of all, however, relates to the pusillanimous servant Michael: 'Note here the force of feare and a troubled conscience'. Holinshed in several places points out Michael's fear of
Black Will (which is the reason that he locks the doors and thereby
prevents one attempt on Arden's life), but the chronicler never
endows him with even a suggestion of the 'troubled conscience'
that becomes one of the 'conflicting' claims with fear in Michael's
impressive soliloquy of scene iv.

Although postulating other sources is unnecessary, for whatever
appears in the play that cannot be found in the chronicle is not
beyond the limits of the playwright's capacity for invention, the
slim possibility exists that what may have been 'the instructions
deliuered' to Holinshed were also available to him. Holinshed, it is
known, had acquired much manuscript material from his pub-
lisher, Reginald Wolf, that the noted antiquary Leland originally
had collected. After Holinshed died in 1580, much of this material
came into the possession of the chronicler John Stow, who, along
with others, was one of the editors of the 1587 edition of the
Chronicles.[1] Among Stow's papers in the British Museum is a manu-

---

[1] Holinshed, to be accurate, was the leading editor of a group of editors
who compiled the 1577 edition, just as Abraham Fleming was of the 1587

script (Harley MSS. 542, ff. 34–37B) entitled: 'The history of a most horible murder comytyd at ffevershame in Kent'—almost identical in wording and in organization with the Holinshed narrative; comparison with the published version reveals only what a fine editor Holinshed was. The manuscript is somewhat repetitious, particularly at the end, which it repeats twice; and it begins with an amusing, though irrelevant, anecdote about Arden's aged mother in Norwich whose habit of going abegging shamed even her rapacious son, who 'assayde all meanes posseble to Kepe hir from it, whiche wowld not be'. But from this point on the two narratives are similar.[1] In some minor details, however, it bears some interesting comparisons with the play:

(1) Both Holinshed and the manuscript make the point that Arden would not fight with Mosby no matter how greatly he had been provoked. In scene xiii of the play, however, Arden at last becomes enraged enough to fight after Mosby calls him (l. 82) a 'hornèd beast' (i.e., a cuckold). Only the manuscript contains this information: 'for he [Mosby] had piked a qwarrell w^t hym [Arden] rydynge to or from london & callynge hym Knave, vyllane & cokeolde'.

(2) Holinshed mentions, of course, the footsteps in the snow that led to the detection of Arden's body; but with xiv. 355–60 only the manuscript offers a close comparison: 'In ye meane tyme there fell a great snowe in so muche y^t they comynge in a gayne into ye howse thowght that ye snow woulde have coveryd theyr fotynge (but sodeynly by ye good provydence of god, who wuld not suffar so

---

edition; convenience and tradition have dictated the rather misleading reference to the one editor.
[1] The manuscript is occasionally clearer on a point than the published version. Holinshed edits out the interesting detail—probably for political reasons—that Arden's wife was 'the lord northes wyves dowghtar' although he retains the fact that Mosby was his servant (in the manuscript: 'one of the chefeste gentlemen about ye lord northe'). The manuscript is also more explicit as to why Arden tolerates his wife's infidelity with Mosby, even permitting the latter to sleep in the house: Arden 'was yet so greatly gyven to seek his advauntage, and caryd so litle how he came by it that in hope of atteynynge some benefits of the lord northe by meanes of this mosby who could do muche w^t hym, he winked at that shamefull dysordor'; Holinshed says simply that Arden did not want to offend Alice's 'freends' (i.e., relatives).

detestable a murther longe hydden) it stint snowynge / they not consyderynge ye same, but thinkynge all had bene sure.'

(3) Less significantly, Holinshed observes that Reede's wife wished 'many a vengeance to light vpon' Arden; the manuscript has 'vengeaunce & plage', both of which words are echoed in Dick Reede's curse (xiii. 31, 49).

A curious omission from the manuscript and from the play is the statement in Holinshed that Alice and Mosby 'both receiued the sacrament on a sundaie at London, openlie in a church there', even before the murder of Arden. In the play, however, Arden does refer to Mosby's wearing the ring that he had given her (i. 17–18); and on two occasions Mosby, with Alice concurring, refers to himself as her 'husband' (i. 638; xiv. 271).

Whether the dramatist relied on a source for his knowledge of Shakebag's fate is unknown.[1] Holinshed reports that after the murder of Arden he fled and was 'neuer heard of', and the Wardmote Book mentions only that 'George losebagg escaped at that tyme'. His place in Franklin's epilogue to the play must just be a device to finish off a character whose role had been greatly expanded from that in the source.

Finally, the Earl of Sussex's Men performed a play at court in 1579 called *Murderous Michael*. The work is no longer extant, but E. K. Chambers and others have thought that *Arden* might possibly be a recasting of it.[2] E. H. C. Oliphant, however, is surely right in claiming that 'the suggestion does not seem very plausible' since 'Michael is far from being either the most important or the most murderous character in the drama'.[3]

3. DATE

Assigning a date for the composition of *Arden of Faversham* involves trying to bridge the gap between the publication of the

[1] See scene xv and Epilogue, ll. 2–5. The 1633 ballad also mentions his fate, but it is dependent upon the play for this information.
[2] E. K. Chambers, *The Elizabethan Stage* (1923), IV. 4, 96. See also the recently published *The English Drama 1485–1585* by F. P. Wilson (1969), p. 146.
[3] 'Problems of Authorship in Elizabethan Dramatic Literature', *M.P.*, VIII (1911), 420.

first edition of Holinshed's *Chronicles of England, Scotland, and Ireland*, its presumed source, in 1577, and Edward White's entry of the play in the Stationers' Register on 3 April 1592. There is a distinct possibility, as we saw, that the playwright may have worked from the 1587 edition of Holinshed. The marginal glosses to the Arden story in this later edition do not furnish, of course, conclusive evidence for setting an upward limit in dating; but they are dramatically suggestive in a way that the Holinshed narrative by itself is not and do illuminate certain aspects of the play. With the possibility, then, of a 1587 date should be coupled the suggestion of M. P. Jackson that Arden's 'unusual expression "play the man in the moon" [xi. 27–8] may (as well as being bawdy) glance at John Lyly's "Endimion, the Man in the Moone. Playd before the Queenes Maiestie at Greenewich on Candelmas day at night, by the Chyldren of Paules", as the title-page of the first edition (1591) has it'.[1] The only 'Candelmas day at night' on which Paul's Boys could have performed at Court was, as E. K. Chambers has discovered, on 2 February 1588.[2] A. F. Hopkinson noted in his 1907 edition of *Arden* that 'the Euphuism of the whole scene . . . seems to me distinctly . . . under the influence of Lyly,' and verbal parallels have been pointed out, in fact, between the two plays.[3]

A customary lapse in time between a play's first production and its publication might suggest a date earlier than 1592; but to attempt to date *Arden* more precisely, especially within the limits of 1587 or 1588 and 1591 or 1592, on the basis of parallel passages or 'inter-play borrowings'—most of them commonplace and from bad texts that have been doubtfully dated themselves—is impossible. The relationship of *Arden*, for example, to *Soliman and Perseda* (entered in the Stationers' Register on 20 November 1592; the earliest extant text printed in 1599) or to Shakespeare's *Henry VI*

---

[1] Jackson, p. 77; see also L. Cust, '*Arden of Feversham*', *Archaeologica Cantiana*, XXXIV (1920), 121.

[2] *The Elizabethan Stage*, III. 415. See also J. W. Bennett, 'Oxford and *Endimion*', *P.M.L.A.*, LVII (1942), 363–4, who dates the play 1587 or earlier, but 'no earlier than mid-1586'.

[3] By Jackson, in scene xi as well as a possible parallel at i. 98; see also what he observes is 'one of the very few classical similes in *Arden*'—the allusion to Endymion and Diana at xiv. 149–53.

trilogy is certainly not clear; in both cases parallels of varying quality are extensive (see Appendix I). A recent editor of the former 'would conjecturally date the play 1587, a date which does not, however, exclude the possibility of later revision', possibly in 1591.[1] A. S. Cairncross, the editor of the Arden Series texts, dates the trilogy in 1590–1; but the parallelisms in *Arden* have greater relevance to the corrupted texts of those plays (*The Contention* and *The True Tragedy of Richard Duke of York*, printed in 1594 and 1595 respectively)—which may argue possibly for an earlier date for *Arden* if the reporters of these 'bad quartos' are recollecting it in their reconstructions. On the other hand, just as scene xi of *Arden* seems to parody *Endymion*, so Michael's letter at the beginning of scene iii seems to parody Lyly's *The Woman in the Moon* (entered on 22 September 1595 in the Stationers' Register, printed in 1597), which has been dated 1591–3;[2] if we could be sure of this dating, a later date would have to be inferred for *Arden*. As it is, a half-confident assertion in limiting *Arden* to 1588–91 is probably warranted in the light of present knowledge; assignment of a definite year, even conjecturally, would be rash. Assessing parallelisms only demonstrates the affinity of *Arden*'s text to the plays of this period; it establishes no precise dates, even where priorities among parallels seem likely.

4. STAGE HISTORY

From its Epilogue it is evident that *Arden of Faversham* was intended to be acted before a live audience, but no record exists of an actual performance before the eighteenth century. There are several indications, however, that the play enjoyed an active stage history before its publication in 1592 and continuously thereafter. Foremost among these is, of course, the evidence itself of a memorially reported text; and the 'inter-play borrowings' or parallelisms with known Pembroke plays at least associates *Arden* with that group of actors who organized themselves at one point

[1] '*The Tragedye of Solyman and Perseda*', ed. J. J. Murray, unpubl. New York Univ. diss. (1959), p. xvi.

[2] By R. W. Bond, ed., *The Complete Works of John Lyly* (1902), III. 234. Chambers, *The Elizabethan Stage*, III. 416–17, dates the play 1590< >5 (?).

under the aegis of the Earl of Pembroke.[1] Furthermore, Edward White's strange entry of 'the tragedie of Arden of Feuersham & blackwill' in the Stationers' Register on 3 April 1592 attests to the popularity of the important but secondary role of the braggart comic villain, as does the introduction later of Black Will's name into a passage in *The True Tragedy of Richard the Third* (a 'bad quarto', registered and printed in 1594, and suffering severe memorial contamination) for no reason, apparently, other than to recall this popular figure.[2] Samuel Rowley's *When You See Me, You Know Me* (registered and printed in 1605) has as one of its villainous characters a Black Will. In fact, as more recent stage history will show, Black Will often is the most popular character with the audience—to the detriment of the rest of the production. Finally, the successive publications of the play in 1599 and again in 1633, along with the ballad of Mistress Arden's 'complaint and lamentation', based on the play, in that same year, testify to a continuing early interest in *Arden*.[3]

[1] See p. xxv, n. 4, above, and Jackson, p. 79. Chambers, *The Elizabethan Stage*, II. 128 (and ff.) records 'an isolated record of a Pembroke's company at Canterbury in 1575–6'. In 1592–3 a company by that name made appearances at Court and in the provinces but soon fell on bad times, even being forced to sell its apparel. A Pembroke company reappears in London and in the provinces from 1597 to 1600. In 1594 and 1595 four plays bearing the Pembroke name were published: *Edward II, Titus Andronicus* (in association with Derby's and Sussex's Men), *The Taming of a Shrew*, and *The True Tragedy of Richard Duke of York*. A. S. Cairncross, in 'Pembroke's Men and Some Shakespearian Piracies', *Sh.Q.*, XI (1960), 349, judges that 'it is . . . likely that Pembroke's, under whatever name or with whatever organization, existed before 1592, probably as early as 1589, and that it was then Shakespeare's company, as it was, for a time at least, Kyd's and Marlowe's.'

[2] 'I warrant you sir, they [the two hired murderers] are such pittilesse villaines, that all London cannot match them for their villainie, one of their names is Will Sluter, yet the most part calles him blacke Will, the other is Iack Denten, two murtherous villaines that are resolute' (ed. W. W. Greg for the Malone Society, 1929, ll. 1213–17). As Jackson points out (p. 74), 'Sluter . . . is not elsewhere referred to as "Black Will" ' and 'The braggadocio of Will in *The True Tragedy of Richard III* is very similar to that of Will in *Arden* and there are even verbal parallels.' F. G. Fleay, who first called attention to this passage in *A Biographical Chronicle of the English Drama 1559–1642* (1871), II. 28–9, dated the play in 1585–6 and associated it with the Queen's Men on grounds that have since been disputed; he dated *Arden* as earlier in 1585.

[3] See comment of John Taylor, the water poet, p. xxxviii above.

From the late fifteen-eighties on into the nineties, London companies frequently toured the southern provinces, with stopovers at
Faversham; and it would be surprising if they did not take *Arden*
on tour with them when it came into the repertoire, especially since
it very early seems to have become Faversham's (and the local
area's) own 'passion play'.[1] One writer has even suggested that the
business of Jack Fitten and the stolen plate in scene ii (and maybe
the allusion to 'Jack of Faversham' at ix. 26) may have been introduced as a topical reference 'which could only be of interest to the
natives of the county'.[2] Be that as it may, certainly by the early
eighteenth century a tradition had been established. The antiquarian John Lewis observed in 1727 that the memory of Arden's
murder 'is still preserved by the Inhabitants in their acting this in-
humane Tragedy on the Stage';[3] and Jacob, as we noted before,
lamented in the Preface to his 1770 edition the way the Faversham
'Inhabitants have till of late, at a few Years interval, doubly murdered it, by the excessive bad Manuscript Copies they used, and
their more injudicious acting'. One such manuscript, the Southouse
text (dated 1716) is probably a transcript, as Nosworthy has demonstrated, of a 'prompt copy used by provincial or local players'
around 1650.[4]

References abound throughout the eighteenth century to productions in Kent of 'the ever popular *Arden*', the first on record
being an amateur performance at 'the Roe-buck joining the Place'
at Faversham on 2 January 1730.[5] It is impossible to tell whether
some of these are the original version, a local adaptation, the version
adapted by Mrs Heywood for the Little Theatre on the Haymarket
and performed there in January 1736, puppet versions,[6] or, after

---

[1] Even down to recent times: the reviewer of a professional London production for *The Times* (29 September 1954) notes that the play 'was produced at Faversham two years ago by amateurs'. For the early touring
companies, see J. T. Murray, *English Dramatic Companies 1558–1642*
(1910), 2 vols., *passim*.

[2] Cust, p. 119.   [3] Lewis, p. 26.   [4] See pp. xxiii–xxiv above.

[5] Sybil Rosenfeld, *Strolling Players and Drama in the Provinces 1660–
1765* (1939), p. 219.

[6] Rosenfeld records an announcement from a 1736 Faversham newspaper 'that Mr Henry Collyer with his Puppet Show has acted ARDIN for
several Nights with great Applause being perform'd after a curious

1759, the Lillo-Hoadly version. As Sybil Rosenfeld observes, 'Local interest in the Arden story caused it to be acted with great success in many forms during the period.'[1] In 1799 Sadler's Wells transformed *Arden* into a ballet.[2]

The Arden story had a natural attraction for George Lillo, the author of the most famous domestic tragedy of its day, *The London Merchant; or, The History of George Barnwell* (1731). He did not live to complete his version, but Dr John Hoadly undertook the task; and on 12 July 1759 a single performance took place at Drury Lane with a cast that included Havard as Arden, Bransby as Mosby, Scrase as Franklin, Wignell as Michael, Packer as Green (*sic*), Phillips as Black Will, Vaughan as George Shakebag, Miss Barton as Maria (Susan of the original version), and 'a young Gentlewoman' as Alicia. The stage historian Genest refers to the Lillo-Hoadly version as 'only an alteration of an old play of the same name',[3] but it was altered almost beyond recognition. Comparison of the Prologue written for the performance with its appeal 'not to the head, but to the heart' and to 'The melting tear'[4] with the steadfast appeal to 'simple truth' in Franklin's Epilogue in the original reveals the measure of distance between the two versions. Most notably missing is the complexity of characterization: Mosby is totally the driving force behind the crime whereas Alicia repents early in the play and is thereafter a mere passive victim forced to watch the plot proceed. Lillo's mediocre verse likewise lacks the power of the original (however imperfectly that may be conveyed in Q's corrupt text).

In 1765 a local Kent company advertised a production of *Arden* 'as originally written' 'in opposition to the Chatham Company— who advertised Lillo's version'.[5] But it was this latter version that

---

manner. . .' (pp. 226–7); in 1742 'another company exhibiting German puppets toured Kent, playing *Arden*' (p. 237).

[1] P. 219.

[2] A. Nicoll, *A History of English Drama 1660–1900*, vol. III: *Late Eighteenth Century Drama 1750–1800*, 3rd ed. (1952), p. 319.

[3] John Genest, *Some Account of the English Stage from the Restoration in 1660 to 1830* (1832), IV, 553.

[4] Quoted from *The Works of Mr. George Lillo* (1775), II, 223. The original acting cast is cited from this edition.

[5] Rosenfeld, p. 264.

was reprinted frequently from 1762 down through the nineteenth
century, just as it was this version—reduced to three acts—that
was staged for a benefit performance for Mr Holman at Covent
Garden on 14 April 1790. The new prologue written especially for
that occasion promised 'Tonight a story of domestic woe' that
'Shall cause the tear of sympathy to flow'. The *European Magazine*
of April 1790 noted that the play 'was well performed by Mr.
Holman, Mr. Hartley, and Mrs. Pope, who represented Arden,
Mosby, and Mrs. Arden'.

The success of this production is verified by a torn, undated, and
fragmentary handbill in the Harvard Theatre Collection announ-
cing a benefit for Mr Keys to be performed 'for Rochester, Chatham,
Strood, and the Vicinity'. Claiming to be using the manuscript of
Mr Holman's benefit 'five seasons before', it also observes that the
play was performed at that time 'five successive nights after, before
the first nobility and persons of fashion in the kingdom, with the
most unbounded applause'. Its description of the impression that
the new Alicia was making upon her audience is worth quoting:
'[She] displays great feeling for his approaching fate, and en-
deavours to frustrate the designs of his murderers, and though, in
many instances, she was culpable, yet in viewing this sad scene,
every human breast must feel for her situation, and drop a tear at
her untimely fate. In short, the whole piece forms such a scene of
domestic distress, as is scarcely to be equalled in the annals of the
British Drama'.

The handbill also notes that since 'that plaintive and excellent
author', Lillo, the play 'has undergone several alterations to make
it a favorite representation for the London Stage'. Apparently it
was, but by 1852 the reviewer for *The Athenaeum* of 2 October pre-
dicted after seeing the 'revival' of 'Lillo's "Arden of Faversham"'
at Sadler's Wells on 24 and 25 September that 'this unfortunate
play has now probably had its last trial; as notwithstanding that on
this occasion it was efficiently acted, it yet proved powerless to
excite the least manifestation of feeling on the part of the audience.'
Aside from 'first-rate' characterizations of Black Will and Shakebag
and the perfection of the 'mechanical arrangement' (the building
up of suspense), he found that 'the mediocrity of Lillo's genius in

D

the delineation of character, in the expression of sentiment, and in poetic diction, could not enable him to lift up either his theme or his persons to the proper dramatic elevation, which nevertheless the artificial style of the dialogue perpetually suggested.'

Faversham, however, was not yet prepared to give 'this unfortunate play . . . its last trial'. Bullen concluded the introduction to his 1887 edition of the original version by observing:

> In recent years the play has been frequently acted, doubtless in Lillo's wretched version, at the Faversham Theatre. But wretched as is Lillo's recast of the old play, it produced on one occasion, according to Campbell, so magnetic an effect of terror on the audience that the representation had actually to be suspended. To see the noble tragedy acted in its integrity, with all its wealth of passion and poetry, would indeed be a rare and high delight.[1]

It would be some time, however, before Bullen's passionate plea was heard anywhere (and then never fully implemented); in the meantime, even worse was to come in William Poel's 'abridgement' (if it could be called that), *Lilies that Fester*.[2] Produced for the Elizabethan Stage Society at St George's Hall, Langham Place, London, on 9 July 1897, on a double bill that included another 'abridged' play from the Shakespeare Apocrypha, *Edward III*, the principals were D. L. Mannering as Arden, Leonard Outram as Mosby, and Miss Alice Isaac as Alice. The reviews were universally —and, apparently, deservedly—negative, William Archer complaining that 'they had quite literally made a hash of it, or rather a mash, a senseless stirabout', that 'the stage-management was utterly hopeless', and that only Arthur Broughton as Black Will showed 'any real talent'.[3] The play must have been impossible to follow; for it began with scene vii, was cut ruthlessly, and almost all exposition was omitted. Clarke was turned into a fop who believed that Alice was in love with him; Dick Reede, the ferryman, and the

---

[1] P. xix. See also the note on the Faversham Theatre (which 'originally stood where the entrance gates to the Railway Station are now placed') in *An Essay on the Tragedy of 'Arden of Feversham'* by C. E. Donne (1873), p. 18.

[2] Published by Bullen in 'The Playhouse Series' (1906).

[3] In *The Theatrical 'World' of 1897* (1898), p. 228.

apprentice were omitted; and Bradshaw's role became merely that
of a dinner guest. The reviewer for *The Morning Post* (10 July 1897)
complained of the 'unhappy tradition of the Society to drawl or
deliver slowly all their sentences and words, even in passages that
ought to be full of fire'.[1]

An anonymous all-male cast of the Marlowe Dramatic Society at
last attempted to stage the original version seriously (in five acts and
nineteen scenes) at Cambridge on 3 August 1921. Sydney W.
Carroll, the *Sunday Times*' critic of 7 August, found that the production 'seemed to be stressed just a little too much upon its comic
side . . . but in the scene of the actual murder the comedy element
was suitably restrained, with a really thrilling result'. A report from
a correspondent to *The Times* of 5 August affirms that the role of
Alice Arden was 'convincingly played by an undergraduate'.

On 7 and 18 December 1923 an unnamed group of players from
the Literary Society of Birkbeck College of the University of London produced *Arden* in five acts at the College theatre. One reviewer
objected to the Heywood interlude and the use of 'too much Elizabethan music' but found the whole affair 'a good deal more satisfy-
ing than the empty thrills of many a modern "crook-play" ' and
that 'it points its moral with a naturalistic force that good acting can
still convey.' This time Shakebag was singled out as a particularly
good ruffian.[2]

Trying to make amends for his earlier production, Poel staged
'a more or less complete version' at the Scala (West) for the
Renaissance Theatre on 6 and 7 December 1925. Ernest Milton as
Arden led 'a much stronger cast' this time, including D. L.
Mannering as Mosby, D. A. Clarke-Smith as Franklin, Geoffrey
Wilkinson as Michael, G. Melville Cooper as Black Will, Percy
Walsh as Shakebag, and Miriam Lewes as Alice.[3] The reviewer for

---

[1] Quoted from R. Speaight, *William Poel and the Elizabethan Revival*,
(1954), p. 122.

[2] From a review by 'S.R.L.' (undated and unassigned) in the Harvard
Theatre Collection; almost certainly, however, by S. R. Littlewood (about
whom, see *Who's Who* for 1947). For dates of production, see H. Child,
'Revivals of English Dramatic Works, 1901–1918, 1926', *R.E.S.*, III (1927),
175.

[3] Speaight, p. 122.

The Sunday Times of 13 December found, however, that Poel was
'not too well served by his actors, many of whom were insuffi-
ciently audible'; and he also objected to the treatment of the play
'as a roaring farce'.[1] The setting, which was influenced by the
theories of W. J. Lawrence's *The Elizabethan Playhouse* (1912–13),
consisted, as the programme pointed out, of 'three stationary
localities on the stage': 'Arden's parlour; the High Road near
Rainham Down; a street in London with an entrance to Franklyn's
House'. Milton later recalled, in his *Stratford Dossier*, how well the
setting worked: 'There was a constant lapping over of times and
places which provided continual movement and excitement, without slurring or distraction or overbrusqueness.' His commentary
on the way that Poel wanted him to play Arden is also interesting:
'He had the strange idea of putting the weak, sad, doomed, un-
popular Thomas Arden into pink tights, and it had the strange
effect of showing perhaps what the man, Arden, might have been,
as of some hidden frivolity in his nature, or some exquisite sup-
pressed libido.'[2]

A version much influenced by the mysticism of H.-R. Lenor-
mand, who, as the programme claimed, 'reconstituted' *Arden*
'around its original uneven beauties', was produced by Gaston
Baty on 9 October 1938, at the Théâtre Montparnasse, with
Georges Vitray as Arden, Lucien Nat as Mosby, and Marguerite
Jamois as Alice. The play was now divided into a Prologue (by 'le
Poète') and ten *tableaux*, one of a St Valentine's Fair with *commedia
dell'Arte* characters ('le charlatan', 'un saltambique', 'la patiente').
The reviewer for *Le Feuilleton du Temps* of 24 October found that
the latter at least relieved the boredom that he felt from watching
the repeated attempts on Arden's life.[3]

'A most intelligent recent production', wrote Raymond Chapman, who particularly admired the social implications of Joan
Littlewood's Theatre Workshop Company production of *Arden* at

[1] *The Boston Transcript* of 8 January 1926 headlined its delayed review:
'Murder-Mystery Play of Elizabethan Days Acted in London—What Was
Tragic Is Now Comic'.
[2] Quoted in Speaight, p. 123.
[3] A. Mantaigne's judgement in *Le Mois*, VIII (1938), 228, was that
'l'interprétation du Théâtre Montparnasse est médiocre'.

the Theatre Royal, Stratford-atte-Bowe, in September of 1954.[1]
Her version was shortened, however, at the end so that the play
unfortunately concluded with the arrest rather than with the
repentance of Alice. As Kenneth Tynan observed, a 'false
economy' marred the production. George Cooper followed the
natural tendency to overact the role of Black Will; but, in Tynan's
words, 'the rampant *Bovarysme* of Barbara Brown's Alice could
hardly be bettered, and Harry Corbett plays Mosbie with a dark,
cringing bravura'.[2] *The Times*' reviewer of 29 September, while
objecting to the single setting of the London scenes 'which does not
sufficiently suggest the alternation of interior and exterior scenes',
found the Faversham scenes, 'set on a gloomy stage dominated by
a triangle of huge black trees without branch or leaf, an effective
symbol of the tragic triangle of the tragedy'. During the following
May the production was transported to the Paris drama festival
where, *The Times* reported (25 May 1955), it became 'a popular
success'.[3]

Since then England has witnessed a fair number of amateur and
professional presentations. One of the more successful appears to
have been the Collyer's College, Horsham, production, whose
director, J. Hanratty, has written so sensitively on the problems of
producing *Arden* that future directors would do well to consult his
article.[4] As for the Black Will and Shakebag roles, which so frequently engulf a production, he observes that 'played in the right
spirit', the murderers can produce a very subtle O'Caseyish combination of comedy and cruel desperation.'

This sympathetic understanding of the proper perspective of
comic and tragic elements in the play did not characterize William
Gaskill's production for the Arts Theatre, Cambridge, 20–5 November 1961. *The Times*' reviewer of 21 November acutely observed

[1] See Chapman's '*Arden of Feversham*: Its Interest Today', *English*, XI
(1956), 15–17.
[2] From a review in *The Observer*, reprinted in *Curtains* (1961), pp. 81–3.
[3] The review also points out that '*Arden of Faversham* was already
familiar to French audiences, having been given here in French in recent
years'; in the introduction to their translation (p. 75), Brunius and Bellon
record that selections translated by André Gide were given by Jean
Marchat and Marcel Herrand in 1937.
[4] '*Arden of Feversham*', *The Use of English*, XI (1960), 176–80.

that here 'the easy road is taken of treating Black Will, the hired
killer, as a comic figure all through' and thus forestalling 'unwanted
laughs at the price of reducing suspense to nothing'. Similarly, by
stripping Michael, Arden's servant, of any importance whatsoever,
Gaskill's version made 'it difficult to take the murder seriously'.
The reviewer also objected to the 'weakening of the social background' but reserved highest praise for Susan Engel's Alice, who
'demonstrates even in the crude incident when Arden is served a
breakfast of poison soup' (i. 360 ff.) 'what could be done with the
play': 'It brings no laugh because her sense of urgency infects the
audience.'

The Tavistock Repertory Company performed *Arden* seven
times from 19 to 27 October 1961, and Raymond Raikes produced
the play for the B.B.C. Home Programme on 29 January 1962. Of
the former, M. P. Jackson has written that its 'realism was carried
to inordinate lengths in the simulation of the fog on Rainham
Down', so that 'Arden's line, "I am almost stifled with this fog"
[xi. 31] might have been spoken by any member of the audience'.
The latter presentation he found 'suffered from unintelligent cut-
ting and reorganization, and from pointless insertions which even
the adaptation to a new medium did not excuse'.[1] Jackson modestly
refrains from commenting on the serious production which claims
his loyalty: the outdoor presentation at Oxford in June 1961, by the
Merton College Drama Society; but he does record the 'burlesque
version of the tragedy [inflicted] upon the patrons of some two
dozen public houses in London and elsewhere during the last three
months of 1961' by 'a troupe of untalented amateurs called the
Taverners, directed by Henry McCarthy'.

The Margate Stage Company brought its April 1962 production
to the Lyric Theatre, Hammersmith, during the following February; and Bernard Levin of *The Daily Mail* (7 February) found it
'inadequate at virtually every point'. *The Times*' review of the same
date pointed out that 'the actors, for some inscrutable reason, are
given startlingly non-realistic white makeup, but they are dressed
and act in a fairly routine naturalistic style, and only the comic
villains are broadly (although not very funnily) burlesqued.'

[1] Jackson, p. 87; see also pp. 86–8.

Jackson observed that 'the original text had been badly mangled.'[1]

The post-war years not surprisingly have found in the Arden story a temperamentally suitable expression of a world loose from moral anchorage, as witnessed by Alexander Goehr's opera, *Arden Must Die (Arden Muss Sterben)*, commissioned by the Hamburg State Opera in 1967, and by the more recent La Mama theatre-of-cruelty production. Erich Fried's witty and trenchantly ironic libretto for Goehr's opera admits to being a free adaptation and interpretation of the Holinshed material and 'in no sense a translation or imitation' of the play; and it openly raises the question of responsibility for guilt—a question that the Mayor lightly passes off near the end of the work, just after he agrees to appointing Black Will and Shakebag to fill the hangman's post, when he proclaims:

> For those who are contrite the law holds out no terrors.
> With true deeds they may strive to wipe out ancient errors.

The Epilogue, spoken by Michael, frontally assaults the audience: 'you yourselves / Are not guilty of murder or indeed of any other crime'.[2] The reaction on opening night (5 March) almost seems to have been calculated as a cheering audience fought off the loud booing of an alleged neo-Nazi faction. Goehr himself was praised for his 'act of creative will and intelligence' (*The Observer*, 12 March), and *The Times*' critic reported (on 6 March) that 'a cleverly chosen cast, led by Kerstin Meyer, radiant and comely as the besotted Mrs. Arden, Ronald Dowd singing strongly and looking ridiculously hirsute as her lover, and Toni Blankenheim hilariously antisexual as the paunchy, money-grubbing booby of the title-role, Falstaff, disguised as Little Lord Fauntleroy, made perfect sense of the given material.'

For the La Mama Experimental Theatre Club (New York) production in February 1970 a young Rumanian director, Andrei Sherban, saw beyond the literal text of the original play a vision of

---

[1] A production of *Arden* at the University of California (Berkeley) was offered through the facilities of the Department of Dramatic Art in April 1969. Spectators with whom this editor has conferred remember most vividly the comic scenes of Black Will and Shakebag.

[2] From the libretto, trans. G. Skelton (1967); the complete score of the opera has been published by Schott & Co. Ltd (London).

excruciating cruelty—'a view of the world', Clive Barnes wrote in
his *New York Times*' review of 17 February, 'so savage in its necessi-
ties that survival itself becomes the solitary virtue'. Both Barnes
and Henry Hewes of *The Saturday Review* (7 March) found the
evening a deeply moving experience, the latter praising Sherban for
'evoking remarkably intense and imaginative performances from
the eager La Mama actors', who included Lou Zeldis as Arden,
Michele Collison as Alice, and Patrick Burke as Mosby.[1] In his
review Hewes describes how 'instead of illustrating the formal
dialogue, they perform subconscious visceral responses to the
play's situations'—as when Arden brutally beats Mosby even as he
is verbally forgiving him or when Mistress Arden castrates her
husband after the murder. Fittingly enough, perhaps, this *Arden*
was the second feature on a double bill that began with that pre-
cursor of the modern Theatre of Cruelty, Jarry's *Ubu Roi* (1896),
a frontal attack on bourgeois mediocrity.

Sherban's absurdist cruelty may appear to have more in common
with the violent, amoral universe pictured in the original than
Lillo's sentimental version has, but it also suggests an attempt
by a director to shock at any cost. For that reason alone, one can
sympathize with Michael Billington's review for *The Times* of
7 November 1970 of the Royal Shakespeare Company's production
that month at the Roundhouse theatre, London, when he writes:
'After the confused, blood-boltered mess that the Cafe la Mama
Company recently made of this Elizabethan domestic tragedy, it's
gratifying to find a revival that puts its trust in the text.' But the
director, Buzz Goodbody, simplified the text in her own way,
according to John Russell Brown, who reviewed the production for
the *Stratford-upon-Avon Herald* (13 November) and found that 'In
my view . . . a strong, complicated and daring play . . . has been
staged boringly.' Emrys James's Arden, David Bailie's Mosby, and
Dorothy Tutin's Alice interpreted their roles as if they had been
purposely instructed 'to simplify motivation and involvement'. The
result, one gathers, is that the characters more closely resembled

---

[1] *Shakespeare Survey*, xx (1967), 130, reports that Sherban, 'who had
not finished his studies', produced 'a widely commended' *Arden* in 1966 at
Piatra Neamţ and afterwards at Bucharest.

Holinshed's one-dimensional melodramatic figures than the ambi-
valently divided characters envisioned by the *Arden* playwright.
Arden, in particular, played as 'taut, cold and dangerous', gave
'scarcely any glimpse' of being 'either in costume or behaviour . . .
the worthy, wealthy and "successful" gentleman of Faversham';
and the always sexually assured Alice 'misses—does not even
attempt—the dramatic dynamite of a confession of love for her
husband, as her self-assurance at last fails'. Billington observed
that what the production 'seems to overlook is the play's incessant
harping on class distinctions', so that one is not made to feel, as the
playwright had intended, that Mosby's 'crime is not merely that
he's a murderous adulterer but that he's base-born with it'.
Geoffrey Hutchings's Black Will and Peter Geddis's Michael were
the only ones who managed to convey any sense of contradiction.

After more than eighty years, Bullen's dream that *Arden* would
one day be 'acted in its integrity, with all its wealth of passion and
poetry', still remains a dream.[1]

5. THE PLAY

The annals of English drama frequently accord *Arden of Faversham*
the distinction of establishing the genre of domestic homiletic
tragedy. Plays within this classification deal with protagonists
'below the ranks of nobility' (domestic), inculcate 'lessons of

---

[1] As this edition was going through the proofing stages, Keith Sturgess
was seriously attempting to turn Bullen's dream into reality in his production for the Department of English of the University of Lancaster on
4–6 December 1972, in the University's Nuffield Theatre Studio. Black
Will and Shakebag were not allowed to overwhelm the play, and the
experienced actor who played Arden as a man whose ruling passing was a
concern for appearances seemed finally to have forced the audience to
identify with the character by the death scene. In the first scene, Arden's
capitulation to Alice evoked laughter; a similar moment in scene xiii, the
scene before the murder, clearly puzzled, even upset, the spectators. The
main innovation was the creation of a narrator who, in modern dress and
purporting to read from Holinshed, opened and closed the play and
appeared also before scenes ii and xiii. His function, Mr Sturgess writes
(privately), 'was to establish the authenticity of the story in as matter-of-
fact a way as possible (lending a kind of documentary air) in order to
allow the bolder, more poetic and more melodramatic effects of the play as
great a heightening as possible'.

morality and religious faith in the citizens who [come] to the
theatres by offering them examples drawn from the lives and customs of their own kind of people' (homiletic), and end 'in death for
the protagonist' (tragedy).[1] *Arden*, however, has evoked such con-
tradictory responses regarding its aims—whether as tragedy
(domestic or otherwise) or as dramatized homily—that it seems
wiser not to worry too precisely over the definition of its type but
rather to take the play on its own terms. Although morality plays
had established the tradition of presenting sin and violence alle-
gorically in relation to a 'realistic social background' and history
plays currently were establishing 'a most intimate connection between the events on the stage and the audience' by dealing with
known personages against a national background,[2] no one really
disagrees that *Arden* brings something new to the English stage in
its serious treatment of the affairs and passions of ordinary and near-
contemporary Englishmen. The disarming, even modest, apology
in the Epilogue for 'this naked tragedy' suggests that the playwright
was fully aware of the extent to which he was experimenting with a
new form for the basically self-conscious romantic stage of his contemporaries. Not for him, at least in this play, the 'stately written
Tragedie . . . fitting Kings, / Containing matter, and not common
things' or the exploits of remarkable personages 'threatning the
world with high astounding tearms',[3] but instead the 'simple
truth', with 'no filèd points . . . foisted in', of average, non-heroic
men, such as the actual Master Thomas Arden of Faversham in
Kent 'who', as the title-pages of the three early quartos inform us,
'*was most wickedlye murdered, by* the meanes of his disloyall and
wanton *wyfe*'.

 To see the outlines of the Agamemnon story repeating itself in
a provincial port town some forty-seven miles east of London in the

---

[1] The definition of H. H. Adams in *English Domestic Or, Homiletic
Tragedy, 1575–1642* (1943), pp. viii–ix, who places *Arden* squarely in the
homiletic tradition; see also pp. 1–2, as well as M. Doran, *Endeavors of Art*
(1954), p. 143. *Arden* is the first extant play of its type. Two that are not
extant, *Murderous Michael* and *The Cruelty of a Step-Mother*, both of the
late 1570s, may be forerunners.
[2] See, respectively, J. M. R. Margeson, *The Origins of English Tragedy*
(1967), p. 67, and H. S. Davies, *Realism in the Drama* (1934), p. 46.
[3] From *Sp.T.*, IV. i. 158–60 and *1 Tamb.*, Prologue, 5, respectively.

middle of the sixteenth century[1] may seem far-fetched. Men like
Arden do not article with the gods, shake the fabric of state, or
attempt to go beyond good and evil to embrace tragedy with heroic
defiance. Nevertheless, they often wander, haplessly and unques-
tioningly, into tragic relationships in their everyday domestic
affairs. Even with its display of violently savage passions, its stark
coincidences and miraculous escapes, and its climactic scene of
cold-blooded murder, 'realistic' rather than 'melodramatic' more
aptly describes the Arden story. For its original audience the play
most likely had the impact that a sensational newspaper story
would have today: the known facts were a source of common
wonder and gossip for decades after the murder took place,[2] and
the points at which the facts left off and the playwright's imagination took over were probably not always discernible to the spectators.

The author of *Arden* has been criticized, in fact, for adhering
much too closely to his source, for refusing 'to alter the "simple
truth" of Holinshed'.[3] But whereas the narrated 'facts' of the
Chronicles read, strangely enough, like melodramatic fiction, the
enacted fiction of the play reproduces more of the sense of life's
complexity because the playwright imaginatively has explored the
facts of their significance. The Elizabethan stage—an open-air
platform employing no scenery and the bare minimum of properties and extending directly into the audience—did not permit

[1] So M. J. Wolff, 'Zu *Arden von Feversham*', *Die Neueren Sprachen*,
XXXV (1927), 426, who would consider the play 'bourgeois' only in the
sense that it gives us *real* human beings; otherwise, in treatment and in
form he sees it as inspired by Seneca and classical ideals of tragedy. Many
writers have alluded to Alice as a latter-day 'bourgeois Clytemnestra' and
to Mosby as 'a modern Ægisthus' (see, for instance, J. A. Symonds,
Shakspere's Predecessors in the English Drama [1884; new ed., 1900], p. 451;
Cust, p. 123). Cf., however, T. S. Eliot, 'Seneca in Elizabethan Translation' in *Selected Essays* (3rd ed., 1951), p. 81, who finds 'no token of
foreign or classical influence'; so, too, M. Praz, *The Flaming Heart* (1958),
p. 146.
[2] See p. xxxviii above.
[3] F. W. Moorman, 'Plays of Uncertain Authorship Attributed to
Shakespeare', in *The Cambridge History of English Literature*, V (1910), 242.
Cf.: 'artlessly realistic' (Thorndike, p. 110) and '[pressing] too closely upon
reality without daring to correct it' (trans. from A. Mézières, *Prédécesseurs
et Contemporains de Shakespeare* [2nd ed., 1863], p. 102).

the photographically realistic illusion of actual life that we associate with nineteenth- and twentieth-century domestic plays that
were written to be performed behind a proscenium arch in a
darkened, indoor theatre; it imposed upon the playwright the more
difficult task of rendering the *sense* of actual life. Topical allusions
(as, probably, to Jack Fitten's theft in scene ii); references to known
persons (Sir Anthony Cooke, Sir Anthony Aucher ['Ager']), com-
munities (Bocton, Rochester, Southwark, etc.), places (the Nag's
Head and the Salutation inns in London); vignettes of the bookseller's apprentice in St Paul's churchyard (scene iii) and of the
ferryman (scenes xi and xii); more general references as to the gos-
siping of neighbours, 'the knights and gentlemen of Kent'—most of
these are not in the source, but they all buttress the feeling of everyday reality in the play; however, as Charles Knight rightly claimed,
the playwright 'aimed at producing something higher than a literal
copy of everyday life'.[1] That 'something higher' was distinctly not
a morality play.

Readers who take moral summaries as the meaning of *Arden*
are probably misled by the original title-page, which the bookseller Edward White must have designed as an advertising come-
on: 'THE LAMENTABLE AND TRVE TRAGEDIE . . .
Wherin is shewed the great mallice and discimulation of a wicked
woman, the vnsatiable desire of filthie lust and the shamefull end
of all murderers'. The whole tone of the play belies this facile and
melodramatic description. Other 'news plays' (as they sometimes
are called) influenced by the example of *Arden*—as *A Warning for
Fair Women*, based on an actual murder of 1573 and published in
1599, and *The Yorkshire Tragedy*, also based on an actual murder
of 1604 and published with almost unseemly haste the following
year—do point a simple moral in a very heavy hand; but one of the
more remarkable features of *Arden*, especially in this earlier period
of Elizabethan drama, and given the nature of its material, is its
lack of didacticism. Louis Gillet has observed:

> What is most astonishing is that the author refrains from judging:
> he never declaims nor moralizes in any way. In this horrible affair

---

[1] Knight, p. 267. Cf. Bullen (p. xv): 'He worked in the sphere of realism,
but it is realism of no vulgar sort.'

of conspiracy and murder, he keeps throughout the unified and transparent tone of simplicity; he shows all these impurities, these follies, as they appear in the bright light of intelligence. We are astonished to find them so natural.[1]

When Franklin turns to the audience at the end to deliver the play's Epilogue, he does not, like the Doctor at the end of *Everyman*, exhort it, as he might be expected to do in his role as a choral character, to observe and to learn from the fate of the various characters. Instead, he concludes the narrative thread of the drama by accounting for the remaining characters not touched upon in the final scene and then apologizes for the author's lack of 'glozing stuff' to adorn the play. In this respect, the ending also differs from a work like Marlowe's *Doctor Faustus*, in which the final Chorus urges the 'gentles' of the audience to 'regard' the protagonist's 'hellish fall'.

Not to moralize is not, of course, the same as taking no view of life at all; but neither the literal 'facts' from the *Chronicles* nor the imposed didacticism of a homiletic glossarist were meaningful enough by themselves to the more sophisticated writer of the play.[2] Like Holinshed, the playwright comes to no specific conclusions about life; but, unlike the chronicler, he sees the isolated murder of a provincial customs official in a much broader social context, as symptomatic of larger and considerably more frightening forces let loose in contemporary society than of 'the great mallice and dis-cimulation of a wicked woman', so that even minor characters in the

[1] *'Arden of Feversham'*, trans. M. Bluestone, in *Shakespeare's Contemporaries*, ed. M. Bluestone and N. Rabkin (1961), p. 154. P. Edwards considers that 'Perhaps the most interesting quality of *Arden of Feversham* is its freedom from the moral clichés of the tragedies of its time' (*Thomas Kyd and Early Elizabethan Tragedy* [1966], p. 21). Cf. also: 'The didactic element is entirely lacking in the play' (W. Thorp, *The Triumph of Realism in Elizabethan Drama, 1558–1612* [1928], p. 110, n. 38) and 'the play is a deliberate protest against the current romantic and didactic tendencies in the drama' (S. H. Patterson, 'The Authorship of *Arden of Feversham*', unpubl. Columbia Univ. M.A. thesis [1925], p. 21).

[2] This view differs from M. Doran's, pp. 351–2, that the playwright is torn between 'the conflicting pulls of *prodesse* and *delectare*', between instructing and entertaining, so that the 'indications of the moral are fitful and inconsistent'. Tieck was impressed, however, with 'the deep moral feeling of the play' ('jenes tiefe moralische Gefühl', pp. xxvi–xxvii), and Hopkinson (3) thought that the play embodied 'a high tone of morality' (p. xxix).

play take on a significance that they do not begin to suggest in the source. Raymond Chapman has pointed out that 'the unknown author of *Arden* was acutely aware of the social upheavals which had taken place in his own and his father's lifetime . . . an age which, like our own, has lost its security of continuance and was learning to question all things.'[1] The play takes into account, as the source does not, the widespread dislocation resulting from the dispersal of church property, from the enclosures of small farms by large land-owners, and, above all, from the slow disintegration of a rural economy and its values before the new agrarianism of middle-class entrepreneurs intent on amassing property while disregarding the social obligations that ownership of property entails.[2]

Tawney has described the medieval ideal of the village as 'a fellowship of mutual aid, a partnership of service and protection, "a little commonwealth"';[3] but the playwright, attuned to the social reality of his day, depicts a community where rampant indi-vidualism is destroying that ideal. Far from being the 'little com-monwealth' where all classes of men work in harmony towards the common good, the world of the play is aggressively and self-centredly class conscious. *Arden* is particularly notable at this point in dramatic history, as Chapman observes, 'for the fact that nearly all of its characters are of the peasant or yeoman class'. Lord Cheyne is the only character of the titled nobility to appear, and then just briefly as a *deus ex machina* in scene ix,[4] where his calm assurance and natural gentility as a representative of the highest social class permit him easily to associate with a subject like Arden, whom he invites back to dinner, and at the same time to banter with a known vagabond like Black Will. A point that R. B. Smith makes in his recent study of the relationship between land and politics during this period defines the contrast between a Lord

[1] P. 15.

[2] Cf. R. B. Smith, *Land and Politics in the England of Henry VIII* (1970), p. 259: 'In the dispersal of monastic property we see land not as a sacred trust but as the object of multifarious transactions whose ultimate object was to gain more gain. The King himself set the trend in motion, for it was in order to increase his wealth that he dissolved the monasteries in the first place.'

[3] R. H. Tawney, *Religion and the Rise of Capitalism* (1926), p. 148.

[4] Chapman, p. 16.

Cheyne and an Arden of Faversham: 'Land was but one aspect of gentility in Tudor England, and those who already had an ample estate probably did not attach very high priority to the acquisition of more. . . . The people most likely to spend their money on land were those still rising on the social scale, for whom land was the pre-requisite of acceptance into the gentry.'[1] On the other hand yeomen 'of great devotion', like Greene and Reede in the play, are desperate to protect the 'little land' that traditionally had been their major source of livelihood from the inroads of a new system that has legally justified Arden's rapaciousness. The denunciation by the Puritan Robert Crowley (in the same year as Arden's murder) of the *new* man of the age whose goal was to amass wealth by any means—

> men that live as thoughe there were no God at all, men that would have all in their owne handes, men that would leave nothyng for others, men that would be alone on the earth, men that bee never satisfied—[2]

affords an interesting parallel to Greene's denunciation of Arden (i. 470–7):

> Your husband doth me wrong
> To wring me from the little land I have.
> My living is my life; only that
> Resteth remainder of my portion.
> Desire of wealth is endless in his mind,
> And he is greedy-gaping still for gain;
> Nor cares he though young gentlemen do beg,
> So he may scrape and hoard up in his pouch.

Ironically, Arden, so keen on preserving his reputation among the 'knights and gentlemen of Kent', is as much a social climber as the time-server Mosby, his wife's lover whom he addresses as 'a velvet drudge, / A cheating steward, and base-minded peasant' (i. 322–3) and against whom he scornfully invokes the statute against arti-ficers (i. 311). To add further to the irony, he has socially and economically advanced himself by his marriage just as Mosby, a former tailor and now steward to a noble house, hopes to do by his own marriage with Alice. Greene reminds the audience of Mistress

---

[1] P. 244.
[2] From *The Way of Welth*, quoted by Tawney, p. 148 (from *Select Works of Robert Crowley*, ed. J. M. Cowper [1872], p. 132).

Arden's position in society when, after she has complained of her husband's alleged mistreatment of her, he exclaims:

> Why, Mistress Arden, can the crabbèd churl
> Use you unkindly? Respects he not your birth,
> Your honourable friends, nor what you brought?
> Why, all Kent knows your parentage and what you are.
>
> (i. 488–91)

All Kent knew, of course, that she was the stepdaughter of Sir Edward North—Baron North of Kirtling by the time that the play was written—in whose employ in the Office of Augmentations, created by Henry VIII to arrange for the dispersal of monastic property, Arden had worked before his marriage.[1]

It would be wrong to give the impression that *Arden of Faversham* is some kind of dramatized sociological tract.[2] The economic individualism of an acquisitive society appears in the play as only a manifestation of something far more corrosive and pervasive: the covetousness of the human heart that blindly drives individuals to press for the immediate satisfaction of appetites regardless of social and personal consequences. Covetousness—of land, money, social position, revenge, other people—motivates almost every character; and the collapse of traditional values furnishes the climate for violence in the play in much the same way that the sordid background of war stresses the futility of love in the main plot of Shakespeare's *Troilus and Cressida*. As human beings take on the value only of the market, property to be bought and sold, the taking of life seems incidental; *Arden* is a universe without pity. To acquire land Arden banishes pity (xiii. 27) as readily as 'pitiless Black Will' would 'for a crown . . . murder any man' (ii. 12). The hired assassin finds that murder has become so profitable that he wishes it 'would grow to an occupation . . . without danger of law' (ii. 106–8). To remove 'that block' (i. 137) that stands between her and her lover,

[1] Unfortunately, it has to be admitted, Greene's reference is oblique, and the point is not pursued elsewhere in the play; a modern reader or spectator could hardly be aware of a class distinction between Arden and Alice.

[2] But see the rightful objection of *The Times*' reviewer (p. lvii above) to the Royal Shakespeare Company's production that seemed 'to overlook the play's incessant harping on class distinctions'.

Mistress Arden willingly pays a fee and promises more 'golden harmony' (xiv. 115) after the job is done; but, ironically, even she has to *buy* her love from Mosby by sending him gifts and by promising him her husband's wealth (i. 220–2). To be 'sole ruler' of his own, Mosby plans to set his fellow conspirators on each other and to 'cleanly rid' himself of Alice (viii. 34 ff.). To protect his property a 'religious' man like Greene conspires to murder Arden, 'For', as he says, 'I had rather die than lose my land' (i. 518). Clarke the painter, after commending Mistress Arden for her 'noble mind' in choosing to 'have [her] husband made away', also agrees to 'venture life'—'for my Susan's sake' (i. 267–72). To win Susan's love too, the servant Michael would help to kill Arden and even 'rid my elder brother away' to make the latter's farm his own (i. 172–3); however much he later may reproach himself, he opts out of fear for his own life to 'Let pity lodge where feeble women lie' (iii. 208). Shakebag would 'On Arden so much pity' take 'as the starven lioness, / When she is dry-sucked of her eager young, / Shows to the prey that next encounters her' (iii. 110–13); he would take even less pity on himself if he fails to take vengeance on Michael for having foiled the plot on Arden's life (v. 51–4). One of the play's most recurrent images is that of the maiming and destroying of the human body ('dissevered joints and sinews torn', 'eat the heart', 'make thee crawl on stumps', 'Till Arden's heart be panting in my hand', 'Lop . . . away his leg, his arm, or both', 'Cut . . . the nose from off the coward's face', 'there be butchered by thy dearest friends', 'broken a sergeant's head'); the murder of Arden on stage theatrically realizes this image.

To say that the play presents no character who is a solid force for good is to exaggerate, perhaps, although the strongest candidate, Franklin, is completely ineffectual in saving his friend Arden;[1] and Bradshaw is merely innocent. What is surprising, however, is that in this bleak, amoral world where anarchic wills operate so freely the playwright has created no character of unrelieved evil.

---

[1] See xiii. 135 to the end of the scene. Franklin's advice to Arden to 'make no question of her love to thee' at the beginning of the play is so naive that the latter, in accepting it, observes that 'this abhors from reason' (i. 54); Franklin later condones Arden's treatment of Dick Reede (xiii. 54–8).

A. W. Ward's impression that 'the characters carrying on its action are throughout either repulsive or uninteresting' and that 'vice is painted as nakedly and blackly as it is by the chronicler' is, even for the nineteenth century, the minority view.[1] G. Baldini comes closer to the mark when he observes that not one character is genuinely Machiavellian—a type so pronounced in the drama of the period.[2] The general impression is that *Arden* stands out among its contemporaries for its 'truth to characterization'. J. B. Black's summation for his volume of the *Oxford History of England*—'Prior to the appearance of the Shakespearian plays, *Arden* is the best psychological drama of the period'—is borne out by W. J. Courthope's belief in the playwright's 'profound knowledge of human motives' and M. Bluestone's praise of 'the divided sensibilities of the murderers', as well as 'the divided sensibility of their victim'.[3]

Whereas Holinshed's figures are one-dimensional and strangely devoid of passion, only the playwright can be said to have actually created character. With few exceptions, such as Franklin (mostly a choral character and confidant), Susan, and Clarke (whose characterization probably suffers most from memorial contamination), there is hardly even a minor character, let alone a major, whom he he has not enlivened in some way, sometimes by just a brief touch. The curse that practically ends the play suddenly enlivens the guileless and rather colourless Bradshaw and brings into focus his role: 'My blood be on his head that gave the sentence!' The small yeoman landowner Greene, of whom Holinshed tells us only that he had come to blows with Arden about his property, is turned into a man of religious devotion driven by Arden's avarice to the extreme of murder. The 'needy' sailor Dick Reede, who is mentioned merely as an afterthought in the *Chronicles*, becomes a

---

[1] *A History of English Dramatic Literature*, II (1899, rev. ed.), 218. Cf., too, A. Wynne's impression that 'truth to human nature' is lacking in the play (*The Growth of English Drama* [1914], p. 264).

[2] 'Un Apocrifo Shakespeariano: *Arden of Feversham*', *Annali della Scuola Normale Superiore di Pisa* (Florence), Serie II, XVIII (1949), 100.

[3] See, respectively, Black, *The Reign of Elizabeth, 1558–1603* (1936), p. 251; Courthope, *A History of English Poetry*, IV (1903), 236; Bluestone, 'The Imagery of Tragic Melodrama in *Arden of Feversham*', *Drama Survey*, V (1966), 173. The phrase 'truth to characterization' is adapted from Mézières's 'la vérité des caractères' (p. 103).

pivotal and haunting character in the play with his passionate curse
upon Arden. The spunky bookseller's apprentice of scene iii and
the bawdy ferryman of scenes xi and xii function dramatically—
the former by inadvertently foiling the second attempt on Arden's
life, the latter by underscoring in the 'flat knavery' of his dialogue
the sexual background of the main plot and by grimly hinting
through his very presence at another ferryman, Charon of Hades—
and also add in their brief but lively appearances realistic local
colouring. Both are creations of the playwright.

Among the lesser characters the two hired assassins, Black Will
and Shakebag, and the servingman Michael especially stand out.
Shakebag is almost non-existent in the source, and the original
picture of Black Will only hints at his development in the play. The
dramatist has enlarged their parts considerably, making them
roughly equal; and he has also carefully individualized them:
Shakebag more sinister, more given to Senecan rhetoric; Black
Will more blustering, more cowardly, a kind of 'Ancient' Pistol
type. Chapman has described them as the 'dread' of the period—
'masterless men', unemployed soldiers returning from the wars in
France to take up a life of vagabondage at home.[1] Stage productions
have tended to obscure their grim reality by excessively farcical
treatment—thereby also making them the two most popular stage
figures of the play;[2] the playwright's own comic treatment of them
indicates that murder is not their true occupation. They continually taunt and bully one another to bolster their own spirits; and by
the end of the twelfth scene, after six attempts on Arden's life
have failed, an audience is inclined to agree with Mosby that
'These knaves will never do it; let us give it over.'

The state of the text may have done some damage to Michael's
role. For the most part he is the silly, loutish servant who glibly
swears an oath to help his mistress murder her husband in return

---

[1] Chapman, p. 16. Vagabondage was a crime in Tudor England; but, as
J. D. Mackie points out, in writing particularly about the reign of Edward
VI, 'the causes producing it were little regarded' (*The Earlier Tudors, 1485–
1558* [1952], p. 505).
[2] Criticism tends to confirm the reaction of audiences; cf. 'delineated by a
master's hand' (Tyrrell, p. 376) and 'most masterly character-portraits' (W.
Creizenach, *The English Drama in the Age of Shakespeare* [1916], p. 324).

for her help in winning her maid Susan's (Mosby's sister's) favours, but at a crucial moment (scene iv) he becomes almost a tragic figure as a combination of *a troubled conscience* (ll. 62–3), *self-gratification* (ll. 64–6), and *fear* (ll. 67–71) confusedly drives him to foil the plot. Guilt and fear continue to plague him in later episodes as he invents excuses not to be present when the assassins plan to murder Arden (ix. 60; x. 36–8). A neat touch by the playwright is Michael's simple cry, 'O, mistress!' (xiv. 239), immediately after Alice stabs her husband; even at this moment in which he himself is so very much implicated he is overcome by her cold-blooded indifference.

The dramatic sureness of the playwright is most evident, however, in his characterization of the three main figures, none of whom resembles his or her counterpart in Holinshed. The greatest and most obvious change is in the character of Arden, who in the source is so perverse that sympathy for Alice is not entirely wanting. Although, Holinshed writes, he 'most entirelie loued her all his life time', so greedy was he for property that, not to offend his wife and thereby 'loose the benefit which he hoped to gaine at some of hir freends [i.e., relatives'] hands in bearing with hir lewdnesse, which he might haue lost if he should haue fallen out with hir', he openly sanctioned a *ménage à trois* under his own roof. Just before the murder takes place, Mosby even greets Arden, when the latter returns home from business, wearing a 'night gowne' (i.e., dressing gown). Furthermore, the chronicler has Alice assure her lover that her husband is so hated and cursed by the townspeople of Faversham for having procured the annual St Valentine's Fair, which 'was woont to be kept partlie in the towne, and partlie in the abbeie', to be kept wholly on his own Abbey property that year—and 'so reaping all the gaines to himselfe, and bereauing the towne of that portion which was woont to come to the inhabitants'—that 'not anie . . . would care for his death, nor make anie great inquirie for them that should dispatch him'. The playwright retains Arden's avariciousness, although he underplays it, but turns him into a jealous husband, who is also deeply concerned about his honour and reputation; he drops the business about the Fair completely.[1]

---

[1] Except for an obscure reference to it (possibly the result of textual transmission) at xiv. 42.

Warnke and Proescholdt, like Symonds, thought that the dramatist made a great mistake not to follow Holinshed in having Arden
'contented to winke at [his wife's] filthie disorder' so that he
would appear, as they believed, 'contemptible to his own wife as
well as to the audience for which the play was intended'; his death,
they concluded, is therefore not poetically justified.[1]

Without doubt the Arden of the play represents an entirely
different conception of the character, one who is so altogether
ambivalent that probably no other character in the earlier English
drama—at least before *Julius Caesar*—presents such a critical
problem; almost any statement about him can be contradicted.
Tieck found him 'noble and amiable', and Hugo 'completely sympathetic' in contrast to Holinshed's figure.[2] But a reviewer of the
1938 Paris production wrote that he had 'rarely seen a less sympathetic victim'—a judgement which, regardless of the merits of this
controversial production, is borne out by S. H. Patterson's view of
Arden's 'increasing stupidity' and by A. Mézières's that he should
be played in the manner of one of Molière's jealous husbands if he
is to be believable.[3] Within the play itself Greene's and Reede's
harsh but justifiable judgements of Arden must be set against the
respect in which Franklin and Lord Cheyne hold him, Michael's
acknowledgement of his 'master's kindness', and Alice's admission,
when she is not under Mosby's spell, that 'Arden to me was dearer
than my soul— / And shall be still' (i. 197–8). The fact is that the
playwright purposely makes categorical judgement impossible.
The almost immediate effectiveness of Reede's curse against Arden
—the murder finally comes about in the next scene—leaves no
doubt about Arden's moral guilt, but only the playwright has
thought to make his avarice legally justified (through 'letters
patents from his majesty' and by the 'Chancery seal')—as in his-

[1] Pp. xxi–xxii. Cf. Symonds, p. 445: 'The omission of ['the real Arderne's
contemptible compliance'] enfeebles the dramatic Arden, and blurs the
outline of his character, in which neither uxorious passion nor avarice is
forcibly enough accentuated to explain his conduct'. See below, pp. lxxiv–
lxxv.

[2] Tieck ('edel und liebenswürdig', p. xxv); Hugo ('complètement sympa-
thique', p. 53).

[3] See, respectively, *Le Feuilleton du Temps* (24 October 1938; see above,
p. lii); Patterson, p. 61; and Mézières, p. 104.

torical truth it was—by the very society whose social and spiritual ideal of a community among men he is unconsciously helping to destroy. Even Arden himself seems troubled by his own treatment of Reede as his need to justify himself to Franklin at xiii. 54–7 testifies. Both Arden and Reede are victims simultaneously of the new system of land redistribution.

Arden's relationship with his wife and her lover is marked by similar confusion. His judgement is not blind to their 'wickedness'; but here his own best instincts for affection, generosity, and trust continually reconcile him to Alice and prompt him to forgive Mosby even without his wife's urging (as at i. 338 ff.). He may appear to us naïve, even 'stupid', to do so, but he is not one to seek the role of tragic hero;[1] he does seem, however, to have a tragic premonition that only death is the answer to his 'heart's grief':

> At home or not at home, where'er I be,
> Here, here it lies [*He points to his heart.*], ah, Franklin,
>   here it lies
> That will not out till wretched Arden dies.   (iv. 31–3)

The Mosby of the play, a man who has raised himself from a mender of old clothes to where he himself can 'bravely [jet] it in his silken gown' as the steward of a great house, is also, ironically, like Arden, very much a victim of a system that is beginning to make a virtue out of ambition. The covetousness of both Arden and Mosby is morally wrong, but the playwright's complex and realistic vision of contemporary society sees the system as putting a curb on the one and as legally sanctioning the other: Mosby's inferior birth stands in his way. Neither Holinshed nor, for that matter, the Wardmote Book of Faversham makes Mosby out to be ambitious; both merely refer to him as a former tailor of London and then 'seruant' of Alice's stepfather, Sir Edward North, and as her lover, the chronicler adding that he was 'a blacke swart man' whereas Arden was 'of a tall and comelie personage'. In the source

---

[1] See Gillet, p. 152: 'The remarkable thing is that, even in those angry moments when he loses his patience, he blames not his wife but his rival; he is the opposite of an Othello; Alice is forgiven beforehand. This trait is very rare in the literature of Elizabethan times, when the Spanish code of honor required that the least suspicion be avenged with blood. The author of *Arden* is quite above these barbaric and ferocious customs.'

Mosby is uninteresting, hardly figuring in the main action; all the schemes for the murder are entirely Alice's (even the final and successful one which in the play is his), and near the end she has to plead on her knees for him 'to go through with the matter, as if he loued hir he would be content to doo', for he 'at the first would not agree to that cowardlie murthering of him, but in a furie floong awaie'.

Certainly more vicious than his chronicle counterpart, the playwright's Mosby is also more humanly complex, a mixture of pride and baseness, of arrogance and cowardice; more intriguing, he is an immoral man troubled by conscience. His rebuke to Arden, 'Measure me what I am, not what I was' (i. 321), after the latter has taunted him with being 'a botcher once', is the anguished plea of a man who feels that he deserves better in the world. As he stabs Arden later in the play, he does so not as a lover eliminating his rival but as a scorned inferior taking revenge: 'There's for the pressing iron you told me of' (xiv. 235). Even his despicable retort to the now-repentant Alice in scene viii, 'Go, get thee gone, a copesmate for thy hinds! / I am too good to be thy favourite' (ll. 104–5), is evoked by her having just called him 'a mean artificer, that lowborn name'; earlier (i. 198), she, anticipating her husband (at i. 323), had called him a 'base peasant'. But such are the ironies of the play that, as it turns out, Arden and Alice have measured Mosby for what he is: a shabby lover, as well as a shabby human being, and not the Endymion that his 'bewitched' mistress sometimes sees in him (xiv. 149–53). Swinburne's description of him just after the duel with Arden in scene xiii when he blames Alice for his wound cannot be improved upon: 'Such exhibition of currish cowardice and sullen bullying spite increases rather our wondering pity for its victim than our wondering sense of her degradation.'[1]

Mosby is not, however, without scruples.[2] We can actually witness the deterioration of a character who comes on the scene wanting to break off the liaison with his wedded mistress, who is unwilling shortly thereafter to break his oath to her husband to leave

---

[1] A. C. Swinburne, *A Study of Shakespeare* (1880), p. 139.
[2] Cf. Mézières, p. 105: 'Mosbie appartient à la famille des ambitieux sans scrupules.'

off soliciting her, and who in mid-course (beginning of scene viii) comes to realize that his 'golden time was when [he] had no gold' and the 'night's repose made daylight fresh to' him. Nevertheless, he 'needs must on, although to danger's gate'. As with Arden, he seems to accept death as a kind of relief from 'this hell of grief' (xviii. 12), his divided self.

Realistic portraiture triumphs in Alice Arden. The critical praise of her has bordered on the extravagant, invoking comparisons with Clytemnestra, Lady Macbeth, Racine's Phædra, Anna Karenina, Emma Bovary, Lady Chatterley, and Strindberg's Miss Julie among others.[1] Thorndike expresses the feelings of many critics when he writes that 'the greatest merit of the play lies in the portrait of Alice Arden . . . incomparably the most lifelike evil woman up to this time depicted in the drama.'[2] To a student of the earlier Elizabethan drama coming upon the play for the first time a character, especially a woman, of such a fluctuating variety of moods and emotions, all believable, must be impressive. In scene xiv alone—the murder scene—she moves from total, almost orgiastic abandonment to the scheme to murder her husband to remorse, fear, lack of control, renewed strength and duplicity, and, finally, resignation that hints of her later repentance.

The praise and the comparisons are understandable; the only danger in them is that either they lead one to expect of Mistress Arden a great-souled woman of tragedy, which she is not, or they suggest motivations for her actions—revenge, ambition, sexual frustration, romantic longings, boredom—which might tend to explain away the enormity of her actions. Alice Arden is 'inexplicable'. The judgement is Ulrici's, and he meant it as negative criticism;[3] but the greatest merit of her characterization is that the dramatist offers no explanation for the passion that unremittingly drives her to keep yearning for what she fears. At intervals throughout the play she recognizes the genuine shabbiness of the lover who has become her new religion, and she even taunts him with his baseness (i. 185 ff. and viii. 71–9; see also viii. 118 ff.). She seems

---

[1] See Gillet, p. 154; Tynan, p. 83, as well as the whole host of critics from Swinburne (p. 140) on.
[2] P. 110.   [3] H. Ulrici, *Shakespeare's Dramatic Art* (1846), p. 447.

also to be dimly aware that their reconciliation will mean her 'over-throw' (i. 215–16). Nevertheless, like Arden, who recognizes also that his wife 'is rooted in her wickedness' (iv. 9) but cannot give her up, and like Mosby, who 'needs must on' although his complicity with evil has brought him only deep insecurity and unhappiness, Alice cannot control the covetousness of her heart even with the awareness that her husband is the better man whom she really does not wish to kill (i. 273–6). 'Bewitched' is a word which accurately describes all three characters: Arden at xiii. 153, Mosby at viii. 93, and Alice at viii. 78. And, as with Arden and Mosby, the approach of her own death is for her a unifying experience. One particular change from Holinshed, where Alice is totally and unequivocally an evil woman, illustrates the playwright's deeper conception of the character. The chronicler relates how right after the murder Mistress Arden joined in great revelry with her guests, even causing 'hir daughter to plaie on the virginals' and later enlisting her aid in carrying the body out to a field adjoining the churchyard. By omitting the daughter entirely from the play and also this ghoulish scene, the playwright has seen to it that Mistress Arden never, even at her most terrifyingly obsessive moments, becomes monstrous; in the play she is always a plausible human being.[1]

What gives *Arden*, then, so much of its illusion of reality and makes the easy didactic judgement of the moralist not fully tenable is the ambivalence of characters living in a society whose own attitude towards newly recognized individual ambition and social mobility is itself ambivalent. For instance, a recent critic's statement, 'Arden is the victim of treachery, but he is a victim whose avarice is the justification of his death. . . . *Arden* follows a clear pattern of tragic retribution',[2] simply does not fit our response to

[1] Cf., however, A. Zanco, who suggests that the playwright does not take over the daughter from Holinshed in order to make Alice appear less motherly (in 'Considerazioni sull'*Arden of Feversham*', in *Shakespeare in Russia* [1945], p. 177, and reprinted from *Rivista Italiana del Teatro*, no. 3 [1943]). Cf., too, Bluestone, 'The Imagery of Tragic Melodrama', p. 175: 'From Holinshed's fable of a marriage ending not in fruition but in death, the playwright appropriately omits a daughter of the source Ardens.'

[2] S. Youngblood, 'Theme and Imagery in *Arden of Faversham*', *S.E.L.*, III (1963), 208, who substantially is in agreement with Adams, pp. 104–6,

the play, especially its conclusion. It is true that Providence for-
sakes Arden when he does not yield to Reede's plea 'to restore the
land he has unlawfully acquired',[1] that doubts arise in our own
minds as to his uxoriousness and avarice (see p. lxix, n. 1 above).
But we do not therefore sense any justice in his murder, only the
evil of the murderers. Arden dies unenlightened about any of his
'sins', and the 'justice' that prevails afterwards sweeps the innocent
(Bradshaw; in a sense also Susan, who allows herself to be duped
into becoming a participant after the murder occurs) along with the
guilty in its condemnation.

A moralistic epilogue would be totally out of place with the
harsh, complicated, and totally unsentimental view of life that the
play presents. This is not to say that the evil perpetrated by any of
the characters is ever in question or exculpated in any way. The
actual murder of Arden has none of the romantic grandeur of high
tragedy about it. It appears what murder always appears to be
in life—senseless, messy, brutal. The 'deep moral feeling' that
Tieck found in *Arden* comes from no particular justice meted out
at the end or from any didactic statement or from any single action[2]
but rather from the totality of an action which ultimately reveals

who sees Arden's death as 'the wages of sin' and the murderers 'in the role
of the "scourge of God"'. Cf., too, H. Baker, *Induction to Tragedy* (1939),
pp. 203–4: 'Arden is guilty of avarice and sacrilege: abstract academic
didacticism demands that if he is to suffer he must be unmistakably guilty.
But Shakespearean tragedy will not be content with so simple a scheme of
crime and punishment.'

[1] Adams, p. 105; see also his discussion, pp. 100–8. The law of property
is, of course, no excuse for failure to honour spiritual obligations, as Arden's lying 'murdered in that plot of ground / Which he by force and
violence held from Reede' (Epilogue) testifies; but the playwright does not
simplify the issue when he indicates that Arden 'dearly bought' the land
from Reede and that 'the rent of it was ever' his (sc. xiii). Ulrici, p. 477,
thought that 'Arden is murdered for no offence; at least for none which
poetic justice requires to be punished; for his treatment of Read cannot
deserve such a penalty'.

[2] See p. lxi, n. 2, above. Except for Alice none of the murderers suffers
the pangs of conscience, and even her repentance is not totally convincing:
it comes upon her after she is arrested; her expectations of divine mercy do
not lead her to show mercy to Bradshaw by pleading for his innocence; and
she goes to her execution blaming Mosby for her plight rather than
assuming responsibility for her actions.

that man is not totally self-determining, that there is a universe greater than himself, and that, in S. L. Bethell's fine phrase, he is not 'an adequate cause of his own history':[1] forces greater than himself conspire with his 'weaknesses' to work out his destiny. In the play these forces appear as the operation of Chance (or Coincidence or Fortune); and just as Chance is but another name for the operation of all those mysterious forces which appear so inscrutable to man and which seem to play so large a part in shaping his destiny, so in the play Arden's 'miraculous' escapes and the repeated intentions of the murderers to 'give … over' what is so obviously bringing them no satisfaction lead directly to a crime that when it occurs seems as inevitable as the events leading to it had seemed fortuitous.

The structure of Arden, which Gillet has described as giving 'the impression of happening right before our eyes, of being improvised',[2] metaphorically realizes the way that Chance works itself out in the lives of men. So much, in fact, does the structure of the play resemble the episodic and unstructured quality of life itself that not a few critics have been beguiled into thinking the play 'singularly devoid of constructive art', 'in danger of becoming as dull as life', 'hopelessly disjointed and ineffective', or as following reality too closely 'without daring to correct it'.[3] The last usually means following Holinshed too closely; but, although the chronicle narration has its own peculiar force, derived mainly from the dispassionate voice of the narrator, Holinshed's account is strictly that—an account, an objective narration of the literal facts as the chronicler had been informed of them; it cannot be said to have 'structure' in any normally accepted sense of the word. The playwright, however, has prepared with obvious care the lengthy delay leading to Arden's murder so that the major characters, in scenes of primarily psychological interest, can persuasively evolve in all their ambivalence, and the sense of impending doom can develop in the proper atmosphere of violence and confusion to which the macabre

---

[1] In *Shakespeare and the Popular Dramatic Tradition* (1944), p. 83.
[2] Gillet, p. 151.
[3] See, respectively, Moorman, p. 241; Patterson, p. 16; Brooke, p. xv; and Mézières, p. 102 (trans.).

humour of the farcical scenes contributes.[1] The laughter of farce usually results from the dissociation of sensibility whereby the human becomes inhuman and mechanical, but the prelude of human folly in the antics of Black Will and Shakebag provides chilling laughter to the horror in which the play culminates. Just before the murder finally takes place, Alice's complete disintegration is heralded by her grim association with Black Will:

> Come, Black Will, that in mine eyes art fair;
> Next unto Mosby do I honour thee.   (xiv. 112–13)

The dramatic irony afforded by the comic elements in Elizabethan tragedy is a well-understood critical fact and needs no discussion here;[2] but the broad comic elements, even actual farce (as the 'breaking' of Black Will's head in scene iii and Shakebag's falling into the ditch in scene xii), are so pervasive in *Arden*—unlike the striking introduction of the 'porter scene' in *Macbeth* or the 'gravedigger's scene' in *Hamlet*—as to suggest that despite the tragic waste of human life and energy in the play its structure is closer to that of comedy or tragicomedy than to even the 'mixed' tragedy of the period. *Arden*'s characters from the middle and lower ranks of life who blindly stumble into tragedy and neither question nor learn from the experience may be one reason.[3] Six external accidents save Arden, and a poor production could easily bear out M. C. Bradbrook's impression that 'the spectator feels positively irritated' after a while 'that the murderers do not succeed'.[4] But by

---

[1] Cf. Edwards, p. 20: 'the comedy of Will and Shakebag's repeated failures adds greatly to the sense of enormity'; and R. Rauch (in a seminar term-paper): 'The comic touches of Black Will and Shakebag throw into relief the truly dangerous murderers, the engineers of the plot, Alice and Mosby.'

[2] See the excellent brief discussion of 'multi-consciousness' in Elizabethan drama in Bethell, pp. 108–12.

[3] Cf. Davies, p. 42: 'And we may notice here that the form of tragicomedy is the first form of realistic drama, paving the way for the drama of personages "just like ourselves" by the abolition of the categories of Tragedy and Comedy, which will include only characters worse, or better, than ourselves.'

[4] *Themes and Conventions of Elizabethan Tragedy* (2nd ed., 1952), p. 41. Cf. Hanratty, p. 180, writing from a director's point of view: '. . . the producer must plan carefully to see that his sections build up to each other so that the shape of the play is more clearly marked. After the initial plotting,

the use of this technique resembling incremental repetition—and
not because he merely adheres slavishly to the source version—the
playwright found the ideal means to reveal dramatically how Providence in the guise of Chance operates on the lives of ordinary men
who ought to see, but are finally incapable of seeing, a pattern
emerging that seeks to save them from themselves. The spectator
should come to feel positively irritated and then terrified from wit-
nessing how thin the boundary is between comedy and tragedy in
men's lives.

'Fortune', writes F. S. Boas, 'seeks to save [Alice] from herself by
baffling her and Mosbie's plans to do away with Arden';[1] but the
two lovers equally conspire with Fortune to prevent their breaking
off their relationship or abandoning their plans to murder Arden
(scenes i, viii, xii). Arden, too, through his repeated instances of
spiritual blindness, as much as by his refusal to believe the evidence
of his senses that Alice is no longer worth keeping as by his avarice
that brings Greene into the conspiracy, conspires with Fortune in
his death. Greene comes to see that 'The Lord of Heaven hath preservèd [Arden]' (ix. 142), but revenge proves too strong an attraction, especially when Black Will immediately assures him that only
'The Lord Cheyne hath preservèd him'. Black Will later acknow-
ledges that 'doubtless, he [Arden] is preserved by miracle' (xiv.
28–9), but he finds Mistress Arden's 'golden harmony' more convincing. Each attempt on Arden lessens the number of options
remaining to the characters to reverse their course, and destiny
finally traps even the innocent who have merely brushed evil—
Bradshaw and Susan. The saddest instance of the loss of 'the intel-
lect's good'[2] that reveals to an individual his options is Mosby's
soliloquy that begins scene viii. Nearly half of it reveals his awareness that ambition has brought him only a 'troubled mind . . .
stuffed with discontent'; but, instead of following through with the
logic of this insight, he abruptly breaks off ('But whither doth con-

---

each attempt on Arden's life should be a small climax, rising in pace, pitch,
tenseness, action, volume of sound, and then dropping to nothing—the
whole building up to the big climax of Arden's death.'

[1] *An Introduction to Tudor Drama* (1933), p. 107.
[2] See Dante's *Inferno*, Canto III, ll. 17–18.

templation carry me ?') to affirm that he 'needs must on, although to danger's gate', to find 'where pleasure dwells' and to destroy all who stand in the way ('Then, Arden, perish thou by that decree'). At this moment the now repentant Alice enters, but Mosby prevents her from breaking off their relationship.[1] The scene ends with their destinies prophetically sealed as Mosby exclaims, 'Ay, to the gates of death to follow thee'. The divinity that shapes men's ends may shape them, of course, for good as well as for evil, and *Arden*'s vision is admittedly one-sided; its justness resides in its uncompromising presentation.

That the playwright 'took the hint . . . from the account in Holinshed's *Chronicles*' makes no difference, H. S. Davies justly observed, for '*Arden* has a really poetic plot; the way in which Arden escapes death by accident over and over again, until one almost feels that he is fated to live in spite of his wife, is a truly mythic creation; there are few plays in which one is made to feel the force of destiny so vividly, and yet so subtly'.[2] Thus the poetry is fundamental to *Arden*, part of its very structure. T. S. Eliot's well-known comment on the function of poetry in drama applies to our play:

> . . . I start with the assumption that if poetry is merely a decoration, an added embellishment . . ., then it is superfluous. It must justify itself dramatically. . . . From this it follows that no play should be written in verse for which prose is *dramatically* adequate. And from this it follows, again, that the audience, its attention held by the dramatic action, its emotions stirred by the situation between the characters, should be too intent upon the play to be wholly conscious of the medium.[3]

This view seems indeed surprising since the very idea of bourgeois or domestic drama suggests prose as the natural medium. In such a play one normally does not expect characters to 'embrace actions and feelings of great power'[4] as they do, for instance, in

---

[1] Compare with the first scene of the play when Alice prevents Mosby from breaking off their relationship. Alice's arranging with Greene immediately thereafter to hire assassins to murder Arden without first informing Mosby of her plans obliquely suggests a desperate attempt on her part to bind her lover to her by means of their mutual complicity in the act.

[2] Pp. 60–1.   [3] *Poetry and Drama* (1951), pp. 10–11.

[4] Quotation from M. E. Prior, *The Language of Tragedy* (1947), p. 96.

Shakespeare's History plays. Yet prose could not have been '*dramatically* adequate' for the *Arden* playwright, who faced the sheer technical problem of conveying to his audience the feeling of the larger powers of destiny operating on the anarchic lives of ordinary men and women; his solution was to so modify and essentially re-create the conventional use of blank verse for tragedy that the 'language of the gods' (Ibsen's phrase for poetry) would become the natural expression for his middle- and lower-class characters and at the same time keep the two worlds of men and gods in simultaneous focus. The first two speeches of the play, by Franklin and Arden, illustrate how successfully the playwright has met this problem. On an immediate level of recognition, introduction of character and exposition of theme could not be more rapid and more concise. Just nineteen lines in all introduce at once the theme of acquisition, set forth the major situation of the play (Mistress Arden's adultery), introduce Franklin in his role of friend and confidant, and establish Arden as an ambitious man whose success is in itself bringing him no happiness and as a more complicated private person whose grief finds its source in mixed motives of rejected love, shame, and hurt pride. The tone is conversational: the sentence structure is for the most part of normal word order, and the vocabulary consists almost entirely of one and two syllable words. Only one image occurs in these lines—'this veil of heaven' for 'sky' in line 13—and that so conventional that it barely begins to call attention to itself. The spectator can hardly 'be wholly conscious of the medium'. But something else is happening here: the conversational tone is caught, as it were, within a rhythm that works steadily, almost inexorably, in the patterning of basically end-stopped lines to suggest as an undercurrent that Arden is not only unhappy but also doomed;[1] and the one image is just enough out of the ordinary to suggest quietly the mystery of larger forces that 'sky' would not.

Thus from the start a tone has been set for the rest of the play which naturalizes the poetry but starts up ironic reverberations in the literalism of the dialogue. It could even be argued that the

---

[1] Cf. Hanratty, p. 177: 'If the speaking of the verse is kept "up", this incantatory pattern is the most unifying factor a play can have—engaging the attention like a game which keeps the ball in play continually.'

ethical confusion and 'divided sensibilities' that finally doom most of the characters who look at other people only as objects and who cannot see beyond their own egos are reflected in how literally they use language without being aware of its 'poetic' overtones of a greater, more meaningful world of order. A striking instance, from innumerable in the play, is Alice's comparison of Arden's arms around her to 'the snakes of black Tisiphone' (xiv. 144)—an allusion to the avenger of crime against kin that ironically eludes the speaker completely.[1] Almost as striking are Mosby's avowal to Alice, cited earlier, that he will follow her even 'to the gates of death'; Black Will's telling Shakebag that they are 'almost in hell's mouth' (xii. 2); and Arden's punning reply to the ferryman that the mist they find themselves engulfed in is 'mystical' (xi. 6) and that he is 'almost stifled with this fog' (xi. 31). A grim parody of this unconsciously literal use of language is in Alice's conscious comparison of Arden's blood first to 'the pig's blood we had to supper' and then to 'a cup of wine that Michael shed' (xiv. 388, 402), but initial signs of Alice's repentant mood come in her earlier recognition that Arden's blood has not ceased to flow 'because I blush not at my husband's death' (xiv. 259); here, the literal becomes metaphorical. In Arden's death by strangulation after his haunting dream of being a deer trapped by herdsmen (recounted in scene vi) and in his body's imprint being seen for more than two years after his murder in 'that plot of ground / Which he by force and violence held from Reede' (Epilogue), the poetic becomes visually literal as destiny fulfils itself.[2]

Even though it suffers from memorial contamination, making the language and particularly the versification suspect in many places (large portions of the Black Will–Shakebag scenes were probably written as prose originally), the text as it has come down to us still makes it possible to conclude with S. Youngblood that *Arden* 'is a well-made play which is both good theater and good poetry' and with M. Bluestone that its 'language commands

[1] In a play with few classical images, it is the more forceful also for its isolation and its context.

[2] Cf. Bluestone, 'The Imagery of Tragic Melodrama', p. 179: 'In the end, hyperbole becomes thoroughly and ironically literal. The facile assurances yield to catastrophe, not only for the guilty but for the innocent.'

respect'.[1] The detailed studies of the play's language by these two
writers reveal beyond doubt the consistency with which the language functions dramatically in *Arden*. A network of inverted or
distorted images of nature and religion—of animals, hunting, and
entrapment; of blood, laceration, and death; of decay and 'blighted
generation' (Bluestone)—pictures a world of nature tooth and claw
where only survival matters; at the same time it foreshadows the
'fatalistic progress into evil' (Youngblood) and the inevitable doom
of the characters. Furthermore, it is clear that the playwright is
experimenting with the poetic medium itself to see how far he can
vary its possibilities within the same work for conversational dialogue, soliloquies of psychological introspection, straightforward
narrative development, and volatile displays of passion. The
'naturalness', or appropriateness, of speech throughout the play—
whether when the major characters are speaking in a plain style (as
mostly during the murder scene) or when the comical assassins are
speaking in a lyrical high style (Black Will at iii. 100–3 or Shakebag
at the beginning of scene v)—is the measure of his success.[2] To
Mézières, this fusion of 'a rich and varied language of lyric poetry'
with drama, at the beginning of Elizabethan drama's golden age,
represents 'the drama of the future'.[3] It remains one of the great
ironies of the operation of Chance on human affairs that the name
of the *Arden* playwright has not come down to us.

6. AUTHORSHIP

Did Shakespeare write *Arden of Faversham*? Today, if the matter
of authorship is raised at all, this question is the only one likely to
arouse serious interest. The leading rival claimants of the past,

[1] Youngblood, p. 207; and Bluestone, 'The Imagery of Tragic Melodrama', p. 172.

[2] Cf. Davies, p. 61: 'Thus is seems that the realistic effect is to be achieved
by putting the poetry in the right place, and not by a complete absence of
poetry.' It should be noted that the *Arden* playwright, whom W. Clemen
does not mention on the subject in his *English Tragedy before Shakespeare*
(1961), considerably naturalized the 'absolutely fundamental ingredient of
pre-Shakespearean tragedy' (p. 12)—the set speech: cf. Michael's and
Mosby's soliloquies (scenes iv, viii), Arden's dream (vi), and Franklin's tale
(ix); each of these is fundamentally integrated into the action dramatically.

[3] Mézières (trans.), pp. 109–10.

F

Kyd and, to a lesser extent, Marlowe, no longer compel any strong assent; and there seems to be tacit agreement among scholars that to suggest collaborative authorship is, as Bayne long ago pointed out, 'to shirk the question'.[1] No conclusive external evidence exists to support the claim of any known writer of the period, and the deductions from internal evidence alone have never completely satisfied all readers. In 1963, after an exhaustive review of the literature on the subject, M. P. Jackson presented in his Oxford B.Litt. thesis the most extensively considered case for Shakespearean authorship; but S. Schoenbaum, although he overlooked this particular work, was on the whole justified in asserting in 1966 that 'the conjecturists appear to have given up on *Arden of Feversham.*' 'This shift', Schoenbaum writes, 'may be due in part to changes in sensibility, in part to the recognition of the law of diminishing returns.'[2]

The comparatively recent neglect of a question that has troubled scholars since the Faversham antiquary Edward Jacob edited the play in 1770 and attributed it in his preface to Shakespeare has been a good thing for the play itself, for it has tended to focus closer attention upon its merits as a work of dramatic literature. One unintentional result, however, of this benign neglect has been to bring Shakespeare's name in again by the back door, so to speak. Latterday recognition of the play's 'dramatic and poetic power' would even appear once again to strengthen 'the case of advocates of Shakespeare's authorship of the play'.[3] M. Bluestone, for example, observes, 'The play consistently reinterprets the source with Shakespearean forms of complication', and 'Although the imagery in the play never quite achieves Shakespearean prevalence and consistency, it is not less than kin to that language which exposes poor forked animals to tragic torment.' Praising 'the richness of its language, the expertness of its dramaturgy, and the intensity of its characters', he concludes that the author 'deserves the celebration implied in the unproved ascriptions to Shakespeare'.[4]

Schoenbaum is right, of course, when he lays down the rule:

[1] P. ix.
[2] *Internal Evidence and Elizabethan Dramatic Authorship* (1966), p. 137.
[3] Adams, p. 107.
[4] 'The Imagery of Tragic Melodrama', pp. 174–5, 180.

'Intuitions, convictions, and subjective judgments generally, carry no weight as evidence.'[1] But at the very least they confirm the critical tradition in which appreciation of *Arden*, regardless of who was being advocated as author, has far outweighed the contrary.[2] What Kenneth Muir calls 'the best of the [Shakespeare] apocryphal plays'[3] is, in fact, so good a play that its anonymity is as surprising as it is troublesome. Appearing on the threshold of the great flowering of Elizabethan drama in the late 1580s and early 1590s, *Arden* represents, as we saw, a bold experiment in portraying the passions of ordinary Englishmen in the setting of contemporary society and in language appropriate to the characters and theme. And it does so without romanticizing the characters or turning them into moral exemplars. One might have expected that with an apparently active stage history and publication in three or four quarto editions from 1592 to 1633 the play would at one point be linked with a named playwright. Anonymous publication in itself at this time means little since most of the plays that we esteem from this early period were so published—*The Spanish Tragedy*, the two parts of *Tamburlaine*, and most of Shakespeare's early plays to name only famous examples. But for these plays and many others persuasive external evidence pointing to particular authors exists; not so for *Arden*.

Play-catalogues down through Jacob's time (1770) list *Arden* as anonymous, with only one exception, and that an untrustworthy one. In Edward Archer's list of 1656 the play is attributed to the

[1] P. 178. See, however, J. D. Jump's criticism of this 'too harsh' rule in *N. & Q.*, 212 (1967), 238–9.

[2] Typical evaluations are: 'apparently the earliest, and beyond all question, the highest achievement of the Elizabethan age in the field of domestic drama' (Moorman, p. 240); 'one of the finest and most effective tragedies of the period' (Oliphant, 'Problems of Authorship in Elizabethan Dramatic Literature', p. 420); 'superior to any other domestic play of the period' (Davies, p. 51); 'Earliest of the well-known domestic tragedies, it remains the finest' (Adams, p. 108); 'the great anonymous play . . . is transmuted [from Holinshed] into moving tragedy, a masterpiece of psychological interpretation, which foreshadows *Macbeth*' (H. Craig, *A History of English Literature* [1950], p. 221); 'an impressive play which anticipates many later developments in Elizabethan and Jacobean tragedy. . . . The story is presented with remarkable psychological realism' (D. Daiches, *A Critical History of English Literature* [1960], I. 234).

[3] *Shakespeare as Collaborator* (1960), p. 3.

Puritan clergyman and translator of Terence, Richard Bernard; but W. W. Greg has demonstrated convincingly that this is a printing-house error for Shakespeare's name, which appears, wrongly aligned with Peele's *Arraignment of Paris*, just above.[1] Although the listing appears more than half a century after the original publication of the play, Archer, still fairly close to the original tradition, may have had solid evidence for his attribution; but his authority in general is so disreputable that one hesitates to accept him. As Greg points out, 'while Archer shows occasional signs of rather unexpected knowledge, his blunders, whether due to carelessness or ignorance, are so many and so gross that very little reliance can be placed upon any particular ascription he may make.'[2] In 1661 the bookseller Francis Kirkman, working from Archer's list, removed the attribution and returned the play to anonymity. Above all, the omission of *Arden* from the First Folio of Shakespeare in 1623, as well as from the 1664 second issue of the Third Folio, which includes a supplement of plays attributed to Shakespeare, is important negative, even if not conclusive, evidence against Shakespeare's authorship.

Arden entered the Shakespeare Apocrypha with Jacob's edition in 1770. In his preface the historian of Faversham claimed that the play 'bids fair ... for being [Shakespeare's] earliest theatrical Production now remaining'; and, although he did not think himself 'qualified to determine magisterially', he felt confident 'that it will be found superior to any of an earlier date in our language'. That Shakespeare was drawn to the material in the first place by the name of Arden (his mother's maiden name) seemed likely to Jacob, who also thought it possible that Heminges and Condell omitted the play from the First Folio because it belonged to a different company. 'To justify the Editor's opinion', he appended a brief list of parallel passages from the canonical plays; but, as Stephen Jones was to point out in the 1812 edition of *Biographica Dramatica* (III, 35), the proof was 'ridiculous', consisting mostly of Elizabethan commonplaces. In 1823, however, Ludwig Tieck translated the play into German and unequivocally attributed it to Shakespeare.

---

[1] 'Shakespeare and *Arden of Feversham*', *R.E.S.*, XXI (1945), 134–6.
[2] P. 135.

Since then, the literature has grown extensively; but, the only evidence coming from the text itself, preconceptions about authorship tend to colour its interpretation.[1] To those who feel that the play could have been written only by Shakespeare, the 'proof' is at hand; so is it for those who think the contrary. As long as objections can be raised on either side of the question, a healthy scepticism is, of course, justifiable. To speak with certainty of an author's style is to isolate precisely those factors which are peculiar to him and to no other writer—a notoriously difficult task considering the common stock of stylistic devices in Elizabethan drama.

Moreover, in the case of the *Arden* playwright the difficulty is compounded by the reportorial nature of the text. To judge from the better portions of the text, *Arden* is written in predominantly end-stopped iambic pentameter verse. But so is almost every extant play of this period, including those by Shakespeare, Marlowe, and Kyd. Studies of vocabulary, imagery, and particularly image-clusters that seem to recur unconsciously in the works of a writer would appear to put us on a surer footing. In considering *Arden* for her study of Marlowe's imagery, M. B. Smith was 'struck even more by the resemblances to the imagination of still another playwright—Shakespeare'. 'Again and again', she writes, 'an image calls to mind his early work, especially in the Histories'—for example, images from the categories of Daily Life (archery, riding, bird-snaring), Nature (animals, especially helpless victims), and the Garden (notably the unweeded or blighted garden) that C. F. E. Spurgeon earlier had found so characteristic of Shakespeare. Besides, Smith finds 'not only single images, but whole passages remind the reader of early Shakespeare'; she quotes in full Arden's dream in scene vi and Clarence's in *Richard III*, I. iv, to enable her readers to observe for themselves the similarities.[2] M. P. Jackson's deeper, more extensive study confirms Professor Smith's obser-

---

[1] A complete review of the entire authorship debate can be found in Jackson; briefer ones in E. A. Taylor, 'Elizabethan Domestic Tragedies', unpubl. Univ. of Chicago Ph.D. diss. (1925), pp. 31–65, in Patterson, and in J. Levenson's forthcoming bibliography (see Preface).

[2] *Marlowe's Imagery and the Marlowe Canon* (1940); see all of chapter IV, pp. 125–36. See also C. F. E. Spurgeon, *Shakespeare's Imagery and What It Tells Us* (1935), *passim*.

vations and brings to our attention other categories of images, further image-clusters, examples of word-play and punning, and the frequent recurrence of adjectival compounds (as 'narrow-prying', 'deep-fetched', hunger-bitten')—all of which are characteristic of Shakespeare's canonical works.[1]

Yet, well-documented though these studies are, the persistence of doubt is understandable; for in dealing with a corrupt text we cannot be absolutely sure that we are isolating features individual to the writer in question. For instance, Jackson clearly shows that *Arden* compares favourably with Shakespeare's known use of adjectival compounds. But I. Koskenniemi's *Studies in the Vocabulary of English Drama, 1550–1600*, which excludes Shakespeare and Jonson from consideration, notes that the use of this form was widely spread among Elizabethan playwrights because it helped them 'to give condensed expression to subtle and complex thoughts and feelings' and also 'compactness and power of expression . . . in colloquial or vulgar speech'.[2] And, although the images of *Arden* are characteristic of Shakespeare, we have to be reasonably sure, as M. Prior reminds us, 'that in its most characteristic form the image is not likely to occur in the work of another writer'.[3] Image-clusters, or the recurrent linking of the same images, would seem to afford a higher degree of statistical probability for determining authorship; but even these ultimately must be related to the dramatic context in which they occur. E. A. Armstrong, who coined the phrase and first proposed the method of studying an author's 'image-clusters', warned that 'it is extremely difficult to show in any instance that [they] owe [their] origin to emotional experiences per-

---

[1] See Jackson, pp. 177–254.

[2] (1962), pp. 15 *et passim*. In *Shakespeare and the Homilies* (1934), pp. 232–6, A. Hart demonstrates that Shakespeare used a higher percentage of compound words than his fellow dramatists. This observation may be true, but the point is that they were in frequent use by all the contemporary dramatists. Jackson (pp. 200–1) observes that *Arden* 'contains seventeen which were also used by Shakespeare'; Koskenniemi shows (Appendix 1 of her book) that several of these occur in other writers, often much earlier.

[3] 'Imagery as a Test of Authorship', *Sh.Q.*, VI (1955), 384. Cf. R. A. Foakes, 'Suggestions for a New Approach to Shakespeare's Imagery', *Sh.S.*, V (1952), 82: 'much of Shakespeare's imagery is borrowed, proverbial or commonplace.'

sonal to the poet as distinct from participation in more general emotion.'[1]

The 'evidence' for Kyd or Marlowe or their joint authorship fails to persuade for the same reasons. 'Some of our brightest intellects', in the words of E. H. C. Oliphant, have succumbed to 'the baleful influence' of 'the deadly parallel'—including, alas, even Oliphant himself.[2] In Kyd's case, most of the 'parallels' are to *Soliman and Perseda*, the authorship of which is extremely debatable, and, to a lesser degree, to *The Murder of John Brewen*, a pamphlet of 1592 about an Arden-type murder which is now completely discredited as Kyd's.[3] Advocates of either author have cited 'typical' words and phrases and have employed the usual 'tests', but they have brought us no closer to certainty. Marlowe's origins in Kent and the probability of Kyd's having been for a time a scrivener (and thus familiar with legal terminology) and a servant (like Mosby) in a large household counter Shakespeare's possible interest in the Arden name; the known circumstance of Kyd and Marlowe's sharing a chamber in 1591 takes on the glow of external evidence for joint authorship. It should be observed that the so-called 'Pembroke group' of plays referred to earlier includes works by all three writers.

Other suggestions for full or partial authorship have not been wanting—Peele, Greene, Anthony Munday, Samuel Rowley,

[1] *Shakespeare's Imagination* (1946), p. 157.

[2] 'How Not to Play the Game of Parallels', *J.E.G.P.*, XXVIII (1929), 13. See Appendix I and also Oliphant's 'Marlowe's Hand in *Arden of Feversham*: A Problem for Critics', *New Criterion*, IV (1926), 76–93; the argument here is repeated in the introduction to his anthology editions of the play in 1929 and in 1931. Fleay, II, 29, tentatively attributed *Arden* to Kyd on the basis of parallel passages at iv. 87–8 and at ix. 39 to *Sp.T.*; but the first elaborate case was presented by C. Crawford, with lengthier and more detailed arguments subsequently set forth by W. Miksch, H. D. Sykes, and P. V. Rubow (see Abbreviations and Appendix I).

[3] See R. M. Gorrell, 'John Payne Collier and *The Murder of John Brewen*', *M.L.N.*, LVII (1942), 441–4, and also S. A. Tannenbaum, *The Booke of Sir Thomas Moore* (1927), p. 50, n. 17. In the preface to one of the most recent works on Kyd, P. B. Murray writes: 'Of the works attributed to Kyd, the most interesting are *Soliman and Perseda* and *Arden of Feversham*. I have made a close study of the language of these plays, however, and cannot convince myself that they are the work of the author of *The Spanish Tragedy*' (*Thomas Kyd* [1969]).

Robert Yarrington, Thomas Heywood, even the 17th Earl of
Oxford, the 6th Earl of Derby, and George Wilkins.[1] None of these
carries any conviction. William Archer's fanciful idea that *Arden*
might 'have been written by some local gentleman (like the Lord
Cheiny introduced into it), who took a special interest in this particular theme, and made no other excursion into letters', is perhaps
the most engaging.[2]

Appearances, then, would still seem to justify Tucker Brooke's
pessimistic assertion, made earlier in this century, that 'in such
cases, not to advance is to recede hopelessly'.[3] When external evidence does not exist, even the soundest of texts, which *Arden* is far
from being, can provide, at best, only *probability* of authorship.
There are, however, degrees of probability. Attribution is, after all,
not an exact science, and interpretations of evidence vary; but the
nature of the evidence itself can be evaluated. Thus, although the
possibility always exists that *Arden* is a single creative effort of an
unknown playwright (or the collaborative achievement of unknown
playwrights or actor-playwrights—see Appendix I), of all the cases
presented for and against various known playwrights that for
Shakespeare emerges as the strongest. As befits discussion from
internal evidence alone, considerations of characterization, structure, underlying theme, and appropriateness of language figure
more prominently and more suggestively with him than they do
with any other writer proposed. As Jackson has pointed out, some
of the very critics who remain doubtful as to the play's author yet
stress certain Shakespearean qualities about the play or even venture to suggest that Shakespeare must have had a part in it. J. A.
Symonds, for example, was 'loth in the absence of any external
evidence' to attribute the play to Shakespeare, but he asked, on the
basis of its 'dramatic skill, [its] tragic force': 'Was there any other
playwright capable of producing work so masterly before the date

[1] Levenson and Jackson (see Preface) cite the full scholarship on the
authorship question. See Swinburne's mocking appendix to *A Study of
Shakespeare* which purports to be the 'First Report of the Newest Shakespeare Society'; in it Ben Jonson is cited as the author of *Arden*, his intention being to make fun of Black *Will Shake*bag and Murderous Michael
(Drayton).
[2] P. 235.   [3] *Apocrypha*, p. xv.

of 1592 ?'[1] Over and over again *Arden*'s strong characterization and
the psychological depth of particular scenes (especially Michael's
soliloquy at the end of iv, Arden's dream in vi, and the quarrel between Alice and Mosby in viii) are singled out for praise.[2] These are
features which do not readily associate themselves with playwrights
or with anonymous plays before 1592; Shakespeare is the only
name that they bring to mind right away. Jackson's detailed analysis
of scene viii confirms the Shakespearean quality of its language;
and, to use Prior's distinction, even if we cannot be sure that particular expressions and images are not likely to occur in their most
characteristic forms in the works of other writers, we can be sure at
least that the style is consistent with what we know of early Shakespeare.[3] In fact, the frequent recurrence of the image of the mud-
died or troubled fountain in the latter's work is behind a widely
accepted emendation of a major crux at viii. 133.

A persistent attitude is that, although *Arden* 'would, in point of
absolute merit, have done no discredit to the early manhood of
Shakespeare himself; . . . both in conception and execution, it is
quite unlike even his earliest manner'.[4] John Masefield has gone so
far as to say: 'It bears no single trace of Shakespeare's mind. It
could not have been written by him at any stage in his career.'[5] For
evidence to the contrary, and without at all trying to press for
Shakespearean authorship, one need seek no further than Shakespeare's first tetralogy, the three *Henry VI* plays and *Richard III*,
which, like *Arden*, have their source in the chronicles. Bayne was
the first to point out the similarities in prose style between the
Black Will–Shakebag scenes and the Jack Cade scenes of *2 Henry*

---

[1] Pp. 418, 459.

[2] See, for example, Ulrici, p. 447; Knight, pp. 269–71, 275–6; Mézières,
pp. 104–7; Bullen, p. xvii; Warnke and Proescholdt, p. xxii; G. Saintsbury,
A History of Elizabethan Literature (1887), p. 425; Ward, II. 218; Courthope, IV. 239; Moorman, p. 242.

[3] Jackson, pp. 227–54; see also pp. 48–51 for the 'fence of trouble' crux
at viii. 133, which is referred to next.

[4] Anonymous reviewer in *The Edinburgh Review*, LXXI (1840), 471, who
also admits that, 'on the other hand, the date cannot possibly be removed
so far back as the time before which [Shakespeare's] own style had demon-
strably been formed.'

[5] *William Shakespeare* (1925), p. 239.

VI; but if the overall poetic effect of the tetralogy is more decoratively rhetorical, more ornate and suited to the language of the noblest figures of the realm, the conscious intent of the *Arden* author, expressed in the Epilogue, was to suit his language to the 'naked tragedy' of commoners. More important, the power-hungry, self-seeking, blind, ruthless, amoral world of *Arden's* commoners expresses the same vision as these early history plays, in which the highest peers and their ladies, Queen Margaret herself, set an example of moral confusion for Jack Cade and his rebellious peasants and artisans. In both *Arden* and the tetralogy human life counts for nothing when it stands in the way of personal ambition; moral and social laws are constantly being abrogated for expediency; and mutual trust breaks down when men swear oaths which they know in advance that they will violate. In *Arden* the effect of words is to 'bewitch' (see p. lxxiii above); and what the Duke of Burgundy, who switches sides and breaks oaths, says of Joan of Arc in *1 Henry VI* (III. iii. 58–9) could well stand as an epigraph for all these plays:

> Either she hath bewitch'd me with her words,
> Or nature makes me suddenly relent.[1]

Black Will's 'Tush, I have broken five hundred oaths!' (*Arden*, iii. 89) finds no mere mechanical parallel in the future King Edward's 'I would break a thousand oaths to reign one year' (*3 Henry VI*, I. ii. 17). Even the good King Henry breaks his oath, not with guile, to be sure, to marry Margaret of Anjou instead of the Earl of Armagnac's daughter to whom he is betrothed. Arden's infatuation for Alice is not unlike Henry's for Margaret; and the two women are instrumental with their lovers in bringing about the ruin of their husbands; in both cases, they also wreak havoc in the com-

---

[1] Cf. M. M. Mahood, *Shakespeare's Wordplay* (1957), pp. 174–5: 'In Shakespeare's lifetime the old hierarchy of delegated verbal authority was breaking up, and many words which had once seemed to hold magical efficacy were losing their connotative power. . . . It is typical of Shakespeare's own linguistic scepticism in the early History plays that in each case the conflict is settled by expediency—that daily break-vow, Commodity. Neither the Murderer's fealty nor his faith [in *Richard III*] weighs anything against the word *reward*—which has a more immediate and tangible referent than either the King's warrant or the tables of the law.'

munity—the provincial society of Faversham, the great kingdom of England.

One of the most recent commentators on the History plays, H. A. Kelly, has written that 'Shakespeare's great contribution was ... to unmoralize [the] moralizations of his contemporaries' and to create a kind of characterization that 'eliminates simplistic evaluations of complex moral situations'[1]—precisely the view taken of *Arden* in this introduction. The episodic structure of *Arden* and of the plays in the tetralogy (more so the *Henry VI* plays) involves characters in an intricate web in which their own weaknesses concur with Fortune to bring about their ruin and the ruin of others. The good are weak, ineffectual, or naïve. Gloucester can no more save Henry from himself than Franklin can save Arden from himself. And the evil, through self-betrayal and distrust of one another, destroy themselves. The role of Providence in all these plays is extremely difficult to assess. It is not at all clear that Henry's loss of his kingdom is divine retribution upon the Lancastrians; it is equally not clear that Arden's murder is in any way a fulfilment of Reede's curse. A voice that echoes King Henry's at the worldly Cardinal Beaufort's death-bed seems pervasive throughout *Arden* and the early Histories: 'Forbear to judge, for we are sinners all' (*2 Henry VI*, III. iii. 31). Reality is too complicated.

Earlier in this century Oliphant wrote: '*Arden*'s claim to rank among even the Shakspere apocrypha is on external evidence absolutely *nil*; nor is it his on the internal evidence.'[2] In view of Edward Archer's untrustworthy ascription of the play to Shakespeare in

---

[1] *Divine Providence in the England of Shakespeare's Histories* (1970), pp. 304–5; see individual chapters on the plays of the tetralogy. Cf. too, J. Winny, *The Player King* (1968), pp. 17–18: 'However it may have developed later, Shakespeare's early interest in history was not activated by a sense of moral retribution working itself out through political disorder and bloodshed. . . . An imaginative view of life does not necessarily exclude a moral awareness, but homiletic commentary on the events of history is alien to Shakespeare's creative purpose.' As for characterization. M. C. Bradbrook, *Elizabethan Stage Conditions* (1932), pp. 84–5, observes that 'there is not a single play of Shakespeare where the motivation for every character is quite sufficient'; H. T. Price, 'Construction in Shakespeare', *Univ. of Michigan Contributions in Modern Philology*, XVII (1951), 22, observes that irony is Shakespeare's 'principle of construction'.

[2] 'Problems of Authorship in Elizabethan Dramatic Literature', p. 420.

1656 we have to accept the first half of this statement, but surely internal evidence at least qualifies it for the apocryphal works. Until finer means, however, are perfected for evaluating internal evidence, to admit *Arden* among the canonical works would be, as Dr Johnson put it in his great *Preface to Shakespeare*, to succumb to 'all the joy and all the pride of invention' which conjecture offers.

Editions

---

[1] The University of Illinois (Urbana) library has in its possession a nineteenth-century manuscript copy of Jacob's edition, briefly annotated and sporadically collated with the 1633 quarto. A few changes in spelling, punctuation, and lineation, as well as several obvious corrections, have been introduced into the text; but the manuscript is totally without textual authority.

Tyrrell	*The Doubtful Plays of Shakespere*, ed. H. Tyrrell, 1851.
Delius	*Arden of Feversham*, ed. N. Delius, 1855 (*Pseudo-Shakspere'sche Dramen*, Vol. II).
Bullen	*Arden of Feversham, a Tragedy*, ed. A. H. Bullen, 1887.
Warnke and Proescholdt [*W-P* in collation]	*Arden of Feversham*, ed. K. Warnke and L. Proescholdt, 1888 (*Pseudo-Shakespearian Plays*, Vol. V).
Hopkinson (1)	*Arden of Feversham*, ed. A. F. Hopkinson, 1890.
Bayne	*Arden of Feversham*, ed. R. Bayne, 1897 (*The Temple Dramatists*).
Hopkinson (2)	*Arden of Feversham*, ed. A. F. Hopkinson, 1898 (*Shakespeare's Doubtful Plays*).
Hopkinson (3)	*Arden of Feversham* ed. A. F. Hopkinson, 1907 (*Shakespeare's Doubtful Plays*, rev. and enl.).
Brooke, *Apocrypha* [*Brooke* in collation]	*The Shakespeare Apocrypha*, ed. C. F. Tucker Brooke, 1908.
Thorndike	*The Minor Elizabethan Drama*, Vol. I: *Pre-Shakespearian Tragedies*, ed. A. Thorndike, 1910 (*Everyman's Library*)
Farmer	*Arden of Feversham*, ed. J. S. Farmer, 1911 (*Tudor Facsimile Texts*).
Schelling	*Typical Elizabethan Plays*, ed. F. E. Schelling, 1926.
Oliphant	*Shakespeare and His Fellow Dramatists*, ed. E. H. C. Oliphant, 1929 (reprinted in the same editor's *Elizabethan Dramatists Other Than Shakespeare*, 1931).

Baskervill
[*B-H-N* in collation]
Elizabethan and Stuart Plays, ed. C. R. Baskervill, V. B. Heltzel, and A. H. Nethercot, 1934 (reprinted in *Elizabethan Plays*, 1971).

McIlwraith
Five Elizabethan Tragedies, ed. A. K. McIlwraith, 1938 (*The World's Classics*).

Macdonald and Smith
[*M.S.R.* in collation]
Arden of Feversham 1592, ed. H. Macdonald and D. N. Smith, 1947 (*The Malone Society Reprints*, 1940).

Gassner
Elizabethan Drama, ed. J. Gassner, 1967 (*Bantam World Drama Editions*).

Sturgess
Three Elizabethan Domestic Tragedies, ed. K. Sturgess, 1969 (*The Penguin English Library*).

Anon.
The Lamentable and True Tragedy of M. Arden of Faversham 1592, 1971 (Scolar Press facsimile).

(D) TRANSLATIONS

Tieck
Shakspeare's Vorschule, ed. L. Tieck, 1823, Vol. I.

Doring
Supplemente zu allen Ausgaben, Shakespeare's Sämtliche Schauspiele, ed. H. Doring, 1840, Vol. I.

Ortlepp
Nachträge zu Shakspeare's Werken von Schlegel und Tieck, ed. E. Ortlepp, 1840, Vol. III.

Thalès
B. Thalès, 'Un nouveau drame de Shakespeare, *Arden de Feversham*, tragédie', *Revue des races latines*, XVIII (1860), 337–99.

Hugo
Œuvres Complètes de William Shakespeare, Vol. XVII: *Les Apocryphes*, ed. F.-V. Hugo, 1867.

Kuitert	*Meesterstukken onder Shakespeare's Pseudo-Drama's,* ed. G. B. Kuitert, 1882.
Halling	*Tre Pseudo-Shakespeareske Skuespil,* ed. A. Halling, 1913.
Angeli	*Opere Attribuite a Shakespeare,* ed. D. Angeli, 1934, Vol. I (*Shakespeare, Teatro Completo,* Vol. XXXVIII).
Baldini	*Teatro Elisabettiano,* ed. M. Praz, with translation by G. Baldini, 1948.
Messiaen	*Théâtre anglais,* ed. P. Messiaen, 1948.
Carrère	*Arden de Feversham,* ed. F. Carrère, 1950 (parallel texts).
Brunius and Bellon	*Arden de Faversham,* ed. L. Brunius and L. Bellon, 1957 (*Répertoire pour un théâtre populaire,* 9).
Somlyó	*Angol reneszánsz drámák,* ed. M. J. Szenczi, with translation by G. Somlyó, 1961, Vol. I.
Cosmos	*Arden de Faversham,* ed. J. Cosmos, 1964.

(E) SELECTIONS

Lamb	*Specimens of English Dramatic Poets who Lived about the Time of Shakspere,* ed. C. Lamb, 1808.
Knight	*The Pictorial Edition of the Works of Shakspere,* ed. C. Knight, 1839–43, Vol. VII.
Schack	*Die Englischen Dramatiker vor, neben und nach Shakespeare,* ed. A. F. von Schack, 1893.
Gide	Selections translated by A. Gide in *Cahiers du Sud,* XX (1933), 107–17.

ARDEN OF FAVERSHAM

THE
LAMENTA=
BLE AND TRVE TRA-
GEDIE OF M. AR-
DEN OF FEVERSHAM
IN KENT.

Who was most wickedlye murdered, *by*
the meanes of his disloyall and wanton
wyfe, who for the loue she bare to one
Mosbie, hyred two desperat ruf-
fins Blackwill and Shakbag,
to kill him.

Wherin is shewed the great mallice and discimulation of a wicked woman, the vnsatiable desire of filthie lust
and the shamefull end of all
murderers.

Imprinted at **London** *for* **Edward**
White, dwelling at the lyttle North
dore of Paules Church at
the signe of the
Gun. 1592.
✳

[*LIST OF CHARACTERS*
in order of appearance

THOMAS ARDEN, *a Gentleman of Faversham.*
FRANKLIN, *his friend.*
ALICE, *Arden's wife.*
ADAM FOWLE, *landlord of the Flower-de-Luce.*
MICHAEL, *Arden's servant.*
MOSBY, *lover of Arden's wife.*
CLARKE, *a painter.*
GREENE, *a tenant.*
SUSAN, *Mosby's sister and Alice's servingmaid.*
BRADSHAW, *a goldsmith.*
BLACK WILL ⎫
           ⎬ *hired murderers.*
SHAKEBAG ⎭
A Prentice.
LORD CHEYNE *and his* Men.
A Ferryman.
DICK REEDE, *sailor and inhabitant of Faversham.*
A Sailor, *his friend.*
Mayor of Faversham *and the* Watch.]

LIST OF CHARACTERS] *adapted from S.MS. and M.S.R., with elaboration from Tieck and Tyrrell; not in Qq.*

3

The Tragedy of Master Arden
of Faversham

[Sc. i]

Enter ARDEN *and* FRANKLIN.

Franklin. Arden, cheer up thy spirits and droop no more.
  My gracious Lord the Duke of Somerset
  Hath freely given to thee and to thy heirs,
  By letters patents from his majesty,
  All the lands of the Abbey of Faversham.   5

Title. Faversham] *Q1c(H)* (Feuershame); Feueshame *Q1u(M, D).*   Sc. i]
Hugo; not in Qq; ACT I. SCENE I. *A Room in* Arden's *House.* Tyrrell, *after*
Tieck.   3. thy] *Q1;* thine *Q2–3.*   4. patents] *Qq;* patent *S.MS., Tyrrell.*
from] *Q1–2, S.MS.;* of *Q3.*

Sc. i] See Intro., p. xxxv.
    1. Franklin] probably just a familiar name (in English common law, a
franklin is a freeholder or one who owns a small landed estate).
    spirits] monosyllabic, as is *given* in l. 3.
    2–5.] Deeds preserved at Rockingham Castle, formerly part of the Abbey
of Faversham, and recorded by Cust ('*Arden of Feversham*', p. 103), indi-
cate that Sir Thomas Cheyne (see sc. ix), who had been granted 'the site
of yᵉ monastery of ffaversham withall ye premisses within yᵉ walls' by
Henry VIII on 16 March 1540, had arranged for the sale and transfer of
the 'lands' to Arden—probably some five or six years before the time of the
play.
    2. *Duke of Somerset*] At the time of Arden's murder in 1551, Edward
Seymour, the Duke of Somerset, served as Lord Protector (l. 34) to
Edward VI (l. 7), then only thirteen years old. The *D.N.B.*'s estimate of his
character provides an apt commentary on Arden's, as well as on the historical background of the events of the play (see Intro., pp. lxi–lxiv): 'The
chief blot on Somerset's career is his rapacity in profiting by the dissolution
of the monasteries, the abolition of the chantries, and sale of church lands.'
    4. *letters patents*] open letters or documents, and therefore publicly
recorded, 'usually from a sovereign... to confer some right, privilege, title,
property, or office' (*O.E.D.*). Although the phrase is now used customarily
in the singular (*letters patent*), the plural form was common during this
period (see Abbott 338).

Here are the deeds,   *[He hands over the papers.]*
Sealed and subscribed with his name and the king's.
Read them, and leave this melancholy mood.

Arden. Franklin, thy love prolongs my weary life;
And, but for thee, how odious were this life,   10
That shows me nothing but torments my soul,
And those foul objects that offend mine eyes—
Which makes me wish that for this veil of heaven
The earth hung over my head and covered me.
Love letters passed 'twixt Mosby and my wife,   15
And they have privy meetings in the town.
Nay, on his finger did I spy the ring
Which at our marriage day the priest put on.
Can any grief be half so great as this?

Franklin. Comfort thyself, sweet friend; it is not strange   20
That women will be false and wavering.

Arden. Ay, but to dote on such a one as he
Is monstrous, Franklin, and intolerable.

Franklin. Why, what is he?

Arden. A botcher, and no better at the first,   25
Who, by base brokage getting some small stock,

6–7.] *so Delius; one line in Qq; divided in Sturgess at* subscribed / With.
6. S.D.] *Bayne; not in Qq.*   13. makes] *Qq;* make *S.MS., Tyrrell.*
14. over] *Qq;* o'er *Tyrrell.*   15. passed] *Qq* (past); pass *S.MS., Tyrrell;*
post *Knight.*   17. spy the] *Qq;* espy a *Sturgess.*   18. day] *Q1–2; not in Q3.*

---

11. *shows*] accords or grants (favour, honour, grace, etc.) (*O.E.D., v.,* 20).
13. *makes*] The singular verb form with plural subjects is a regular feature of Elizabethan English (see Abbott 333, 336).
for this veil of heaven] instead of the sky.
19.] Cf. *Con.,* I. iii. 58 ('Can any griefe of minde be like to this'; not in 'good' quarto of *2H6*). Arden's distraction here is, as Bayne points out, at variance with the description in Holinshed ('he was contented to winke at hir filthie disorder') and in the Wardmote Book of Faversham ('All whiche things thesaid Thomas Ardern did well knowe and wilfully did permytt and suffred the same').
25. *botcher*] 'a tailor who does repairs' (*O.E.D.,* 2.b).
at the first] literally: at his beginnings; since he was born.
26. *base brokage*] pimping. (*O.E.D.* cites for definition the dedicatory

Crept into service of a nobleman,
And by his servile flattery and fawning
Is now become the steward of his house,
And bravely jets it in his silken gown.   30

Franklin. No nobleman will count'nance such a peasant.

Arden. Yes, the Lord Clifford, he that loves not me.
But through his favour let not him grow proud;
For, were he by the Lord Protector backed,
He should not make me to be pointed at.   35
I am by birth a gentleman of blood,
And that injurious ribald that attempts

---

31. count'nance] *Q1–2;* countenance *Q3, S.MS.*   33. not him] *Qq;* him
not *Jacob.*   37. ribald] *Q3;* riball *Q1–2, S.MS.*

---

epistle of Spenser's *The Shepheardes Calender*, 1579: 'it serued well
Pandares purpose, for the bolstering of his baudy brocage'.)

29. *steward*] an important official in a nobleman's household because all
domestic arrangements and expenditures were entrusted to him. Webster's
Duchess of Malfi, it will be recalled, marries her steward. Cf. Arden's contempt for Mosby's status to Sir Toby's for Malvolio's: 'Art any more than
a steward?' (*Tw.N.*, II. iii. 108–9).

30. *bravely jets it*] handsomely struts about. Cf. Holinshed: 'Then went
Mosby to the dore, and there stood in a nighte gowne [i.e., dressing gown]
of silke girded about him.'

32. *Lord Clifford*] The sources are agreed that Mosby was 'seruant' to
Lord North (Sir Edward at the time of the play's action). There being 'no
Lord Clifford at the date of the murder', Cust suggests (p. 144) that the
alteration was 'probably made to prevent scandal in the North family'. See
Intro., p. xxxvi, n. 1.

33. *his favour*] i.e., Lord Clifford's.
him] Mosby.

36. *a gentleman of blood*] well born, of a good family. The technical distinction cited by the *O.E.D.* (under *gentleman,* 1)—'properly, one who is
entitled to bear arms, though not ranking among the nobility'—may have
bearing on Arden's contemptuous reply to Mosby's challenge at ll. 310–11
below.

37–40.] Rubow compares Kyd's *Hovsholders Philos.* (p. 255, ll. 31–4):
'for if hee himselfe doo not first *violate* the bandes by so *defiling of the
marriage bedde*, he shall doubtles much confirme the womans *chastitie*'
(italics added).

37. *injurious*] harmful, insulting.
ribald] base, dissolute fellow. Until the 1640's, the term also applied in
England to 'a menial or dependent of low birth' (*O.E.D., sb.,* †1), a meaning
equally in keeping with the tenor of Arden's scorn. Hopkinson (3) suggests

To violate my dear wife's chastity
(For dear I hold her love, as dear as heaven)
Shall on the bed which he thinks to defile   40
See his dissevered joints and sinews torn
Whilst on the planchers pants his weary body,
Smeared in the channels of his lustful blood.

Franklin. Be patient, gentle friend, and learn of me
To ease thy grief and save her chastity.   45
Entreat her fair; sweet words are fittest engines
To raze the flint walls of a woman's breast.
In any case be not too jealous,
Nor make no question of her love to thee;
But, as securely, presently take horse,   50
And lie with me at London all this term;
For women when they may will not,

---

47. raze] *Qq* (race).   48. jealous] *Q3;* Jelyouse *Q1;* iealious *Q2.*
49. no] *Qq;* a *Jacob.*   question] *Qq;* mention *S.MS.*   51. lie] *Qq;*
be *S.MS.*

---

that the original quarto spelling might also be taken to read *rebel,* but the
emendation is unnecessary.

42. *planchers*] floor planks; hence, the floor itself.

44–5. *Be patient ... ease thy grief*] Cf. *S. & P.,* I. iv. 126 ('Come therefore, gentle death, and ease my griefe').

46. *Entreat*] treat.

engines] contrivances or instruments used in war (*O.E.D.,* 5.a).

47. *flint walls of a woman's breast*] Cf. the proverb, 'A heart as hard as
flint' (Tilley, H311). The idea recurs frequently in Shakespeare: see *R2,*
v. i. 3 ('flint bosom'); *2H6,* III. ii. 99 ('thy flinty heart'); *Tit.,* v. iii. 88 ('My
heart is not compact of flint nor steel'); *Mer.V.,* IV. i. 31 ('rough hearts of
flint'); and *Tw.N.,* I. v. 270 ('his heart of flint') and v. i. 118 ('marble-
breasted tyrant'). See also xiii. 8 below.

48. *jealous*] suspicious, mistrustful. Probably trisyllabic in Q1–2 spelling;
see, however, Intro., p. xxxiv, n. 2.

49. *Nor ... no*] The double negative is common in Elizabethan English
(see Abbott 406).

50. *as securely*] confidently, without misgiving.

presently] immediately, at once.

51. *lie*] lodge, stay over.

term] one of the yearly sessions of the law courts.

52–3.] Cf. Tilley, W721, 'Women will be quiet when they are well
pleased'; W723, 'Women will have their wills.'

But, being kept back, straight grow outrageous.

Arden. Though this abhors from reason, yet I'll try it,
And call her forth, and presently take leave.—   55
How, Alice!

Here enters ALICE.

Alice. Husband, what mean you to get up so early?
Summer nights are short, and yet you rise ere day.
Had I been wake, you had not rise so soon.

Arden. Sweet love, thou know'st that we two, Ovid-like,   60
Have often chid the morning when it 'gan to peep,

55–6.] *so Delius; one line in Qq.*   56.1. *enters*] *Q2–3; entes Q1.*   57. get
up] *Q1–2, S.MS.;* rise *Q3.*   59. wake] *Qq;* awake *S.MS.;* 'wake *Tyrrell.*
rise] *Qq;* ris *Delius;* rose *Tyrrell;* risen *W-P, Brooke.*   60. know'st] *Qq;*
knowest *S.MS., Jacob.*   61. often] *Qq; omitted Bullen.*   when it] *Qq;*
when't *Jacob.*   'gan] *Qq;* Came *S.MS.*

---

53. *outrageous*] furious. The line reads metrically if *being* is pronounced
monosyllabically and *outrageous* tetrasyllabically.

54. *abhors from*] is repugnant to, is at variance with (*O.E.D., v.,* †6).

59. *wake*] obsolete past participle of *to wake*.

rise] pronounced *riz*; obsolete variant of past participle of *to rise* (see *ris,*
O.E.D.).

60–4.] Warnke and Proescholdt compare these lines to Ovid's thirteenth
Elegy from the first book of the *Amores*, which Marlowe translated as
follows:

Now ore the sea from her old Loue comes she
That drawes the day from heauens cold axeltree.
Aurora whither slidest thou? . . .
Whither runst thou, that men, and women loue not?
Hold in thy rosy horses that they moue not. . .
Would *Tithon* might but talke of thee a while,
Not one in heauen should be more base and vile.
Thou leauest his bed, because hee's faint through age,
And early mountest thy hatefull carriage.
But heldst thou in thine armes some *Cephalus,*
Then wouldst thou cry, stay night and runne not thus.

(ll. 1–3, 9–10, 35–40)

61. *often*] Bullen's reason for omitting this word is that 'the compositor's
eye caught the word *often* from the following line'; but, as Oliphant
remarks, 'the sense, but not the meter, requires the first; the meter, but not
the sense, requires the second.' The line, like many others in the play, is a
perfectly fine alexandrine.

And often wished that dark Night's purblind steeds
Would pull her by the purple mantle back
And cast her in the ocean to her love.

But this night, sweet Alice, thou hast killed my heart: 65
I heard thee call on Mosby in thy sleep.

Alice. 'Tis like I was asleep when I named him,
For being awake he comes not in my thoughts.

Arden. Ay, but you started up and suddenly,
Instead of him, caught me about the neck.   70

Alice. Instead of him? Why, who was there but you?
And where but one is how can I mistake?

Franklin. Arden, leave to urge her overfar.

Arden. Nay, love, there is no credit in a dream.

Let it suffice I know thou lovest me well.   75

Alice. Now I remember whereupon it came:
Had we no talk of Mosby yesternight?

Franklin. Mistress Alice, I heard you name him once or twice.

Alice. And thereof came it, and therefore blame not me.

---

62. Night's purblind steeds] *Qq;* night, purblind Steed, *S.MS.*   67. I
(2)] *Q1–2; not in Q3.*   68. in] *Q1–2, S.MS.;* to *Q3.*   73. leave] *Qq;*
forbeare *Jacob.*   75. lovest] *Qq;* lov'st *Tyrrell.*   77. yesternight] *Qq;*
yesterday *S.MS.*   78. heard] *Q2–3;* hard *Q1.*   79. and] *Qq;*
omitted Tyrrell.   not me] *Qq;* me no more *S.MS.*

---

62. *purblind*] totally blind.
69–74.] Symonds (*Shakspere's Predecessors*, p. 452) compares this
passage to *Oth.*, III. iii. 423–31:

    Iago. . . . In sleep I heard [Cassio] say 'Sweet Desdemona,
          Let us be wary, let us hide our loves;'
          And then, sir, would he gripe and wring my hand,
          Cry 'O sweet creature!' and then kiss me hard, . . .
    Oth. O monstrous! monstrous!
    Iago.   Nay, this was but his dream.
73. *leave*] cease.
74.] Cf. *Con.*, I. ii. 37 ('Nay *Nell*, Ile giue no credit to a dreame'; omitted
2H6). Cf. also Tilley, D587, 'Dreams are lies.'
76. *whereupon it came*] how it came about (Sturgess).
79.] Tyrrell's omission of *and* to regularize the line, as well as similar
changes throughout the text by him and other editors, is not necessary
since Renaissance theorists of prosody allowed the addition of a syllable
before the caesura (in this case, *it*) as a permissible variation (see Intro.,
p. xxix, n. 2.)

Arden. I know it did, and therefore let it pass.   80
    I must to London, sweet Alice, presently.
Alice. But tell me, do you mean to stay there long?
Arden. No longer than till my affairs be done.
Franklin. He will not stay above a month at most.
Alice. A month? Ay me! Sweet Arden, come again   85
    Within a day or two or else I die.
Arden. I cannot long be from thee, gentle Alice.
    Whilst Michael fetch our horses from the field,
    Franklin and I will down unto the quay,
    For I have certain goods there to unload.   90
    Meanwhile prepare our breakfast, gentle Alice,
    For yet ere noon we'll take horse and away.

                        Exeunt ARDEN *and* FRANKLIN.
Alice. Ere noon he means to take horse and away!
    Sweet news is this. O, that some airy spirit
    Would in the shape and likeness of a horse   95
    Gallop with Arden 'cross the ocean
    And throw him from his back into the waves!
    Sweet Mosby is the man that hath my heart;
    And he usurps it, having nought but this,

---

83. than] *S.MS.* (then); there *Qq.*   be] *Qq;* are *S.MS.*   94. airy] *Qq;*
angry *S.MS.*   96. 'cross] *Qq;* across *Tyrrell.*

---

80. *let it pass*] pay no attention. Note recurrence of this popular tag
phrase at i. 539, 585, 589; ii. 32; v. 32.
    83. *than*] S.MS.'s reading is independently supported by M.P. Jackson's
argument that ' "then", which is the normal Elizabethan spelling of
"than", could easily have been misread as "there" [in Qq], particularly
under the influence of "there" in the previous line' ('An Emendation to
Arden of Feversham', N. & Q., CCVIII [1963], 410).
    88. *Whilst Michael fetch*] See Abbott 302 for *while* with the subjunctive
in Elizabethan English. *Whilst* may mean *till.*
    89–90.] Arden was chief comptroller of his majesty's customs of the port
of Faversham, but the point is not made in the play's sources.
    94. *airy spirit*] Rubow cites the phrase in Kyd's *Corn.*, III. i. 103; but it
is, of course, a commonplace. At least Puck in *MND.* (where the phrase is
used at III. i. 147) refers to his assuming the likeness of a horse (l. 101 of the
same scene).
    96.] Possibly *ocean* was meant to be trisyllabic (as is *marriage* in l. 100).
    99. *he*] i.e., Arden.

That I am tied to him by marriage.   100
Love is a god, and marriage is but words;
And therefore Mosby's title is the best.
Tush! Whether it be or no, he shall be mine
In spite of him, of Hymen, and of rites.

Here enters ADAM *of the Flower-de-Luce.*

And here comes Adam of the Flower-de-Luce.   105
I hope he brings me tidings of my love.—
How now, Adam, what is the news with you?
Be not afraid; my husband is now from home.
Adam. He whom you wot of, Mosby, Mistress Alice,
Is come to town and sends you word by me   110
In any case you may not visit him.
Alice. Not visit him?
Adam. No, nor take no knowledge of his being here.
Alice. But tell me, is he angry or displeased?

---

103. be or no] *Qq;* be so or not *Tyrrell.*   104.1] *Qq;* after l. *106 Hopkinson*
(*2*).   Flower-de-luce] *Q3* (*Flowre-de-luce*); Flourdeluce *Q1–2.*   105.
comes] *Q1–2;* come *Q3, S.MS.*   108. husband is] *Qq;* husband's *Delius.*
109. wot] *Qq;* thought *S.MS.*   110. sends] *Qq;* hath Sent *S.MS.*
113. take no knowledge] *Qq;* take knowledge *Jacob.*   114. displeased] *Qq;*
Pleased *S.MS.*

98–100.] Cf. *Mas.P.*, 665–6:
      Sweet *Mugeroune*, tis he that hath my heart,
      And *Guise* vsurpes it, cause I am his wife.
Cf., too, *End.*, I. iv. 35 ('*Endimion*, sweet *Endimon* is he that hath my hart').
   104. *Hymen*] god of marriage.
   104.1. Flower-de-Luce] 'an Inn, formerly situated in Abbey Street,
nearly opposite Arden's house' (Donne, *An Essay on the Tragedy of 'Arden
of Feversham'*, p. 15). The Fleur-de-Lis Public House stands now in
Preston Street, and there is some argument as to whether it was in fact in
Preston Street or in Abbey Street at the time of the murder. Some present-
day inhabitants of Faversham believe that Globe House, a private residence
opposite Arden's House in Abbey Street that was once an inn, is actually
the original Fleur-de-Lis. (The *O.E.D.* observes that 'The prevailing form
[*fleur de lis*] . . . is scarcely found in Eng. before the 19th c. . . . The form
flower-de-luce survives as a poetical archaism'.)
   107. *what is the news*] another recurrent catch-phrase; cf. l. 537 below.
   109. *wot*] know.
   111. *in any case*] Cf. iii. 38; ix. 48; xiii. 66; and xiv. 352.

Adam. Should seem so, for he is wondrous sad.   115
Alice. Were he as mad as raving Hercules,
    I'll see him. Ay, and were thy house of force,
    These hands of mine should raze it to the ground
    Unless that thou wouldst bring me to my love.
Adam. Nay, and you be so impatient, I'll be gone.   120
Alice. Stay, Adam, stay; thou wert wont to be my friend.
    Ask Mosby how I have incurred his wrath;
    Bear him from me these pair of silver dice
    With which we played for kisses many a time,
    And when I lost I won, and so did he—   125
    Such winning and such losing Jove send me!
    And bid him, if his love do not decline,
    To come this morning but along my door
    And as a stranger but salute me there.
    This may he do without suspect or fear.   130

115. Should] *Qq;* It should *S.MS., Jacob.*   117. Ay] *Qq* (I), *Delius;*
I *Tyrrell.*   118. raze] *Q3;* race *Q1–2, S.MS.*   120. and] *Qq;* if *S.MS.*
121. stay] *Qq;* omitted *Jacob.*   124. we played] *Qq;* we have played
S.MS.   128. To come] *Q2–3, S.MS.;* Come *Q1.*

115.] The line may be defective in the original, but initial truncation of
the basically decasyllabic iambic pentameter line was considered permissible in Elizabethan metrics (see Intro., p. xxix, n. 2); in this case, the
truncation makes for a more colloquial reading.

116. *mad as raving Hercules*] The most illustrious of Greek heroes went
raving mad and committed suicide after having suffered extreme torments
brought about by a poisoned blood-stained shirt that his wife, Deïanira,
had innocently sent her faithless husband on the advice of the centaur,
Nessus, who, to take revenge for the mortal wound that Hercules had given
him, claimed that it had the magic power to win him back. Ironically, the
blood on the centaur's shirt had been poisoned by the very arrow that
Hercules himself had used to kill the Hydra (about whom, see iv. 13, n.).

117. *house of force*] i.e., of strength; a fortified house. Cf. *Woodstock,*
I. iii. 197 ('Would I had tears of force to stint this fire!').

120–1.] *Nay . . . stay*] Cf. iii. 134–5.

120. *and*] if.

121. *Stay . . . stay*] See Intro., pp. xxvii–xxviii.

123. *Bear him . . . silver dice*] Cf. Holinshed, App. II, p. 148.

128.] Q1's reading may be merely another truncated foot; but, since the
entire passage is metrically smooth, Q2's emendation is accepted.

129. *as*] as if he were.

130. *suspect*] suspicion.

Adam. I'll tell him what you say, and so farewell.

Alice. Do, and one day I'll make amends for all.—   *Exit* ADAM.

I know he loves me well but dares not come

Because my husband is so jealous

And these my narrow-prying neighbours blab,   135

Hinder our meetings when we would confer.

But, if I live, that block shall be removed;

And Mosby, thou that comes to me by stealth,

Shalt neither fear the biting speech of men

Nor Arden's looks. As surely shall he die   140

As I abhor him and love only thee.—

Here enters MICHAEL.

How now, Michael, whither are you going?

Michael. To fetch my master's nag. I hope you'll think on me.

Alice. Ay; but, Michael, see you keep your oath

---

132. S.D.] *so Hugo; after l. 131 Qq.*   134. jealous] *Q3;* Jelious *Q1;* ielious *Q2.*   135. neighbours blab,] *Qq;* neighbours' blab *Delius.* 136. Hinder] *Qq;* Hinders *Jacob.*   would] *Q1;* should *Q2–3.*   138. comes] *Q1–2, S.MS.;* comest *Q3;* com'st *Delius.*   141. only] *Q1;* none but *Q2–3, S.MS.*   143.] *so Hopkinson (2); two lines in Qq, divided at* nagge, / I.   nag] *Qq;* Horse *S.MS.*

---

131. *and so farewell*] See Intro., p. xxvii. For numerous examples of this catch-phrase in just scene i, see ll. 204, 408, 416, and 534.

135. *narrow-prying*] The original of Q1 is certainly more striking metaphorically than that of Q2–3 and may be the correct one. A similar construction appears in *S. & P.*, v. ii. 14 ('Such is the force of marrow burning loue') and in *Ven.*, l. 741 ('the marrow-eating sickness'). In both cases, however, the context makes it clear that the phrase refers to the Elizabethan medical belief that the marrow of the bones is a sexual provocative (see '*The Tragedye of Solyman and Perseda*', ed. Murray, p. 148). With Q2's emendation, accepted here, should be compared *Shr.*, III. ii. 142 ('The narrow-prying father, Minola').

135–6. *blab, | Hinder*] i.e. blab and so hinder. Delius's reading of *neighbours* as genitive with *blab* as a noun taking the verb *Hinder* may be right.

138. *comes*] Third-person verbs are common in Elizabethan English in relative clauses 'though the antecedent be in the *second* or *first*' (Abbott 247). This usage occurs frequently in *Arden*.

141. *only*] Q2's reading of *none but* represents a remarkable change in the text, but it is the only one of its type and not enough to warrant the suggestion that Jeffes's illegal edition was consulted (see Intro., p. xxi, n. 4).

And be as secret as you are resolute.   145

Michael. I'll see he shall not live above a week.

Alice. On that condition, Michael, here is my hand;

None shall have Mosby's sister but thyself.

Michael. I understand the painter here hard by

Hath made report that he and Sue is sure.   150

Alice. There's no such matter, Michael; believe it not.

Michael. But he hath sent a dagger sticking in a heart,

With a verse or two stolen from a painted cloth,

The which I hear the wench keeps in her chest.

Well, let her keep it! I shall find a fellow   155

That can both write and read and make rhyme too;

And, if I do—well, I say no more.

I'll send from London such a taunting letter

As she shall eat the heart he sent with salt

And fling the dagger at the painter's head.   160

Alice. What needs all this ? I say that Susan's thine.

Michael. Why, then I say that I will kill my master

Or anything that you will have me do.

Alice. But, Michael, see you do it cunningly.

Michael. Why, say I should be took, I'll ne'er confess   165

That you know anything; and Susan, being a maid,

---

147. here is] *Qq; here's Tyrrell.*   148. thyself] *Qq; yourself S.MS.*
149. here] *Qq; omitted S.MS.*   150. is] *Q1–2; are Q3, S.MS.*   157. I
say] *Qq; I [will] say Hopkinson (2).*   159. she] *Delius; not in Qq, S.MS.*
161. that] *Q1–2; not in Q3.*   163. that] *Q1–2; not in Q3.*   165. ne'er]
Qq (nere); not S.MS.; never Jacob.

---

147. *here is my hand*] Cf. i. 261, 528.

148.] Cf. Holinshed, App. II, p. 151: 'The cause that this Michaell conspired with the rest against his maister, was: for that it was determined,
that he should marrie a kinswoman of Mosbies.'

149. *hard by*] close by.

150. *sure*] betrothed, engaged. For the *is sure* construction see note to
l. 13 above.

153. *stolen*] 'borrowed', plagiarized.

painted cloth] tapestry, with a love story and appropriate inscription
painted into it.

159. *As*] that.

166–7. *Susan . . . shrieve*] alluding to the popular belief that a virgin
might save a condemned man from the gallows by offering to marry him.

May beg me from the gallows of the shrieve.

Alice. Trust not to that, Michael.

Michael. You cannot tell me; I have seen it, I.
But, mistress, tell her whether I live or die   170
I'll make her more worth than twenty painters can;
For I will rid mine elder brother away,
And then the farm of Bolton is mine own.
Who would not venture upon house and land
When he may have it for a right-down blow?   175

Here enters MOSBY.

Alice. Yonder comes Mosby. Michael, get thee gone,
And let not him nor any know thy drifts.—   *Exit* MICHAEL.
Mosby, my love!

Mosby. Away, I say, and talk not to me now.

Alice. A word or two, sweetheart, and then I will.   180
'Tis yet but early days; thou needest not fear.

Mosby. Where is your husband?

---

167. shrieve] *Qq* (Shriefe); sheriff *S.MS.*, *Tyrrell*.   170. mistress] *Qq;*
Madam *S.MS.* (*normally in manuscript*).   172. mine] *Q1–2;* my *Q3*.
173. Bolton] *Qq;* Bocton *Jacob;* Boughton *Hopkinson* (2).   177. drifts]
Qq; drift *Tyrrell*.   177. S.D.] *After Michael's exit, Tyrrell adds new scene:*
ACT I. SCENE II. *Before* Arden's House. *Enter* Alice *from the House, meeting*
Mosbie.   181. days] *Qq;* day's *Delius*.   needest] *Q1–2;* need'st *Q3;*
needs *S.MS.*

---

167. *shrieve*] sheriff.

171. *worth*] wealthy, prosperous. Bayne suggests that 'perhaps *worth*
should be omitted' although the line stands as an alexandrine.

172. *rid . . . away*] get rid of, kill.

173. *Bolton*] 'Probably we should read with Jacob, Bocton. The place
intended is Boughton-under-Blean, a village in Kent, a few miles West of
Canterbury on the Pilgrims Road' (Sugden, p. 68, who quotes a letter of
Cranmer to Cromwell, 'written in 1558', in which 'he speaks of a farm at
Bowghton under the Blayne which his servant Nevell "had of the Abbot
and Convent of Feversham" ').

175. *right-down*] downright.

177. *drifts*] schemes, plots.

181. *early days*] early in the day. Cf. *Troil.*, IV. v. 12 ('Tis but early
days.')

needest] monosyllabic.

Alice. 'Tis now high water, and he is at the quay.
Mosby. There let him be; henceforward know me not.
Alice. Is this the end of all thy solemn oaths ?   185
      Is this the fruit thy reconcilement buds ?
      Have I for this given thee so many favours,
      Incurred my husband's hate, and—out alas!—
      Made shipwreck of mine honour for thy sake ?
      And dost thou say, 'Henceforward know me not' ?   190
      Remember, when I locked thee in my closet,
      What were thy words and mine ? Did we not both
      Decree to murder Arden in the night ?
      The heavens can witness, and the world can tell,
      Before I saw that falsehood look of thine,   195
      'Fore I was tangled with thy 'ticing speech,
      Arden to me was dearer than my soul—
      And shall be still. Base peasant, get thee gone,
      And boast not of thy conquest over me,
      Gotten by witchcraft and mere sorcery.   200
      For what hast thou to countenance my love,

---

186. this] *Q1–2; not in Q3.*   188. and . . . alas!] *Qq; omitted S.MS.*
191. thee] *Q2–3; the Q1.*   195. falsehood] *Qq;* false *S.MS.*   196.] *Qq;*
omitted S.MS.

---

183. *high water*] high tide.
185–6.] Cf. *Sp.T.*, IV. i. 1–3:
            Is this the loue thou bearst *Horatio* ?
            Is this the kindnes that thou counterfeits ?
            Are these the fruits of thine incessant teares ?
and *E2*, 832–3:
            Is this the loue you beare your soueraigne ?
            Is this the fruite your reconcilement beares ?
186–9.] Cf. train of images in *1H6*, v. v. 7–9:
            So am I driven by breath of her renown,
            Either to suffer *shipwreck* or arrive
            Where I may have *fruition* of her love.
186. *buds*] causes to bud, i.e., the quarrel between them.
191. *closet*] private room or chamber.
194.] Cf. similar expressions of this commonplace at ll. 319, 329, 350
below, and xiii. 116.
199–200.] Cf. viii. 78.
200. *mere*] absolute, downright.
201. *countenance*] 'be in keeping with' (*O.E.D., v.,* †6).

Being descended of a noble house
And matched already with a gentleman
Whose servant thou may'st be ? And so farewell.

Mosby. Ungentle and unkind Alice, now I see   205
That which I ever feared and find too true:
A woman's love is as the lightning flame
Which even in bursting forth consumes itself.
To try thy constancy have I been strange.
Would I had never tried but lived in hope!   210

Alice. What needs thou try me whom thou never found false ?

Mosby. Yet pardon me, for love is jealous.

Alice. So lists the sailor to the mermaid's song;
So looks the traveller to the basilisk.
I am content for to be reconciled,   215
And that I know will be mine overthrow.

Mosby. Thine overthrow ? First let the world dissolve!

Alice. Nay, Mosby, let me still enjoy thy love;
And, happen what will, I am resolute.
My saving husband hoards up bags of gold   220
To make our children rich, and now is he
Gone to unload the goods that shall be thine,
And he and Franklin will to London straight.

Mosby. To London, Alice ? If thou'lt be ruled by me,

211. needs] *Qq;* needst *S.MS.*   never] *Qq;* ne'er *Tyrrell.*   found] *Qq;*
foundest *S.MS.;* found'st *Delius.*   212. jealous] *Q3;* Jelious *Q1;*
iealious *Q2.*   213. lists] *Q3;* list *Q1–2.*   mermaid's] *Q1* (Marmaids).
218. me] *Q1, S.MS.;* him *Q2–3.*

207–8.] Cf. viii. 48–9.
209. *strange*] distant, unfriendly.
213–14. *lists . . . looks*] Cf. collation at ix. 34 for a similar change in the
persons of the verb in Q1.
213. *mermaid's song*] The mermaid was frequently associated with the
classical Siren, whose melodious song lured sailors to their destruction.
214. *basilisk*] a fabled serpent whose glance alone was reputed to be fatal.
218. *still*] always.
221.] No Arden children are introduced into the play, but Holinshed
writes that following the murder and 'After supper, mistres Arden caused
her daughter to plaie on the virginals'.
222. *Gone . . . goods*] See note to ll. 89–90 above.
223. *straight*] straightway; without delay.

H

We'll make him sure enough for coming there.   225
Alice. Ah, would we could!
Mosby. I happened on a painter yesternight,
 The only cunning man of Christendom,
 For he can temper poison with his oil
 That whoso looks upon the work he draws   230
 Shall, with the beams that issue from his sight,
 Suck venom to his breast and slay himself.
 Sweet Alice, he shall draw thy counterfeit,
 That Arden may, by gazing on it, perish.
Alice. Ay, but, Mosby, that is dangerous;   235
 For thou or I or any other else,
 Coming into the chamber where it hangs, may die.
Mosby. Ay, but we'll have it covered with a cloth
 And hung up in the study for himself.
Alice. It may not be; for, when the picture's drawn,   240
 Arden, I know, will come and show it me.
Mosby. Fear not; we'll have that shall serve the turn.

        [They cross the stage.]
 This is the painter's house; I'll call him forth.
Alice. But, Mosby, I'll have no such picture, I.
Mosby. I pray thee leave it to my discretion.—   245
 How, Clarke!

225. for] *Qq;* 'fore *Sturgess.* 237.] *so Qq; two lines in Brooke, divided at*
hangs, / May. 242. we'll] *Qq* (weele)*; we will S.MS., Jacob.* 242.1.]
B-H-N; not in Qq. 244. I] *Q1–2;* not I *Q3; omitted S.MS.* 245–6.] *so*
Delius; one line in Qq. 246. How] *Qq;* How now *S.MS.;* Ho *Delius.*

---

 225. *for*] to prevent (him) from (*O.E.D.,* 23. †d.).
 228. *only*] most.
 231–2.] For the contemporary theory that there issue 'out of the eye
bright beames or a certaine light which should reach vnto the object, and
thereby cause vs to see it,' see Chapter x of M. Andreas Laurentius, *A*
Discovrse of the Preservation of the Sight (London, 1599; reprinted in
Shakespeare Association Facsimiles No. 15 [Oxford, 1938]).
 233. *counterfeit*] portrait.
 235–7.] See Intro., p. xxviii.
 236. *any other*] anyone.
 242.1.] The dialogue indicates the nature of the staging at this point.
Alice and Mosby cross over to one of the doors at the rear of the stage. (See
Intro., p. xxxv.)

Here enters CLARKE.

O, you are an honest man of your word; you served me well.
Clarke. Why, sir, I'll do it for you at any time,
    Provided, as you have given your word,
    I may have Susan Mosby to my wife.   250
    For, as sharp-witted poets, whose sweet verse
    Make heavenly gods break off their nectar draughts
    And lay their ears down to the lowly earth,
    Use humble promise to their sacred Muse,
    So we that are the poets' favourites   255
    Must have a love. Ay, Love is the painter's Muse,
    That makes him frame a speaking countenance,

247.] *Qq; two lines in Tyrrell, divided at* word, / You.   250. to] *QI;*
for *Q2–3*, S.MS.

246.1. *CLARKE*] Holinshed does not identify the painter by name,
which here is solely the playwright's invention. The Wardmote Book of
Faversham gives the name as William Blackborne.

247.] See Jackson, p. 35, n. 1: 'Possible support for the theory of con-
taminating transcription from [authorial] foul-papers is provided by [this
line]. Mosby has been speaking verse and continues to do so in his next
speech. If the redundant phrase "of your word" be omitted and "you are"
elided, we are left with a regular pentameter. Both "honest" and "of your
word" may have stood in the foul-papers, the latter imperfectly crossed out.
Alternatively, the scribe may have copied down "honest" correctly but
added the synonymous phrase from his own memory, which had been
disturbed by "your worde" [QI spelling] two lines further on.'

251–6.] F. S. Boas, *Christopher Marlowe* (1940), p. 199, thinks that this
passage 'might be a pendant to the passage' in *1 Tamb.*, 1942–71, that
begins 'If all the pens that euer poets held' and includes the lines:
        That which hath st⟨o⟩opt the tempest of the Gods,
        Euen from the fiery spangled vaile of heauen,
        To feele the louely warmth of shepheards flames,
        And martch in cottages of strowed weeds.
Cf. also Ovid's *Tristia*, II. 69–76. J. Bakeless, *The Tragicall History of
Christopher Marlowe* (1924), II. 289, parallels 'the lowly earth' (l. 253) to
E2, 1999 ('the lowly earth') and 397 ('the lowlie ground').

251. *sharp-witted*] The 'wit' of a poet refers to his inventive or imaginative powers (as inspired by his 'sacred Muse').

255–6. *So . . . love.*] to whom we can express 'humble promise' in return
for inspiration (?). *Poets' favourites* alludes to the Renaissance critical
commonplace (ultimately derived from Horace) that poetry is a 'speaking
picture'.

A weeping eye that witnesses heart's grief.

Then tell me, Master Mosby, shall I have her?

Alice. 'Tis pity but he should; he'll use her well.   260

Mosby. Clarke, here's my hand; my sister shall be thine.

Clarke. Then, brother, to requite this courtesy,

You shall command my life, my skill, and all.

Alice. Ah, that thou couldst be secret!

Mosby. Fear him not. Leave; I have talked sufficient.   265

Clarke. You know not me that ask such questions.

Let it suffice I know you love him well

And fain would have your husband made away,

Wherein, trust me, you show a noble mind,

That rather than you'll live with him you hate   270

You'll venture life and die with him you love.

The like will I do for my Susan's sake.

Alice. Yet nothing could enforce me to the deed

But Mosby's love. Might I without control

Enjoy thee still, then Arden should not die;   275

But, seeing I cannot, therefore let him die.

Mosby. Enough, sweet Alice; thy kind words makes me melt.—

[*To Clarke.*] Your trick of poisoned pictures we dislike;

---

258. witnesses] *Q1;* witnesseth *Q2–3, S.MS.*   265. not. Leave; I] *Qq*
(not, leaue, I)*; not, love, I Tyrrell.*   269. show] *Q1–2* (shew)*; beare Q3.*
273. the] *Qq;* this *Hopkinson* (2).   276.] *Q1, 3; not in Q2, S.MS.*
277. makes] *Q1;* make *Q2–3, S.MS.*   278. S.D.] *Sturgess; not in Qq.*

258.] Cf. the ironic overtones of this line with Arden's own expression
of his genuine 'heart's grief' at l. 19 above and at iv. 19.

260. *but*] but that, unless.

use] treat.

261. *here's my hand*] Cf. l. 147 above.

265. *Leave*] cease.

sufficient] i.e., sufficiently. Adjectives for adverbs are common in
Elizabethan English (see Abbott 1); other instances in this play are usually
not annotated.

266. *questions*] trisyllabic.

268. *fain*] willingly, gladly.

270. *That*] in that.

274. *control*] restraint.

276. *seeing*] monosyllabic.

277. *words makes*] See note to l. 13 above.

Some other poison would do better far.

Alice. Ay, such as might be put into his broth,   280
    And yet in taste not to be found at all.

Clarke. I know your mind, and here I have it for you.
    Put but a dram of this into his drink,
    Or any kind of broth that he shall eat,
    And he shall die within an hour after.   285

Alice. As I am a gentlewoman, Clarke, next day
    Thou and Susan shall be marrièd.

Mosby. And I'll make her dowry more than I'll talk of, Clarke.

Clarke. Yonder's your husband. Mosby, I'll be gone.

Here enters ARDEN *and* FRANKLIN [*and* MICHAEL].

Alice. In good time, see where my husband comes.   290
    Master Mosby, ask him the question yourself.   *Exit* CLARKE.

Mosby. Master Arden, being at London yesternight,
    The Abbey lands whereof you are now possessed
    Were offered me on some occasion
    By Greene, one of Sir Antony Ager's men.   295

---

282. it] *Q1–2; not in Q3.*   288. I'll] *Qq* (ile)*; I will S.MS.*   289.1. *and*
MICHAEL] *Sturgess; not in Qq.*   295. Ager's] *Delius;* Agers *Qq;* Agers'
Tyrrell.

282–5.] Cf. Holinshed, App. II, p. 149. In the source, Alice later forgets
to take the painter's advice to put the poison 'into the bottome of a
porrenger' before adding milk—a circumstance omitted by the *Arden* playwright but made use of by the author of *Brewen.*

289.1. and *MICHAEL*] Arden's address to Michael at l. 363 below and
the latter's subsequent *exit* at l. 416.1 necessitate this addition to the
stage direction.

290. *In good time*] at the opportune moment; luckily (*O.E.D., Time,
sb.*, 42.†c.). Alice suddenly switches the conversation to make it seem as if
Mosby came purposely to talk to her husband on business matters. Mosby
catches on at once and responds accordingly.

292. *yesternight*] last night. (*O.E.D.*, A., *adv.*: 'In early use not necessarily
restricted to the night.')

293. *you are*] in practice elided.

295. *Sir Antony Ager's*] referring to Sir Anthony Aucher, whom the
D.N.B. refers to as a 'knight, of Hautsbourne in Kent'. The spelling is
Holinshed's, but this particular encounter between Arden and Mosby is
strictly the playwright's invention.

I pray you, sir, tell me, are not the lands yours?
Hath any other interest herein?

Arden. Mosby, that question we'll decide anon.—
Alice, make ready my breakfast; I must hence.   *Exit* ALICE.
As for the lands, Mosby, they are mine   300
By letters patents from his majesty.
But I must have a mandate for my wife;
They say you seek to rob me of her love.
Villain, what makes thou in her company?
She's no companion for so base a groom.   305

Mosby. Arden, I thought not on her; I came to thee,
But rather than I pocket up this wrong—

Franklin. What will you do, sir?

Mosby. Revenge it on the proudest of you both.

                Then ARDEN *draws forth Mosby's sword.*

Arden. So, sirrah, you may not wear a sword!   310
The statute makes against artificers.
I warrant that I do. Now use your bodkin,

---

297. herein] *Q1–2;* therein *Q3, S.MS.*   301. from] *Q1–2;* of *Q3.*
304. makes] *Q1–2;* makest *Q3;* mak'st *Delius.*   307. I] *Q1;* Ile *Q2–3,*
S.MS.   pocket] *Q1–2, S.MS.;* put *Q3.*   wrong—] *Q3;* wrong. *Q1–2.*

301.] Cf. 1. 4 above.

304. *makes thou*] are you doing.

305. *groom*] 'fellow', in contemptuous sense; but *O.E.D.*, 3., is relevant,
too, in light of Arden's remarks at ll. 25–30: 'a man of inferior position; a
serving-man; or man-servant', which Mosby literally is. Malvolio, even
though a steward (like Mosby), had to be reminded that he was, after all,
'the fellow of servants' (*Tw.N.*, II. v. 138). Cf. *E2*, 588 ('Thinke me as base
a groome as *Gaueston*?').

306. *on*] of.

307. *pocket up*] meekly submit to.

310. *sirrah*] 'A term of address used to men or boys, expressing contempt,
reprimand, or assumption of authority on the part of the speaker' (*O.E.D.*).
'Ordinary form of address to inferiors; when used otherwise it implies
disrespect' (Onions).

311. *The statute*] 37 Edward III, c. 9 (so Bullen), which forbade the
wearing of swords by anyone under the rank of gentleman (see note to l. 36
above).

makes against] decrees against.

312. *warrant that*] have warrant or authorization for that which. (See

Your Spanish needle, and your pressing iron,
For this shall go with me. And mark my words—
You goodman botcher, 'tis to you I speak—   315
The next time that I take thee near my house,
Instead of legs I'll make thee crawl on stumps.

Mosby. Ah, Master Arden, you have injured me;
I do appeal to God and to the world.

Franklin. Why, canst thou deny thou wert a botcher once?   320

Mosby. Measure me what I am, not what I was.

Arden. Why, what art thou now but a velvet drudge,
A cheating steward, and base-minded peasant?

Mosby. Arden, now thou hast belched and vomited

---

323. and base-minded] *Qq;* and a base-minded *S.MS.*, Sturgess.

Abbott 244 for the omission of the relative pronoun in Elizabethan
English.)

313. *Spanish needle*] Whether the Spanish needle differed from an
ordinary tailor's needle is uncertain; but the *Encyclopædia Britannica*
(11th ed., 1911) notes that although 'steel needles were introduced into
Europe by the Moors . . . . In England their manufacture was established
about 1650'—thus making it an item of exceedingly rare value, as the antics
involving the loss of one in *Gammer Gurton's Needle* (*c.* 1563) reveal.
Bullen cites from Howe's edition of Stow's *Annals* (1631), p. 1038: 'The
making of Spanish needles was first taught in England by Elias Crowse a
Germane about the eight yeere of Queene Elizabeth, and in Queen Maries
time there was a Negro made fine Spanish Needles in Cheape-side, but
would neuer teach his Art to any.'

pressing iron] mentioned by Holinshed (see xiv. 235).

315. *goodman*] prefixed, usually without satirical intention, to the names
of persons under the rank of gentleman (see *O.E.D.*, †3.†b., for its ironical
use, as here).

317. *of legs*] i.e., of on legs.

320-2.] Jackson (p. 42), arguing for a freer handling of the text, would
emend to:

> *Franklin.* Canst thou deny thou wert a botcher once?
> *Mosby.* Measure me what I am, not what I was.
> *Arden.* Why, what are thou but a velvet drudge, . . .

321.] 'Mosbie was a tailor by trade, and here he talks like one; allusions
to his calling are frequent in the play' (Hopkinson [3]).

322. *velvet drudge*] 'menial in velvet livery' (Sturgess). (*O.E.D.* cites the
passage for figurative use of *velvet.*)

323. *base-minded*] Cf. Alice's own rebuke to Mosby at l. 198 above.

324-5.] Rubow compares *Corn.*, v. 205 ('When they haue vomited theyr
long-growne rage'), and *S. & P.*, III. ii. 14-15 ('swolne hearts greefe'; see

The rancorous venom of thy misswoll'n heart,   325
Hear me but speak. As I intend to live
With God and His elected saints in heaven,
I never meant more to solicit her;
And that she knows, and all the world shall see.
I loved her once—sweet Arden, pardon me.   330
I could not choose; her beauty fired my heart.
But time hath quenched these overraging coals;
And, Arden, though I now frequent thy house,
'Tis for my sister's sake, her waiting-maid,
And not for hers. Mayest thou enjoy her long!   335
Hell-fire and wrathful vengeance light on me
If I dishonour her or injure thee.

Arden. Mosby, with these thy protestations
The deadly hatred of my heart is appeased,
And thou and I'll be friends if this prove true.   340
As for the base terms I gave thee late,
Forget them, Mosby; I had cause to speak
When all the knights and gentlemen of Kent
Make common table-talk of her and thee.

Mosby. Who lives that is not touched with slanderous tongues?

---

333. now] *Q1–2; not in Q3.*   335. Mayest] *Q1–2* (maiest); maist *Q3;*
May'st *Delius.*   338. protestations] *Q1, 3, S.MS.;* protestation *Q2.*
339. heart is] *Qq;* heart's *S.MS., Jacob.*   341. thee late] *Qq;* thee
lately *Jacob;* thee [of] late *Hopkinson* (2).   345. slanderous] *Qq* (slaun-
derous); sland'rous *Hopkinson* (2).

---

l. 258 above). Bakeless (p. 287), however, thinks that l. 325 'might well be
an imitation of' Marlowe's 'swolne with the venome of ambitious pride'
(*E2*, 238). But cf. *Con.*, I. i. 86 ('The big swolne venome of thy hatefull
heart'), a line which has no equivalent in the 'good' quarto of *2H6.* An
actor-reporter's memory seems to be behind at least some of these passages.

   335. *Mayest*] monosyllabic.

   336–7.] Hart, *S.S.C.*, parallels *Con.*, III. ii. 143 ('Hell fire and vengeance
go along with you'—a line which appears in 'corrected' form in *2H6,* III. ii.
300, as 'Mischance and sorrow go along with you!'). Parallels to *S. & P.,*
II. i. 114 ('all vengeance light on me'), and v. ii. 74 ('And mischiefe light on
me, if I sweare false') have been pointed out, but this latter construction
seems commonplace (cf., too, *1 Tamb.*, 903: 'And fearefull vengeance light
vpon you both').

   341. *late*] i.e., lately; but now.

Franklin. Then, Mosby, to eschew the speech of men,   346
    Upon whose general bruit all honour hangs,
    Forbear his house.

Arden. Forbear it! Nay, rather frequent it more.
    The world shall see that I distrust her not.   350
    To warn him on the sudden from my house
    Were to confirm the rumour that is grown.

Mosby. By my faith, sir, you say true.
    And therefore will I sojourn here awhile
    Until our enemies have talked their fill;   355
    And then, I hope, they'll cease and at last confess
    How causeless they have injured her and me.

Arden. And I will lie at London all this term
    To let them see how light I weigh their words.

Here enters ALICE.

Alice. Husband, sit down; your breakfast will be cold.   360

Arden. Come, Master Mosby, will you sit with us?

Mosby. I cannot eat, but I'll sit for company.

Arden. Sirrah Michael, see our horse be ready.

                  [*Exit* MICHAEL *but returns soon after.*]

---

346. eschew] *Qq;* avoid *S.MS.*   352. to] *Q2-3;* too *Q1.*   grown] *Qq;*
grounded *S.MS.*   353. my faith] *S.MS., Tyrrell;* faith, my *Qq.*
358. lie] *Qq* (ly)*;* be *S.MS.*   359.1.] *Qq;* ACT I. SCENE III. *Room in*
Arden's *House, as before. Enter* Arden, Franklin, Mosbie, Michael, *and*
Alice. *Tyrrell.*   363. S.H.] *Q1-2;* Alice *Q3.*   our] *Q1, S.MS.;* your
Q2-3; my *Tyrrell.*   horse] *Qq;* horses *S.MS.*   363.1] *This ed., after*
Sturgess; *not in Qq.*

---

347. *bruit*] report.

357. *causeless*] without cause.

358.] Cf. l. 51 above.

359.1.] Editors who begin a new scene here have in mind an interior
breakfast scene; but on the open Elizabethan stage tables were carried on,
usually by the actors themselves, in full view of the audience (see *Ant.,* II.
vii, and *Mac.,* III. iv). Here, Arden, who is the only character eating, and
then just briefly, most likely just sat down on one of the stools that stood
about the stage; no change of scene is necessary.

363. *Sirrah*] See note to l. 310 above.

horse] 'the nominative plural was the same as the singular' (*O.E.D.,*
which also notes that its use was uncertain till in the seventeenth century

Alice. Husband, why pause ye ? Why eat you not ?

Arden. I am not well. There's something in this broth   365
    That is not wholesome. Didst thou make it, Alice ?

Alice. I did, and that's the cause it likes not you.

               Then she throws down the broth on the ground.
    There's nothing that I do can please your taste.
    You were best to say I would have poisoned you.
    I cannot speak or cast aside my eye,   370
    But he imagines I have stepped awry.
    Here's he that you cast in my teeth so oft;
    Now will I be convinced or purge myself.—
    I charge thee speak to this mistrustful man,
    Thou that wouldst see me hang, thou, Mosby, thou.   375
    What favour hast thou had more than a kiss
    At coming or departing from the town ?

Mosby. You wrong yourself and me to cast these doubts;
    Your loving husband is not jealous.

Arden. Why, gentle Mistress Alice, cannot I be ill   380
    But you'll accuse yourself ?—
    Franklin, thou hast a box of mithridate;

---

364. ye] *Q1;* you *Q2–3.*   379. jealous] *Q3;* Jelious *Q1;* iealious *Q2.*
380–1.] *so Qq;* Why . . . Alice, / Can . . . yourself ? *Delius;* Why . . . I / Be . . .
your selfe ? *Brooke.*   380. cannot] *Qq;* can't *Jacob.*   382. thou hast a]
Qq; thou, haste! a *Brooke.*

'sometimes *horse* appears as the collective and *horses* as the individual
plural').

    363.1.] necessitated by stage direction in Q at l. 416.1 below.

    367. *likes not you*] pleases you not (as in *Troil.,* v. ii. 101–2: 'but that that
likes not you / Pleases me best'). For the construction of impersonal verbs,
see Abbott 297.

    372. *he*] Mosby.
    cast in my teeth] throw up to me.

    373. *convinced*] convicted, proved guilty (*O.E.D., convince, v.,* II. †4).

    374. *mistrustful*] distrustful or suspicious.

    376–7. 'This would be required by bare civility, as at line [411]' (Mc-
Ilwraith). Cf. *Oth.,* II. i. 98–9, where Cassio kisses Emilia with the excuse
that "tis my breeding / That gives me this bold show of courtesy'.

    382. *mithridate*] 'A composition of many ingredients . . . regarded as a
universal antidote against poison and infectious disease [so called from
Mithridates VI, king of Pontus (died c. 63 B.C.), who was said to have

I'll take a little to prevent the worst.

Franklin. Do so, and let us presently take horse.

My life for yours, ye shall do well enough.   385

Alice. Give me a spoon; I'll eat of it myself.

Would it were full of poison to the brim,

Then should my cares and troubles have an end!

Was ever silly woman so tormented?

Arden. Be patient, sweet love; I mistrust not thee.   390

Alice. God will revenge it, Arden, if thou dost;

For never woman loved her husband better

Than I do thee.

Arden. I know it, sweet Alice. Cease to complain,

Lest that in tears I answer thee again.   395

Franklin. Come, leave this dallying, and let us away.

Alice. Forbear to wound me with that bitter word;

Arden shall go to London in my arms.

Arden. Loath am I to depart, yet I must go.

Alice. Wilt thou to London then, and leave me here?   400

Ah, if thou love me, gentle Arden, stay.

Yet, if thy business be of great import,

Go if thou wilt; I'll bear it as I may.

But write from London to me every week,

Nay, every day, and stay no longer there   405

Than thou must needs, lest that I die for sorrow.

Arden. I'll write unto thee every other tide,

388. and troubles have] *Qq;* be at *S.MS.*   392–3.] *so W-P; one line in Qq.*
393. do] *Qq; omitted Tyrrell.*   395. Lest] *Q3;* Least *Q1–2.*   396. let us]
Qq; let's *Delius.*   398. my] *Q1;* mine *Q2–3.*   406. lest] *Q3;* least
Q1–2.   407. other] *Q1–2; not in Q3.*

rendered himself proof against poisons by the constant use of antidotes]'
(*O.E.D.*).

389. *silly*] helpless, defenceless.

407. *tide*] It is more explicit in Holinshed that the customary way of
travelling to London from Faversham was by way of horse along the old
Pilgrims' Road (from Canterbury), passing through Sittingbourne, Rainham, and Rochester, to Gravesend, from where the journey was continued
by boat along the Thames. The references to this familiar route are frequent throughout the play. See 1575 map, reproduced as endpapers to this
volume.

And so farewell, sweet Alice, till we meet next.

Alice. Farewell, husband, seeing you'll have it so.—

And, Master Franklin, seeing you take him hence,   410
In hope you'll hasten him home I'll give you this.

And then she kisseth him.

Franklin. And, if he stay, the fault shall not be mine.—
Mosby, farewell, and see you keep your oath.

Mosby. I hope he is not jealous of me now.

Arden. No, Mosby, no. Hereafter think of me   415
As of your dearest friend, and so farewell.

Exeunt ARDEN, FRANKLIN, *and* MICHAEL.

Alice. I am glad he is gone; he was about to stay,
But did you mark me then how I brake off?

Mosby. Ay, Alice, and it was cunningly performed.
But what a villain is this painter Clarke!   420

Alice. Was it not a goodly poison that he gave!
Why, he's as well now as he was before.
It should have been some fine confection
That might have given the broth some dainty taste.
This powder was too gross and populous.   425

---

409. seeing] *Qq;* Since *S.MS.*   414. jealous] *Q3;* Jelious *Q1;* iealious *Q2.*
415. of] *Q1-2;* on *Q3.*   416. of] *Q1-2; not in Q3.*   418. brake] *Qq;*
broke *Tyrrell.*   419. and it] *Qq;* and't *Delius.*   420. is this] *Q1;* was the
Q2-3, S.MS.; is that *B-H-N.*   421. Was it] *Qq;* Was't *Delius;* 'Twas
conj. Hopkinson (*3*).   gave!] *McIlwraith;* gave? *Qq.*   425. populous]
Qq (populos)*;* popular *S.MS.;* palpable *Delius.*

---

411. *hasten*] monosyllabic.

418. *brake*] former past tense of *break*.

419.] Taylor compares *J.M.,* 1132 ('True; and it shall be cunningly
performed').

and it] Since *Alice* is generally pronounced monosyllabically in the play,
Delius's emendation is unnecessary whereas in l. 421 the metre justifies the
elision.

421. *Was it*] Hopkinson's suggested emendation obliterates the sarcasm
of Alice's exclamation.

gave !] In Elizabethan English, ? often = !.

425. *gross*] indelicate (to the taste); indigestible.

populous] obvious, perceptible (suggested by Ortlepp's translation into
German: *Es war zu bemerklich*). *O.E.D.* cites the passage under *a.,* 3 ('Of
or pertaining to the populous: = POPULAR *a.,* in various senses'); and

Mosby. But, had he eaten but three spoonfuls more,
   Then had he died and our love continued.
Alice. Why, so it shall, Mosby, albeit he live.
Mosby. It is unpossible, for I have sworn
   Never hereafter to solicit thee   430
   Or, whilst he lives, once more importune thee.
Alice. Thou shalt not need; I will importune thee.
   What ? Shall an oath make thee forsake my love ?
   As if I have not sworn as much myself
   And given my hand unto him in the church!   435
   Tush, Mosby! Oaths are words, and words is wind,
   And wind is mutable. Then, I conclude,
   'Tis childishness to stand upon an oath.
Mosby. Well proved, Mistress Alice; yet, by your leave,
   I'll keep mine unbroken whilst he lives.   440
Alice. Ay, do, and spare not. His time is but short;
   For, if thou beest as resolute as I,
   We'll have him murdered as he walks the streets.

---

428. so it shall] *Q1–2; not in Q3, S.MS.*   albeit] *Qq;* what though *S.MS.*
429. unpossible] *Q1;* impossible *Q2–3.*   431, 440. whilst] *Q2–3;*
whylest *Q1;* while *S.MS.*   434. have] *Qq;* had *Hopkinson* (2).   436. is]
Q1; are *Q2–3.*   437. wind is] *Qq;* words are *S.MS.*   442. beest] *Qq;*
be *S.MS.;* be'st *Delius;* art *Tyrrell.*

Bayne, McIlwraith, and Sturgess, among others, take the word to mean
common, inferior, crude (from *popular = suitable to the common people;* cf.
S.MS. reading). Bullen offers *thick* as a possible definition. Hugo trans-
lates as *répulsive.* None of these definitions thoroughly excludes the others,
but Ortlepp's *bemerklich* seems more directly in keeping with Alice's train
of thought: if the poison did not taste so obviously as poison, Arden would
have gone on eating. The phrase 'gross and palpable' appears in the
Shakespeare apocryphal play of *Edward III,* II. i. 142 ('That line hath two
falts, grosse and palpable' [ed. Brooke, *Apocrypha*]); Delius, however, later
retracted his conjectural emendation (in the introduction to his edition of
The Birth of Merlin [*Pseudo-Shakspere'sche Dramen,* Vol. III (1856), p.
xvii]) on the basis of 'he I plead for / Has power to make your beauty
populous' from Webster's *Appius and Virginia,* II. i. 70–1 (*The Complete
Works,* vol. III [1927], ed. F. L. Lucas, who glosses the word as 'famous
among the people').
   429. *unpossible*] common for *impossible* from about 1400 to 1660 (*O.E.D.*).
   436–7.] Parallels have been cited (see App. I), but the expression is

In London many alehouse ruffians keep,
Which, as I hear, will murder men for gold.   445
They shall be soundly fee'd to pay him home.

Here enters GREENE.

Mosby. Alice, what's he that comes yonder ? Knowest thou him ?
Alice. Mosby, begone! I hope 'tis one that comes
        To put in practice our intended drifts.   *Exit* MOSBY.
Greene. Mistress Arden, you are well met.   450
        I am sorry that your husband is from home
        Whenas my purposed journey was to him.
        Yet all my labour is not spent in vain,
        For I suppose that you can full discourse
        And flat resolve me of the thing I seek.   455
Alice. What is it, Master Greene ? If that I may
        Or can with safety, I will answer you.
Greene. I heard your husband hath the grant of late,
        Confirmed by letters patents from the king,
        Of all the lands of the Abbey of Faversham,   460

---

446. fee'd] *S.MS.* (feed), *Tyrrell;* fed *Qq.*   447. Knowest] *Q1–2;*
knowst *Q3;* know'st *Delius.*   458. hath] *Q1;* had *Q2–3.*   459. patents]
Qq; patent *Tyrrell.*

---

commonplace, as well as proverbial: see Tilley, W833 ('Words are but
wind'), W412, and W439.
    444. *keep*] live, lodge.
    446. *fee'd*] given a fee, as executioners customarily were.
    to pay him home] to pay him directly, i.e., to murder him. Cf. l. 515 below
and note to x. 45. The phrase is commonplace, but it can be argued that
the pun here with *fee'd* is in the Shakespearean manner: cf. *1H4*, I. iii.
286–8:

        The king will always think him in our *debt*,
        And think we think ourselves *unsatisfied*,
        Till he hath found a time to *pay us home*.

    447.] Cf. l. 295 above, where Mosby seems to know who Greene is.
    449.] The following encounter between Alice and Greene expands
Holinshed's account (see App. II, pp. 149–50).
    452. *Whenas*] seeing that, since.
    453.] See App. I.
    454. *full discourse*] fully explain.
    455. *flat resolve*] completely satisfy or make clear to.

Generally intitled, so that all former grants
Are cut off, whereof I myself had one;
But now my interest by that is void.
This is all, Mistress Arden; is it true nor no?

Alice. True, Master Greene; the lands are his in state,   465
And whatsoever leases were before
Are void for term of Master Arden's life.
He hath the grant under the Chancery seal.

Greene. Pardon me, Mistress Arden; I must speak,
For I am touched. Your husband doth me wrong   470
To wring me from the little land I have.
My living is my life; only that
Resteth remainder of my portion.
Desire of wealth is endless in his mind,
And he is greedy-gaping still for gain;   475
Nor cares he though young gentlemen do beg,
So he may scrape and hoard up in his pouch.

---

463. that is] *Qq;* that [deed] is *Hopkinson (2).*   464. nor] *Q1;* or *Q2–3.*
466. were] *Q1–2; not in Q3.*   471. wring me from] *Qq;* wrest from me
S.MS.   473. remainder] *Q1;* remained *Q2–3.*   475. greedy-gaping]
W-P; gredy gaping *Qq;* gredy, gaping *Jacob.*

---

461. *Generally intitled*] deeded or furnished a title without any exceptions.

462. *cut off*] put a stop to, i.e., superseded.

465. *in state*] by right of legal ownership or possession.

467. *term*] the duration.

468. *Chancery seal*] At this time the court of the Lord Chancellor of England was 'the highest court of judicature next to the House of Lords'; 'in civil matters it was a kind of court of appeal' (*O.E.D.*).

470. *touched*] affected, hurt in feelings.

472. *living*] land.

472–3. *only . . . portion*] Only my land is what remains to me of my inheritance. Hopkinson (3) suggests that the legal definition of *remainder* ('an estate limited in lands, tenements, or rents, to be enjoyed after the expiration of another particular estate') is applicable here possibly; but the simpler reading is probably the truer one.

475. *greedy-gaping*] This compound adjective, not recorded in the *O.E.D.*, appears in the anonymous play *The Bugbears*, I. ii. 54 (in *Early Plays from the Italian*, ed. R. W. Bond [1911], who dates the play *c.* 1564–5).
still] always.

477. *So*] so long as (*O.E.D.*, 26).

But, seeing he hath taken my lands, I'll value life
As careless as he is careful for to get;
And, tell him this from me, I'll be revenged   480
And so as he shall wish the Abbey lands
Had rested still within their former state.

Alice. Alas, poor gentleman, I pity you,
And woe is me that any man should want.
God knows, 'tis not my fault. But wonder not   485
Though he be hard to others when to me—
Ah, Master Greene, God knows how I am used!

Greene. Why, Mistress Arden, can the crabbèd churl
Use you unkindly? Respects he not your birth,
Your honourable friends, nor what you brought?   490
Why, all Kent knows your parentage and what you are.

Alice. Ah, Master Greene, be it spoken in secret here,
I never live good day with him alone.
When he is at home, then have I froward looks,
Hard words, and blows to mend the match withal.   495
And, though I might content as good a man,
Yet doth he keep in every corner trulls;
And, weary with his trugs at home,
Then rides he straight to London. There, forsooth,
He revels it among such filthy ones   500
As counsels him to make away his wife.
Thus live I daily in continual fear,

478. taken] *Qq;* ta'en *Bayne.*   494. he is] *Qq;* he's *Tyrrell.*   498. And, weary] *Qq;* And, when he's weary *Bayne.*   501. counsels] *Q1–2;* counsell *Q3.*

---

479. *careful for to get*] solicitous to acquire possessions.
481. *so as*] in such a way that.
488. *crabbèd*] ill-tempered.
489. *unkindly*] improperly; ungratefully.
490. *what you brought*] i.e., as your dowry.
491. *parentage*] See Intro., p. xxxvi.
494. *froward*] ill-humoured, ugly.
495. *mend . . . withal*] bitterly ironic, of course.
497. *trulls*] wenches, prostitutes.
498. *trugs*] same as *trulls.* (*O.E.D.* quotes Florio's 'fustian or roguish word for a trull, a whore, or a wench').

In sorrow, so despairing of redress
As every day I wish with hearty prayer
That he or I were taken forth the world.   505

Greene. Now trust me, Mistress Alice, it grieveth me
So fair a creature should be so abused.
Why, who would have thought the civil sir so sullen?
He looks so smoothly. Now, fie upon him, churl!
And if he live a day he lives too long.   510
But frolic, woman! I shall be the man
Shall set you free from all this discontent.
And if the churl deny my interest
And will not yield my lease into my hand,
I'll pay him home, whatever hap to me.   515

Alice. But speak you as you think?

Greene. Ay, God's my witness, I mean plain dealing,
For I had rather die than lose my land.

Alice. Then, Master Greene, be counsellèd by me:
Endanger not yourself for such a churl,   520
But hire some cutter for to cut him short;
And here's ten pound to wager them withal.
When he is dead, you shall have twenty more;
And the lands whereof my husband is possessed

---

505. forth] *Qq;* from *S.MS.*   508. Why] *Qq; omitted S.MS.*   who
would] *Qq;* who'd *Jacob.*   509. Now] *Qq; omitted S.MS., Jacob.*   510.
live] *Qq;* lives *Jacob.*   516. think] *Qq;* mean *S.MS.*   521. cutter] *Qq;*
cutters *Oliphant.*   short] *Qq;* down *S.MS.*

---

509. *smoothly*] pleasantly, agreeably.
510. *And if*] See Abbott 105 for the phrase as representing both *even if*
and *if indeed* in Elizabethan English; cf. l. 513 below.
511. *frolic*] make merry, cheer up.
512. *Shall*] See Abbott 244 for omission of the relative pronoun ('who')
in Elizabethan English.
513. *interest*] legal right or title to property (*O.E.D., sb.* 1. a.).
515. *pay . . . home*] See note to l. 446 above.
521. *cutter*] cut-throat.
522-3.] Cf. ll. 568-9 below; ii. 103-4; and xiv. 126-7.
522. *wager*] hire, pay wages to (this passage cited by *O.E.D., v.,* ¶4, as a
misusage for WAGE, *v.,* 7).
withal] therewith.

I

Shall be intitled as they were before.   525
Greene. Will you keep promise with me ?
Alice. Or count me false and perjured whilst I live.
Greene. Then here's my hand; I'll have him so dispatched.
 I'll up to London straight; I'll thither post
 And never rest till I have compassed it.   530
 Till then farewell.
Alice. Good fortune follow all your forward thoughts.
 And whosoever doth attempt the deed,
 A happy hand I wish; and so farewell.—   *Exit* GREENE.
 All this goes well. Mosby, I long for thee   535
 To let thee know all that I have contrived.

Here enters MOSBY *and* CLARKE.

Mosby. How now, Alice, what's the news ?
Alice. Such as will content thee well, sweetheart.
Mosby. Well, let them pass awhile, and tell me, Alice,
 How have you dealt and tempered with my sister ?   540
 What, will she have my neighbour Clarke or no ?
Alice. What, Master Mosby! Let him woo himself.
 Think you that maids look not for fair words ?—
 Go to her, Clarke; she's all alone within.
 Michael, my man, is clean out of her books.   545
Clarke. I thank you, Mistress Arden. I will in;

530. And] *Qq;* Ile *S.MS.*   534. S.D.] *so* Hugo, Oliphant; *after l. 531 Qq.*
536.1.] *Qq;* ACT II. SCENE I. *Before* Arden's *House. Enter* Mosbie *and*
Clarke, *meeting* Alice. Tyrrell.   539. them] *Qq;* it *S.MS.*

---

525. *intitled*] See note to l. 461 above.
 528. *dispatched*] killed.
 529. *to London straight*] Note repetition at ll. 223, 499 above, and ll. 570–1
below.
 532. *forward*] zealous, eager.
 539. *them*] i.e., the news (regarded as plural, as also in ll. 550–1, 553,
572–3 below).
 540. *tempered with*] worked upon, i.e., persuaded.
 545.] Cf. the proverb: 'To be in (out of) one's books' (Tilley, B534), i.e.,
to be in (or out of) one's favour or esteem. Petruchio, for instance, asks
Kate to 'put me in thy books!' (*Shr.*, II. i. 221).
 clean] completely, entirely.

And, if fair Susan and I can make a gree,
You shall command me to the uttermost
As far as either goods or life may stretch.   *Exit* CLARKE.

Mosby. Now, Alice, let's hear thy news.   550

Alice. They be so good that I must laugh for joy
Before I can begin to tell my tale.

Mosby. Let's hear them, that I may laugh for company.

Alice. This morning, Master Greene—Dick Greene, I mean,
From whom my husband had the Abbey land—   555
Came hither, railing, for to know the truth
Whether my husband had the lands by grant.
I told him all, whereat he stormed amain
And swore he would cry quittance with the churl
And, if he did deny his interest,   560
Stab him whatsoever did befall himself.
Whenas I saw his choler thus to rise,
I whetted on the gentleman with words;
And, to conclude, Mosby, at last we grew
To composition for my husband's death.   565
I gave him ten pound to hire knaves,
By some device to make away the churl.
When he is dead, he should have twenty more

---

547. can make a gree] *Qq;* can agree *S.MS.,Jacob.*   a gree] *Q1–2;* agree
Q3, M.S.R.   551. They be] *Qq;* It is *S.MS.*   553. them, that] *Qq;*
them, then, that *Jacob;* then, that *Sturgess.*   them] *Qq;* it *S.MS.*
555. land] *Qq;* lands *S.MS., Delius.*   561. whatsoever] *Qq;* whatever
S.MS.,Jacob.   566. pound to] *Qq;* pound [for] to *Hopkinson* (2).

---

547. *Susan*] probably monosyllabic.
make a gree] come to terms (*O.E.D.*, GREE. *sb.*², 2).
556. *for*] in order.
558. *amain*] with all his might.
559. *cry quittance*] be even. Cf. proverb: 'I'll cry quittance with you'
(Tilley, Q18).
561. *whatsoever*] Jacob's emendation is probably correct; Q's reading
may simply be a recollection of l. 533 above.
562. *Whenas*] when.
563. *whetted on*] stirred up, incited.
565. *composition*] agreement (for payment).
568–9.] Cf. ll. 522–3 above; ii. 103–4.

And repossess his former lands again.
On this we 'greed, and he is ridden straight   570
To London to bring his death about.
Mosby. But call you this good news?
Alice. Ay, sweetheart, be they not?
Mosby. 'Twere cheerful news to hear the churl were dead;
But trust me, Alice, I take it passing ill   575
You would be so forgetful of our state
To make recount of it to every groom.
What! to acquaint each stranger with our drifts,
Chiefly in case of murder—why, 'tis the way
To make it open unto Arden's self   580
And bring thyself and me to ruin both.
Forewarned, forearmed; who threats his enemy
Lends him a sword to guard himself withal.
Alice. I did it for the best.
Mosby. Well, seeing 'tis done, cheerly let it pass.   585
You know this Greene; is he not religious?
A man, I guess, of great devotion?
Alice. He is.
Mosby. Then, sweet Alice, let it pass. I have a drift

570. 'greed] *Qq;* agreed *S.MS., Jacob.*   571. London to] *Qq;* London
[for] to *Hopkinson* (2).   576. would] *Qq;* should *S.MS.*   585. cheerly]
Q1–2 (cherely); cheerefully *Q3, S.MS.;* clearly *Tyrrell;* cheerily
McIlwraith; cheer'ly *Sturgess.*   589. sweet Alice] *Q1–2; not in Q3.*

575. *passing*] very, exceedingly.
580. *make it open*] reveal it.
582. *Forewarned, forearmed*] proverbial (Tilley, H54).
585. *cheerly*] cheerily (*O.E.D.*). Cf. textual note and commentary for
haply, l. 602 below.
586. *religious*] pious (in the accustomed sense, as the next line indicates),
as well as conscientious. Schelling's explanation as 'a man of his word' and
Oliphant's 'to be relied upon' are, in view of Mosby's following dismissal
of Greene and his preferred reliance on the painter's device, beside the
mark: Mosby does not believe that a genuinely religious man, one who
formally and devoutly follows religious ceremony, can in fact be relied
upon to engage in the crime that Alice has planned.
589.] Q3's omission of 'sweet Alice' is justifiable, for the phrase is
probably an actor's insertion; without it, the two lines (588–9) form one
iambic pentameter line.

Will quiet all, whatever is amiss.   590

Here enters CLARKE *and* SUSAN.

Alice. How now, Clarke ? Have you found me false ?
     Did I not plead the matter hard for you ?
Clarke. You did.
Mosby. And what ? Will't be a match ?
Clarke. A match, i'faith, sir. Ay, the day is mine.   595
     The painter lays his colours to the life;
     His pencil draws no shadows in his love:
     Susan is mine.
Alice. You make her blush.
Mosby. What, sister ? Is it Clarke must be the man ?   600
Susan. It resteth in your grant. Some words are passed,
     And haply we be grown unto a match
     If you be willing that it shall be so.
Mosby. Ah, Master Clarke, it resteth at my grant;
     You see my sister's yet at my dispose;   605
     But, so you'll grant me one thing I shall ask,
     I am content my sister shall be yours.
Clarke. What is it, Master Mosby ?
Mosby. I do remember once in secret talk
     You told me how you could compound by art   610
     A crucifix impoisonèd,
     That whoso look upon it should wax blind

593–4.] *so Qq; as one line of verse in Tyrrell.*   598–9.] *so Qq; as one line of verse in Tyrrell.*   601. grant] *Qq;* breast *S.MS.*   passed] *Qq* (past).
602. haply] *Delius;* happely *Q1;* happily *Q2–3, B-H-N.*   be grown] *Qq;*
agree *S.MS.*   612. look] *Qq;* looks *S.MS.;* look'd *Jacob.*

---

    596. *lays . . . life*] faithfully reproduces the exact details of life; applies
his colours with life-like vividness.
    601. *in your grant*] i.e., in your authority to grant.
    602. *haply*] perhaps, maybe. (See *O.E.D.*, which lists the variant spelling
happely [Q1] from the fifteenth through the seventeenth century and indicates that 'the form *happely* connects this with *happily*'.) See note to cheerly,
l. 585 above.
    605. *dispose*] disposal.
    610 ff.] not in Holinshed.

And with the scent be stifled, that ere long
He should die poisoned that did view it well.
I would have you make me such a crucifix,   615
And then I'll grant my sister shall be yours.
Clarke. Though I am loath, because it toucheth life,
       Yet, rather or I'll leave sweet Susan's love,
       I'll do it, and with all the haste I may.
       But for whom is it?   620
Alice. Leave that to us. Why, Clarke, is it possible
       That you should paint and draw it out yourself,
       The colours being baleful and impoisoned,
       And no ways prejudice yourself withal?
Mosby. Well questioned, Alice.—Clarke, how answer you that?
Clarke. Very easily. I'll tell you straight   626
       How I do work of these impoisoned drugs:
       I fasten on my spectacles so close
       As nothing can any way offend my sight;
       Then, as I put a leaf within my nose,   630
       So put I rhubarb to avoid the smell,
       And softly as another work I paint.
Mosby. 'Tis very well, but against when shall I have it?
Clarke. Within this ten days.
Mosby. 'Twill serve the turn.—   635
       Now, Alice, let's in and see what cheer you keep.
       I hope, now Master Arden is from home,
       You'll give me leave to play your husband's part.

618. or] *Qq;* then *S.MS.*   I'll] *Q1–2* (Ile); I *Q3.*   625.] *so Tyrrell; two lines in Qq, divided at* Ales, / Clarke.   626–ii. 26] *so Qq; missing in S.MS.* 634–5.] *so Qq; as one line of verse in Tyrrell.*   634. this] *Qq;* these *Jacob.*

618. *or*] than.
620.] Cf. ll. 268–71 above, and see Intro., pp. xxix–xxx.
623. *baleful*] baneful, injurious, noxious.
624. *prejudice*] injure or endanger.
629. *offend*] harm.
631. *rhubarb*] considered to have medicinal properties, as in *Mac.*, v. iii. 55 ('rhubarb, senna, or what purgative drug').
632. *softly as*] comfortably as with (Sturgess).
636. *cheer*] hospitality.

Alice. Mosby, you know who's master of my heart
    He well may be the master of the house.   *Exeunt.*   640

[Sc. ii]

Here enters GREENE *and* BRADSHAW.

Bradshaw. See you them that comes yonder, Master Greene?
Greene. Ay, very well. Do you know them?

Here enters BLACK WILL *and* SHAKEBAG.

Bradshaw. The one I know not, but he seems a knave,
    Chiefly for bearing the other company;
    For such a slave, so vile a rogue as he,   5
    Lives not again upon the earth.
    Black Will is his name. I tell you, Master Greene,
    At Boulogne he and I were fellow soldiers,
    Where he played such pranks
    As all the camp feared him for his villainy.   10
    I warrant you he bears so bad a mind
    That for a crown he'll murder any man.
Greene. [*Aside*] The fitter is he for my purpose, marry!
Will. How now, fellow Bradshaw? Whither away so early?

---

639. heart] *This ed.;* hart, *Qq;* heart; *Sturgess.*   640. He] *Qq; As* Jacob.

Sc. ii] *Hugo; not in Qq;* ACT II. SCENE II. *Country between* Feversham *and*
London. *Tyrrell;* ACT II. SCENE I. *Delius.*   1. comes] *Q1–2;* come *Q3.*
2.1.] *so Qq; after l. 13 in Tyrrell.*   7. name.] *Jacob* (name:); name *Q1;*
name, *Q2–3.*   8, 19. Boulogne] *Qq* (Bulloine).   13. *Aside*] *Tyrrell.*
14.] *so W-P; two lines in Qq, divided at* Bradshaw / Whether.

---

    ii. 7–32.] Cf. Holinshed, App. II, p. 150. Henry VIII captured the sea-
port of Boulogne (on the English Channel, 157 miles from Paris [Sugden]),
in 1544, but his son Edward VI surrendered it back to the French in the
Treaty of Boulogne, 29 March 1550, almost a year before Arden's murder.
Qq's spelling of Boulogne undoubtedly reflects Elizabethan pronunciation.
    11. *warrant*] assure.
    13. Aside] Cf. Holinshed: 'Yea thought Greene (as he after confessed)
such a one is for my purpose'.
    marry !] 'interjection: originally the name of the Virgin Mary used as an
oath or invocation' (Onions).

Bradshaw. O Will, times are changed. No fellows now,   15
  Though we were once together in the field;
  Yet thy friend to do thee any good I can.

Will. Why, Bradshaw, was not thou and I fellow soldiers at
  Boulogne, where I was a corporal and thou but a base
  mercenary groom? 'No fellows now' because you are a   20
  goldsmith and have a little plate in your shop? You were
  glad to call me 'fellow Will' and, with a cursy to the earth,
  'One snatch, good corporal' when I stole the half ox from
  John the victualler and domineered with it amongst good
  fellows in one night.   25

Bradshaw. Ay, Will, those days are past with me.

Will. Ay, but they be not past with me, for I keep that same
  honourable mind still. Good neighbour Bradshaw, you
  are too proud to be my fellow; but, were it not that I see
  more company coming down the hill, I would be fellows   30
  with you once more, and share crowns with you too. But
  let that pass, and tell me whither you go.

Bradshaw. To London, Will, about a piece of service

18–25.] so *W-P; as verse in Qq, lines ending* I / Bulloine: / groome? /
gouldsmith, / shoppe, / Will, / earth, / corporall. / vitler. / fellowes, / night.
22. cursy] *Qq;* curtsey *Tyrrell;* courtesy *Delius.*   24. victualler] *Qq*
(vitler).   amongst] *Q1–2;* among *Q3.*   27–32.] *so W-P; as verse in Q1,
lines ending* me. / still, / fellow, / down / more, / you to. / goe; *ll. 29–31* ('but,
were . . . once more') *as prose in Q2–3; prose to l. 31* ('you too') *Delius.*
27. Ay, but] *Qq* (I but); Ay? But *Delius.*   32. go] *Qq;* are going
S.MS.

---

20. *mercenary*] hired (*O.E.D.*, 2).
22. *cursy*] 'obsolete form of CURTSY' (*O.E.D.*).
23. *snatch*] morsel, small piece.
24. *domineered*] revelled, lived riotously.
30. *more company*] In Holinshed, when Greene and Bradshaw 'came to
Rainham downe, they chanced to see three or foure seruingmen that were
comming from Leeds' and thereafter Black Will and his companion ('an
other with a great staffe on his necke'). 'Then said Bradshaw to Greene;
We are happie that here commeth some companie from Leeds.' Sturgess
(p. 290) suggests that 'Leeds' might be Lidsing, about ten miles south of
the Faversham–Gravesend road.
31. *and share crowns with you*] 'i.e., rob you' (Sturgess).
33. *To London*] In Holinshed, Bradshaw is merely accompanying
Greene, who is going to London, as far as Gravesend. The business that

Wherein haply thou may'st pleasure me.

Will. What is it ?   35

Bradshaw. Of late Lord Cheyne lost some plate,

　　Which one did bring and sold it at my shop,

　　Saying he served Sir Anthony Cooke.

　　A search was made, the plate was found with me,

　　And I am bound to answer at the 'size.   40

　　Now Lord Cheyne solemnly vows,

　　If law will serve him, he'll hang me for his plate.

　　Now I am going to London upon hope

　　To find the fellow. Now, Will, I know

　　Thou art acquainted with such companions.   45

Will. What manner of man was he ?

Bradshaw. A lean-faced, writhen knave,

　　Hawk-nosed and very hollow-eyed,

---

34. haply] *Delius;* happely *Q1;* happily *Q2–3, B-H-N.*   may'st] *Qq*
(maist)*;* mayest *S.MS., Bayne.*   pleasure] *Qq;* Serve *S.MS.*   38–40.]
so Qq; divided in Oliphant at search / Was *and* I / Am.   38. Anthony] *This
ed.;* Antony *Qq.*   41–5.] *so Qq; prose Oliphant.*   41–2.] *so Qq; divided
in W-P at* law / Will.   41. vows] *Qq;* doth vow *S.MS.*   45. com-
panions] *Qq;* Company *S.MS.*   47. writhen] *Qq;* wrinkled *S.MS.*

---

follows about Jack Fitten's theft of the stolen plate is the playwright's
invention. It has been argued that the passage may have local relevance
with which only a Kentish author would have been familiar or that the
actors added it to their prompt copy while on tour in Kent (see Intro.,
p. xlvii and n. 2).

　36. *Lord Cheyne*] pronounced *Chay-nee* (see note to ix. 94.1).

　38. *Sir Anthony Cooke*] 1504–76; tutor to Edward VI and politician
(*D.N.B.*).

　40. *'size*] assize (usually in plural: 'The sessions held periodically in each
county of England, for the purpose of administering civil and criminal
justice . . . circuit courts' [*O.E.D., assize,* 12]).

　45. *companions*] used in contemptuous sense.

　47–59.] The following description of Jack Fitten functions as a kind of
litmus paper in the testing of authorship, except that the results prove, it
seems, what one expects them to prove. The most sustained parallels are to
Err., v. i. 237–41, and to *J.M.,* 1858–60. In 'A Brace of Villains', *M.L.N.,*
L (1935), 168–9, M. Grubb finds a parallel in Spenser's description of
Guyle in *F.Q.,* v. ix. 10, and argues that the *Arden* passage must be the
later one. Such descriptions of villains, however, had come to fit an icono-
graphic pattern; cf. also *Rom.,* v. i. 37–44.

　47. *writhen*] contorted, twisted.

With mighty furrows in his stormy brows,
Long hair down his shoulders curled;   50
His chin was bare, but on his upper lip
A mutchado, which he wound about his ear.

Will. What apparel had he?

Bradshaw. A watchet satin doublet all to-torn
 (The inner side did bear the greater show),   55
A pair of threadbare velvet hose, seam rent,
A worsted stocking rent above the shoe,
A livery cloak, but all the lace was off;
'Twas bad, but yet it served to hide the plate.

Will. Sirrah Shakebag, canst thou remember since we trolled 60
the bowl at Sittingburgh, where I broke the tapster's head
of the Lion with a cudgel-stick?

Shakebag. Ay, very well, Will.

Will. Why, it was with the money that the plate was sold for.

---

49. his] *Q1–2; not in Q3.* 50. down his] *Q1–2;* downe to his *Q3.*
54. watchet] *Qq;* Wreched *S.MS.* all to-torn] *Qq* (all to torne)*;* all torn
S.MS.; all so torn *Jacob;* all-to torn *Hopkinson* (2). 55. greater] *Qq;*
greatest *Jacob.* 57. worsted *Tyrrell;* wosted *Q1, 3, S.MS.;* wosten *Q2.*
stocking] *S.MS., Jacob;* stockin *Qq.* 60–2.] *so Delius; as verse in Qq,*
lines ending remember / Sittingburgh, / Lyon / sticke? 61. Sittingburgh]
Q1–2; Sittingburne *Q3, S.MS.* 62. of] *Q1–2;* at *Q3, S.MS.* 64–6.]
so Delius; as verse in Qq, lines ending for: / him / plate?

49.] See App. I.

52. *mutchado*] moustache.

54. *watchet*] light or pale blue.

all to-torn] completely torn apart. (See *O.E.D.*, ALL, C. *adv.*, †14: '*All*
emphasized the particle combined with a verb: . . . especially the prefix
to = "asunder".')

55.] i.e., more lining was visible than the outer garment.

56. *seam rent*] torn apart at the seams.

57. *worsted stocking*] Hopkinson (2) compares *Lr.*, II. ii. 15 ('filthy,
worsted-stocking knave').

60–1. *trolled the bowl*] handed round the drinking cup.

61. *Sittingburgh*] actually Sittingbourne: 'A town in Kent, 38 miles
South-East of London, and about 9 miles East of Faversham . . . on the
Pilgrims' Road to Canterbury' (Sugden).

61–2. *the tapster's head of the Lion*] i.e., the head of the tapster of the
Lion's Inn (an actual inn where, as Donne, p. 15, notes, 'an entertainment
was given to Henry 5th, as he returned from the battle of Agincourt, in
1415').

—Sirrah Bradshaw, what wilt thou give him that can tell   65
thee who sold thy plate?

Bradshaw. Who, I pray thee, good Will?

Will. Why, 'twas one Jack Fitten. He's now in Newgate for
stealing a horse, and shall be arraigned the next 'size.

Bradshaw. Why then, let Lord Cheyne seek Jack Fitten forth,   70
For I'll back and tell him who robbed him of his plate.
This cheers my heart.—Master Greene, I'll leave you,
For I must to the Isle of Sheppey with speed.

Greene. Before you go, let me entreat you
To carry this letter to Mistress Arden of Faversham   75
And humbly recommend me to herself.

[*He hands over a letter.*]

Bradshaw. That will I, Master Greene, and so farewell.—
Here, Will, there's a crown for thy good news.

Will. Farewell, Bradshaw; I'll drink no water for thy sake
whilst this lasts. (*Exit* BRADSHAW.)—Now, gentleman,   80
shall we have your company to London?

Greene. Nay, stay, sirs.
A little more I needs must use your help,

67.] *Qq; who was it I pray good Will, S.MS.*   68–9.] *so Delius; as verse in
Qq, lines ending* Fitten, / horse, / sise.   71. back] *Q1–2;* goe back *Q3.*
74–6.] *so Qq; prose Oliphant.*   76.1.] *This ed., after Oliphant; not in Qq.*
79–81.] *so Delius; as verse in Qq, lines ending* Bradshaw, / lasts: / London.
80. whilst this lasts] *Q1* (whilest)*; whilst this doth last Q2; while this does
last Q3.*   S.D.] *so Hugo, Oliphant; after l. 78 Qq.*   82–3.] *so W-P; one
line in Qq.*   Sirs. A ... more I] *This ed., after W-P;* sirs, a ... more I *Q;*
sirs, a ... more; I *Sturgess.*

---

68. *Newgate*] a London prison.
69. *arraigned*] charged or indicted.
70–8.] probably prose although an undercurrent of blank verse is
detectable. Jackson (p. 29) 'readjusts' ll. 70–3 as follows:

> Then let Lord Cheiny seek Jack Fitten forth:
> I'll back and tell [him] who robb'd him of his plate.
> This cheers my heart. I'll leave you Master Greene,
> For I must to the Isle of Sheppy with speed.

73. *the Isle of Sheppey*] 'an island in Kent, on the South side of the estuary
of the Thames, separated from the mainland by a branch of the Medway.
... It is just opposite to Faversham' (Sugden).
78. *crown*] 'from the 15th to the 18th century the common English name
for the French *écu*' (*O.E.D.*); see iii. 73 n.

And in a matter of great consequence,

Wherein, if you'll be secret and profound,   85

I'll give you twenty angels for your pains.

Will. How? Twenty angels? Give my fellow George Shakebag and me twenty angels; and, if thou'lt have thy own
father slain that thou may'st inherit his land, we'll kill
him.   90

Shakebag. Ay, thy mother, thy sister, thy brother, or all thy
kin.

Greene. Well, this it is: Arden of Faversham
Hath highly wronged me about the Abbey land,
That no revenge but death will serve the turn.
Will you two kill him? Here's the angels down,   95
And I will lay the platform of his death.

Will. Plat me no platforms! Give me the money, and I'll stab
him as he stands pissing against a wall, but I'll kill him.

Shakebag. Where is he?

Greene. He is now at London, in Aldersgate Street.   100

87–90.] *so Delius; as verse in Qq, lines ending* fellow / Angels, / slaine, / him.
88. own] *Q1–2;* one *Q3.*   91.] *one line in Qq; prose Delius.*   93. highly]
Q1; mightily *Q2–3, S.MS.*   about the Abbey land] *Q1;* about Abby land
Q2–3; about Some Abby lands *S.MS.*   95. Here's] *Qq* (heeres); here is
S.MS.; Here are *Jacob.*   97–8.] *so Delius; as verse in Qq, divided at*
money, / wall, / .

---

85. *profound*] crafty, cunning (the *O.E.D.* cites a 1611 example as 'the
earliest sense in English').

86. *angels*] gold coins, worth ten shillings each during the reign of
Edward VI and so named from 'having as its device the archangel Michael
standing upon, and piercing the dragon' (*O.E.D.*).

94. *That*] i.e., so that (see Abbott 283).
serve the turn] suit my purpose.

96. *platform*] plan or scheme. Warnke and Proescholdt compare *1H6*,
II. i. 77 ('And lay new platforms to endamage them').

97. *Plat me no platforms!*] a common Elizabethan construction to indi-
cate a contemptuous response.

100. *Aldersgate Street*] running south from Aldersgate 'to St. Martin's-
le-Grand, and so into the West end of Cheapside' (Sugden, who notes that
on this fashionable street the Earls of Northumberland, Westmorland, and
Thanet and the Marquis of Dorchester, as well as Franklin, had their town
houses; Milton lived there from 1640 to 1645).

Shakebag. He's dead as if he had been condemned by an Act
of Parliament if once Black Will and I swear his death.

Greene. Here is ten pound; and, when he is dead,
Ye shall have twenty more.

Will. My fingers itches to be at the peasant. Ah, that I might   105
be set awork thus through the year and that murder
would grow to an occupation, that a man might without
danger of law—Zounds, I warrant I should be warden of
the company! Come, let us be going, and we'll bait at
Rochester, where I'll give thee a gallon of sack to handsel   110
the match withal.   *Exeunt.*

[Sc. iii]
Here enters MICHAEL.

Michael. I have gotten such a letter as will touch the painter,
and thus it is:

Here enters ARDEN *and* FRANKLIN *and hears*
MICHAEL *read this letter.*

101–2.] *so Delius; as verse in Qq, lines ending* condemned / I / death.
101. He's dead] *Qq;* He'se as dead *S.MS.*   105–11.] *so Delius; as verse
in Qq, lines ending* pesant, / yeere, / occupation: / law, / company, /
Rochester, / Sack, / with all.   105. itches] *Q1–2;* itch *Q3, S.MS.*
Ah] *Q1;* Oh *Q2–3, S.MS.*   106. awork] *Q1–2* (a worke); at worke *Q3,
S.MS.*   107. might without] *Qq;* might [follow it] without *Hopkinson*
(2).   108. warrant I] *Qq;* warrant you, I *S.MS.*

Sc. iii] *Hugo; not in Qq;* ACT II. SCENE III. London. *A Street near* St.
Paul's. *Tyrrell;* ACT II. SCENE II. *Delius.*   1–2.] *so Delius; as verse in Qq,
divided at* letter, / As; *divided in W-P at* Painter: / And.

103–4.] Cf. verse at i. 522–3.
107. *might*] i.e., might work at his occupation (murder).
108. *Zounds*] = 'Swounds (interjection corrupted from 'By God's
wounds!').
108–9. *warden of the company*] that is, a governor (or member of the
governing body) of the guild ('company') of murderers, a set-up that Black
Will sees as resembling one of the official livery companies of the City of
London.
109. *bait*] stop for food and rest.
110. *sack*] white wine from Spain.
handsel] confirm or inaugurate with an omen of success.

'My duty remembered, Mistress Susan, hoping in God
you be in good health as I, Michael, was at the making
hereof. This is to certify you that, as the turtle true, when   5
she hath lost her mate, sitteth alone, so I, mourning for
your absence, do walk up and down Paul's till one day I
fell asleep and lost my master's pantofles. Ah, Mistress
Susan, abolish that paltry painter, cut him off by the
shins with a frowning look of your crabbed countenance,   10
and think upon Michael, who, drunk with the dregs of
your favour, will cleave as fast to your love as a plaster of
pitch to a galled horseback. Thus hoping you will let my

---

3. Mistress] *Qq;* Mrs. *S.MS., Jacob.*   8. fell asleep] *Qq;* fell fast asleep
S.MS.   10. a] *Q1;* the *Q2–3.*   13. horseback] *Qq;* Horses back
S.MS., Jacob.

3–17.] The 'taunting letter' that Michael had promised to send Susan
from London (i. 158) is an obvious parody of the euphuistic style with its
rhetorical devices of alliteration, sentence balancing, proverbs, and similes
culled from nature and fable. Crawford parallels the opening to Lyly's *The
Woman in the Moone,* v. i. 142–5 (ed. R. W. Bond, *The Complete Works,* III
[1902]):

> *Learchus.* But why broughtest thou me this letter ?
> *Gunophilus.* Onely to certifie you that she was in health, as I was at the
> bringing hereof. And thus being loth to trouble you, I commit you
> to God. Yours, as his owne, *Gunophilus.*

4–5. *as I . . . making hereof*] cited by P. Legouis as an example of the
classical epistolary past in English—that is, where the writer's present is
the recipient's past ('The Epistolary Past in English', *N. & Q.,* CXCVIII
[1953], 111–12.

5. *certify*] inform.

   turtle] turtle-dove. Cf. proverb: 'As true as a turtle[-dove] to her mate'
(Tilley, T624).

7. *walk up and down Paul's*] referring to Paul's Walk (or 'Duke Humphrey's Walk'), the nave or central aisle of St Paul's Cathedral in London,
a convenient and much-frequented meeting-place, particularly for business transactions.

8. *pantofles*] galoshes, presumably being cared for by Michael while
Arden was inside the Cathedral worshipping.

12–13. *plaster . . . horseback*] part of a remedy suggested by Nicholas
Maltby (supposed author) in *Remedies for diseases in Horses* (London,
1576).

13. *galled*] sore.

13–15. *Thus . . . hands*] Crawford parallels Thomas Watson's *The Tears
of Fancie,* Sonnet 43, l. 6 ('And let my passions penetrate thy brest').

passions penetrate, or rather impetrate mercy of your
meek hands, I end.   15
                                  Yours,
                         Michael, or else not Michael.'
Arden [*coming forward*]. Why, you paltry knave,
    Stand you here loitering, knowing my affairs,
    What haste my business craves to send to Kent ?   20
Franklin. 'Faith, friend Michael, this is very ill,
    Knowing your master hath no more but you;
    And do ye slack his business for your own ?
Arden. Where is the letter, sirrah ? Let me see it.—
                    Then he [MICHAEL] *gives him the letter.*
    See, Master Franklin, here's proper stuff: 25
    Susan my maid, the painter, and my man,
    A crew of harlots, all in love, forsooth.—
    Sirrah, let me hear no more of this.
    Now, for thy life, once write to her a word!

      Here enters GREENE, WILL, *and* SHAKEBAG.

    Wilt thou be married to so base a trull ?   30
    'Tis Mosby's sister. Come I once at home,
    I'll rouse her from remaining in my house.—
    Now, Master Franklin, let us go walk in Paul's.
    Come but a turn or two, and then away.
            Exeunt [ARDEN, FRANKLIN, *and* MICHAEL].

---

18. S.D.] *Tyrrell; not in Qq.*   23. ye] *Q1;* you *Q2-3.*   for] *Q1-2; not
in Q3.*   24.1. MICHAEL] *Sturgess, after Hugo; not in Qq.*   27. harlots]
Qq; whores and Rogues and *S.MS.*   29. Now] *Qq;* Nor *S.MS., Jacob.*
32. from] *Q1;* for *Q2-3.*   33. let us] *Qq;* let's *Jacob.*   34.1. ARDEN,
FRANKLIN, *and* MICHAEL] *Ortlepp; not in Qq.*

---

   20. *What haste . . . to Kent*] The meaning seems clear enough (see i. 87),
but the grammar becomes clearer when *to send* is understood as a passive
infinitive (= 'to be sent'; see Abbott 359).
   27. *harlots*] lewd, worthless persons (of either sex).
   29. *Now*] The S.MS.-Jacob emendation, accepted by many editors,
assumes that the line otherwise is unfinished; but the exclamation—with
its implied threat—seems to be what is intended. It can be argued, of
course, that the compositor's eye caught the 'Now' from l. 33 below.

Greene. The first is Arden, and that's his man;   35
　　The other is Franklin, Arden's dearest friend.

Will. Zounds, I'll kill them all three.

Greene. Nay, sirs, touch not his man in any case;
　　But stand close, and take you fittest standing,
　　And, at his coming forth, speed him.   40
　　To the Nag's Head; there is this coward's haunt.
　　But now I'll leave you till the deed be done.   *Exit* GREENE.

Shakebag. If he be not paid his own, ne'er trust Shakebag.

Will. Sirrah Shakebag, at his coming forth I'll run him
　　through, and then to the Blackfriars and there take water   45
　　and away.

Shakebag. Why, that's the best; but see thou miss him not.

Will. How can I miss him when I think on the forty angels I
　　must have more ?

Here enters a Prentice.

Prentice. 'Tis very late; I were best shut up my stall, for here   50

---

35. that's] *Qq;* that is *Delius.*   39. you] *Q1;* your *Q2–3.*   41. there is]
Q1 (ther'is)*; there's *Q2–3.*   this] *Q1–2; not in Q3.*   42.] *so Qq; after*
l. 43 Oliphant.   44–6.] *so Delius; as verse in Qq, lines ending* foorth /
blackfreers, / way.   45. Blackfriars] *Q3* (Blackfriers)*; blackfreers *Q1;*
Blackfrees *Q2.*   48–9.] *so Delius; as verse in Qq, divided at* fortye /
Angels.   50–2.] *so Delius; as verse in Qq, divided at* stall, / For; *lines*
ending in B-H-N at stall, / press / Paul's.   50. stall] *Qq;* shop *S.MS.*

35–8.] Cf. Holinshed, App. II, p. 151.

39. *stand close*] stand concealed; hide yourself.

　standing] i.e., standing-place ('fittest standing' = best place from which
to spring the ambush). See ix. 38.

40, 44. *at his coming forth*] The clumsy repetition suggests corruption of
the text.

40. *speed*] kill.

41. *Nag's Head*] 'A tavern in London, at the East corner of Cheapside
and Friday Street' (Sugden).

43. *paid his own*] Cf. 'to pay him home' (i. 446, n.).

45. *the Blackfriars*] fashionable residential district which still retained,
even after the dissolution of the Dominican monastery there in 1538, the
right of sanctuary; see xv. 12, n.

　take water] cross the Thames by boat.

50. *stall*] i.e., book-stall, which the apprentice manages. Numerous such
stalls lined the walls of St Paul's churchyard, which was the centre of

will be old filching when the press comes forth of Paul's.

Then lets he down his window, and
it breaks Black Will's head.

Will. Zounds, draw, Shakebag, draw! I am almost killed.

Prentice. We'll tame you, I warrant.

Will. Zounds, I am tame enough already.

Here enters ARDEN, FRANKLIN, *and* MICHAEL.

Arden. What troublesome fray or mutiny is this?   55

Franklin. 'Tis nothing but some brabbling, paltry fray,
   Devised to pick men's pockets in the throng.

Arden. Is't nothing else? Come, Franklin, let us away.

Exeunt [ARDEN, FRANKLIN, *and* MICHAEL].

Will. What 'mends shall I have for my broken head?

Prentice. Marry, this 'mends, that, if you get you not away   60
   all the sooner, you shall be well beaten and sent to the
   Counter.

---

52. draw (2)] *Q1; not in Q2–3.*   56. brabbling] *Qq;* babling *Jacob;*
bawbling *Delius.*   58. let us] *Q1;* lets *Q2;* let's *Q3.*   60–2.] *so Q2–3;*
as verse in Q1, divided at away / All.   61. all the sooner] *Qq;* quickly
S.MS.   62. Counter] *Qq;* compter *Tyrrell.*

England's book trade. Title-pages were pasted on posts in front of the stalls
to advertise the books, and such a practice undoubtedly accounts for the
kind of detailed title-page exemplified by *Arden* (see Intro., p. xix), which
was published for the bookseller Edward White, who was set up in business, as the imprint indicates, 'at the lyttle North dore of Paules Church at
the signe of the Gun'.

51. *old filching*] plenty of stealing.

press] crowd.

51.1–2.] Although not too frequently employed, large portable structures
were not unknown on the Elizabethan stage; here, one resembling a
typical book-stall that could be closed by letting down a wooden shutter
had undoubtedly been moved on to the stage for this scene only. (See G. F.
Reynolds, *The Staging of Elizabethan Plays at the Red Bull Theater 1605–
1625* [1940], pp. 80, 115.) Henslowe's list of properties (compiled in 1598)
contains 'i wooden canepie'.

51.2. breaks] grazes or bruises (*O.E.D., v.,* 5.b.).

56. *brabbling*] noisy, wrangling.

paltry] Cf. ll. 9 and 18 above, and see Intro., p. xxvii.

59. *'mends*] amends; recompense or reparation.

62. *Counter*] debtors' prison in Southwark. Tyrrell's note may be of

K

Will. Well, I'll be gone; but look to your signs, for I'll pull
them down all. (*Exit* PRENTICE.)—Shakebag, my broken
head grieves me not so much as by this means Arden hath   65
escaped.

Here enters GREENE.

I had a glimpse of him and his companion.

Greene. Why, sirs, Arden's as well as I. I met him and
Franklin going merrily to the ordinary. What, dare you
not do it ?   70

Will. Yes, sir, we dare do it; but, were my consent to give
again, we would not do it under ten pound more. I value
every drop of my blood at a French crown. I have had ten
pound to steal a dog, and we have no more here to kill a
man. But that a bargain is a bargain and so forth, you   75
should do it yourself.

63–7.] *so Delius; as verse in Qq, lines ending* signes, / all. / much, / escaped. /
[S.D.] / companion.   64. S.D.] *so Hugo, Oliphant; after l. 62 in Qq.*
66.1.] *so Qq; after l. 67 Oliphant.*   67.] *so Qq; attributed to* Greene *in
Jacob, Tyrrell, Delius, Hugo.*   68–70.] *so Delius; as verse in Qq, lines
ending* as I, / ordinary, / it ?; *lines ending in W-P at* met / ordinary. / it ?
69. ordinary] *Qq;* ordinary again *Jacob.*   71–6.] *so Delius; as verse in Qq,
lines ending* againe, / more. / Crowne. / dogge, / man, / foorth, / your selfe.
72. again] *Qq; omitted Jacob.*

interest here: 'Some may be surprised at the insolence of the 'prentice, and
the comparatively submissive manner of the ruffian, Black Will, who is
represented as a man not likely to put up with the slightest injury without
resenting it. But they must remember that the apprentices of London were,
in the age referred to, a very formidable body, and that a cry for "clubs"
would have brought hundreds of these young gentlemen, ever ready for
and delighting in a fray, to the assistance of their comrade.' Dekker's *The
Shoemakers' Holiday* presents a lively illustration of Tyrrell's description
(Act v, sc. ii, in F. Bowers' ed., vol. I [1953]).

63–4. *look . . . down all*] Cf. xiv. 25–7.
65. *as*] as the fact that (Sturgess).
69. *ordinary*] tavern dining-room.
71. *consent to give*] agreement (to murder Arden) to be given (see Abbott
359 for Elizabethan use of the infinitive active in place of the passive, and
cf. l. 20, n., above).
73. *French crown*] the *écu*, worth just under five shillings in England at
this time.

Greene. I pray thee, how came thy head broke ?

Will. Why, thou seest it is broke, dost thou not ?

Shakebag. Standing against a stall, watching Arden's coming,
    a boy let down his shop window and broke his head; 80
    whereupon arose a brawl, and in the tumult Arden
    escaped us and passed by unthought on. But forbearance
    is no acquittance; another time we'll do it, I warrant thee.

Greene. I pray thee, Will, make clean thy bloody brow,
    And let us bethink us on some other place 85
    Where Arden may be met with handsomely.
    Remember how devoutly thou hast sworn
    To kill the villain; think upon thine oath.

Will. Tush, I have broken five hundred oaths!
    But wouldst thou charm me to effect this deed, 90
    Tell me of gold, my resolution's fee;
    Say thou seest Mosby kneeling at my knees,
    Off'ring me service for my high attempt;
    And sweet Alice Arden, with a lap of crowns,
    Comes with a lowly cursy to the earth, 95
    Saying, 'Take this but for thy quarterage;
    Such yearly tribute will I answer thee.'
    Why, this would steel soft-mettled cowardice,

79–83.] *so W-P; as verse in Qq, lines ending* coming, / head. / tumult / on. /
acquittance, / thee.   83. acquittance] *Q1;* quittance *Q2–3, S.MS.*
85. let us] *Qq;* let's *Jacob.*   92. knees] *Qq;* feet *S.MS.*   95. Comes] *Qq;*
Come *Jacob.*   cursy] *Qq;* Curtsie *S.MS., Tyrrell;* courtesy *Delius.*
98. -mettled] *Q1* (metled); melted *Q2–3, S.MS.*

82–3. *forbearance is no acquittance*] proverbial (Tilley, F584).

85.] See l. 117 below and Intro., pp. xxvi–xxvii.

86. *handsomely*] readily, conveniently.

87. *devoutly*] See i. 587, and cf. the irony of Greene's use of the word
here.

92–4.] Hopkinson (3) wonders whether 'from this speech one must suppose something has taken place which has not been shown in the action.
Hitherto Black Will had not met Mosbie or Alice Arden'. Greene, in
hiring him and Shakebag, indicates that he wants revenge because Arden
'Hath highly wronged me about the Abbey land' (ii. 93). Authorial or
textual confusion may be the problem here (see Intro., pp. xxvi–xxvii).

96. *quarterage*] quarterly payment.

97. *answer*] guarantee.

With which Black Will was never tainted with.
I tell thee, Greene, the forlorn traveller   100
Whose lips are glued with summer's parching heat
Ne'er longed so much to see a running brook
As I to finish Arden's tragedy.
Seest thou this gore that cleaveth to my face ?
From hence ne'er will I wash this bloody stain   105
Till Arden's heart be panting in my hand.

Greene. Why, that's well said; but what saith Shakebag ?

Shakebag. I cannot paint my valour out with words;
　　But, give me place and opportunity,
　　Such mercy as the starven lioness,   110
　　When she is dry-sucked of her eager young,
　　Shows to the prey that next encounters her,
　　On Arden so much pity would I take.

Greene. So should it fare with men of firm resolve.
And now, sirs, seeing this accident   115
Of meeting him in Paul's hath no success,
Let us bethink us on some other place
Whose earth may swallow up this Arden's blood.

Here enters MICHAEL.

See, yonder comes his man. And wot you what ?
The foolish knave is in love with Mosby's sister;   120
And for her sake, whose love he cannot get
Unless Mosby solicit his suit,
The villain hath sworn the slaughter of his master.

99. with] *Qq; yet S.MS., Jacob.* 　　101. summer's] *Q1–2;* Summer *Q3.*
105. hence ne'er will I] *Qq;* thence will I not *S.MS.* 　　111. her] *Q1–2;*
not in Q3. 　　117. on] *Qq;* of *Bullen.* 　　118.1.] *so Qq; after l. 124 Tyrrell.*
120. knave is] *Qq;* knave's *Jacob.* 　　121. cannot get] *Qq;* Cant obtain
S.MS.

———————————————————————————

110. *starven*] starved.
117.] Cf. l. 85 above.
119–23.] See note to ll. 92–4 above. Here one might query how Greene
happens to have all this information.
119. *wot*] know.
122. *solicit*] plead.

We'll question him, for he may stead us much.—

How now, Michael, whither are you going?   125

Michael. My master hath new supped,

And I am going to prepare his chamber.

Greene. Where supped Master Arden?

Michael. At the Nag's Head, at the eighteenpence ordinary.—

How now, Master Shakebag?—What, Black Will! God's   130

dear Lady, how chance your face is so bloody?

Will. Go to, sirrah; there is a chance in it. This sauciness in

you will make you be knocked.

Michael. Nay, and you be offended, I'll be gone.

Greene. Stay, Michael; you may not 'scape us so.   135

Michael, I know you love your master well.

Michael. Why, so I do; but wherefore urge you that?

Greene. Because I think you love your mistress better.

[*Michael.*] So think not I. But say, i'faith, what if I should?

---

126. new] *Qq;* now *S.MS.*   129–31.] *so Bayne; as verse in Qq, lines ending*
ordinarye, / Wil, / bloody?   129. eighteenpence] *Qq* (18 pence)*;* 18
penny *S.MS., Tyrrell.*   130–1. God's dear Lady] *Qq;* Gods-life *S.MS.*
132–3.] *so Bayne; as verse in Qq, divided at* it. / This.   132. it. This] *Qq;*
it, this *Tyrrell;* it this *Sturgess.*   133. will . . . knocked] *Qq;* deserves a
knock *S.MS.*   be] *Q1; not in Q2–3.*   139. S.H.] *Q2–3; not in Q1.*

---

127. *prepare . . . chamber*] i.e., for sleeping.

129. *eighteenpence ordinary*] a dining room at the Nag's Head where the
meal has a fixed price of eighteen-pence.

130–1.] Another sign of confusion or corruption in this scene (see notes
to ll. 92–4 and 119–23 above): How does it happen that Michael knows
Black Will and Shakebag? At l. 35 above, Greene points Michael out to the
two cutthroats, who obviously do not know him.

132. *Go to*] 'used to express . . . remonstrance, protest' (Onions).

there . . . in it] it was a bad accident (see note on *chance* at vii. 8). Although
this reading follows Qq's punctuation, Tyrrell's or Sturgess's may be the
better one.

133. *make*] cause (you) to (be).

be] Q2–3's omission makes each of Will's two sentences perfect iambic
pentameter.

knocked] hit; beaten up.

134–5. *Nay . . . Michael*] Cf. i. 120–1. The repetitive phrasing and poor
metre point to memorial confusion in both instances. The second 'stay'
which offsets the metre at i. 121 would, if added here, regularize l. 135.

134. *and*] if.

Shakebag. Come to the purpose, Michael. We hear   140
    You have a pretty love in Faversham.
Michael. Why, have I two or three, what's that to thee?
Will. You deal too mildly with the peasant.—Thus it is:
    'Tis known to us you love Mosby's sister;
    We know besides that you have ta'en your oath   145
    To further Mosby to your mistress' bed
    And kill your master for his sister's sake.
    Now, sir, a poorer coward than yourself
    Was never fostered in the coast of Kent.
    How comes it then that such a knave as you   150
    Dare swear a matter of such consequence?
Greene. Ah, Will—
Will. Tush, give me leave; there's no more but this:
    Sith thou hast sworn, we dare discover all;
    And, hadst thou or shouldst thou utter it,   155
    We have devised a complot under hand,
    Whatever shall betide to any of us,
    To send thee roundly to the devil of hell.
    And therefore thus: I am the very man,
    Marked in my birth-hour by the Destinies,   160
    To give an end to Arden's life on earth;

---

143. You . . . peasant] *so Qq; as aside in Oliphant.*   144. known] *Q2–3,*
kowne *Q1.*   us you] *Qq;* us that you *Jacob.*   149. fostered in] *Qq;*
harboured on *S.MS.*   150. then] *Q1–2; not in Q3.*   155. utter it] *Qq;*
Ever make it known *S.MS.*   156. complot] *Q2–3;* complat *Q1.*   under
hand] *Qq;* against, understand *S.MS.*   158. of hell] *Qq; omitted*
S.MS.

---

151. *a matter . . . consequence*] Cf. ii. 84.
154. *Sith*] since.
  discover] reveal.
156. *complot*] plot, conspiracy.
  under hand] in secret.
158. *roundly*] promptly, without any ado.
159–61.] Cf. i. 511–12, and also *Con.*, IV. i. 17 ('I am the man must bring
thee to thy death'; not in *2H6*) and *Tr.T.*, II. ii. 133–4 ('But like a foule
mishapen stygmaticke / Markt by the destinies to be auoided'; also *3H6*,
II. ii. 136–7).
160. *Destinies*] the three Fates.

Thou but a member but to whet the knife
Whose edge must search the closet of his breast.
Thy office is but to appoint the place
And train thy master to his tragedy;　　165
Mine to perform it when occasion serves.
Then be not nice, but here devise with us
How and what way we may conclude his death.

Shakebag. So shalt thou purchase Mosby for thy friend,
And by his friendship gain his sister's love.　　170

Greene. So shall thy mistress be thy favourer,
And thou disburdened of the oath thou made.

Michael. Well, gentlemen, I cannot but confess,
Sith you have urged me so apparently,
That I have vowed my Master Arden's death;　　175
And he whose kindly love and liberal hand
Doth challenge nought but good deserts of me
I will deliver over to your hands.
This night come to his house at Aldersgate;
The doors I'll leave unlocked against you come.　　180
No sooner shall ye enter through the latch,
Over the threshold to the inner court,
But on your left hand shall you see the stairs
That leads directly to my master's chamber.
There take him and dispose him as ye please.　　185
Now it were good we parted company.
What I have promisèd I will perform.

Will. Should you deceive us, 'twould go wrong with you.

---

162. but] *Qq;* for *S.MS.*　　165. thy] *Q1, 3;* the *Q2.*　　172. made] *Qq;*
mad'st *Delius.*　　173. cannot but] *Qq;* must *S.MS.*　　174. Sith] *Qq;*
Since *S.MS., Tyrrell.*　　181. latch] *Qq;* hatch *S.MS.*

---

162. *member*] helper.
165. *train*] lure.
167. *nice*] squeamish, coy, scrupulous.
174. *apparently*] plainly, evidently.
177. *challenge*] claim.
deserts of] deeds from.
180. *against you come*] in anticipation of your coming.

Michael. I will accomplish all I have revealed.

Will. Come, let's go drink. Choler makes me as dry as a dog.   190

   Exeunt WILL, GREENE, *and* SHAKEBAG. *Manet* MICHAEL.

Michael. Thus feeds the lamb securely on the down
   Whilst through the thicket of an arbour brake
   The hunger-bitten wolf o'erpries his haunt
   And takes advantage to eat him up.
   Ah, harmless Arden, how, how hast thou misdone   195
   That thus thy gentle life is levelled at?
   The many good turns that thou hast done to me
   Now must I quittance with betraying thee.
   I, that should take the weapon in my hand
   And buckler thee from ill-intending foes,   200
   Do lead thee with a wicked, fraudful smile,
   As unsuspected, to the slaughterhouse.
   So have I sworn to Mosby and my mistress;
   So have I promised to the slaughtermen;
   And, should I not deal currently with them,   205
   Their lawless rage would take revenge on me.
   Tush, I will spurn at mercy for this once.

---

193. haunt] *Qq* (hant).   194. advantage to] *Qq;* advantage, for to *S.MS.,*
Tyrrell.   195. how, how hast] *Qq;* how hast *S.MS.,Jacob.*   197. that]
Q1–2; not in Q3.   198. quittance with] *Qq;* quitt thee, with thus
S.MS.   201. wicked] *Q1–2; not in Q3.*   207. will spurn] *Qq;* will not
Spurne *S.MS.*

---

190. *as dry as a dog*] proverbial (Tilley, D433).

190.1. Manet] remains.

191–4.] Clark parallels *3H6*, I. i. 241–2 ('Such safety finds / The
trembling lamb environed with wolves'), but cf. the proverb: 'The lamb is
more in dread of the wolf than of the lion' (Tilley, L36).

191. *securely*] without concern, carelessly.

193. *hunger-bitten*] Cf. the Apocryphal play *Locrine*, IV. ii. 67 (Brooke,
Apocrypha): 'The hunger-bitten dogs of *Acheron*'.

o'erpries] surveys, looks over.

195. *harmless*] guiltless.

how hast thou misdone] what wrong have you done.

196. *levelled*] aimed.

198. *quittance*] requite, repay.

200. *buckler*] defend, shield, protect.

205. *currently*] faithfully, honestly.

Let pity lodge where feeble women lie;
I am resolved, and Arden needs must die.　　*Exit* MICHAEL.

[Sc. iv]

Here enters ARDEN *and* FRANKLIN.

Arden. No, Franklin, no. If fear or stormy threats,
If love of me or care of womanhood,
If fear of God or common speech of men,
Who mangle credit with their wounding words
And couch dishonour as dishonour buds,　　　　　　　　5
Might 'join repentance in her wanton thoughts,
No question then but she would turn the leaf
And sorrow for her dissolution.

Sc. iv] *Hugo; not in Qq;* ACT III. SCENE I. *A Room in* Franklin's *House, at*
Aldersgate. *Tyrrell.*　　2. womanhood] *Qq;* Reputation *S.MS.*　　5.
couch] *Q1–2* (cooch), *Q3* (couch); crop *Delius.*　　8. dissolution] *Qq;*
desolation *S.MS.*

---

iv. 4. *credit*] good name, repute.

5. *couch*] 'cause to germinate' (Brooke, *Apocrypha*) or sprout; hence, to
spread. (Warnke and Proescholdt's comparison with *couch-grass*, or simply
couch, a kind of creeping grass, somewhat like a weed, seems relevant; a
variant spelling and pronunciation at this time are those of the first two
quartos.) The line has baffled most editors, but Brooke's definition of the
word (based on *O.E.D.*, *v*[1]., 5: to promote germination) and his explanation of the line ('scandal mongers nourish the unripe buds of dishonour, as
fast as they appear, till they sprout and grow') have the merit not only of
simplicity but also of keeping to the metaphor of the line and, in fact, to the
imagery of the entire passage ('turn the leaf . . . rooted . . . as rain to weeds
. . . to grow . . . plenished by decay'; cf. also viii. 24–5). Bayne, following
Hopkinson (2), accepts the surgical definition of the word (*O.E.D.* 9: to
remove a cataract) and explains the line thus: 'Cut the bud of dishonour so
that it bursts into flower'. Delius's emendation (as well as Tieck's *ernten* in
German [to harvest, reap]) is unwarranted. Sturgess bases his reading
metaphorically on *O.E.D.* †4.b. ('to embroider with gold thread or the like
laid flat on the surface'); but embroidered dishonour is as metaphorical as
half a virgin. A possible, but more remote, reading might be based on
O.E.D., 15 (to put into words): as Alice's dishonour begins to develop (bud)
the gossips lose no time in giving expression to (or *couching*) it.

6. *'join*] (aphetic form for) enjoin.

7. *No question*] no doubt.

8. *dissolution*] dissoluteness, dissolute living (pronounced penta-
syllabically.)

But she is rooted in her wickedness,
Perverse and stubborn, not to be reclaimed;   10
Good counsel is to her as rain to weeds,
And reprehension makes her vice to grow
As Hydra's head that plenished by decay.
Her faults, methink, are painted in my face
For every searching eye to overread;   15
And Mosby's name, a scandal unto mine,
Is deeply trenchèd in my blushing brow.
Ah, Franklin, Franklin, when I think on this,
My heart's grief rends my other powers
Worse than the conflict at the hour of death.   20
Franklin. Gentle Arden, leave this sad lament.
She will amend, and so your griefs will cease;
Or else she'll die, and so your sorrows end.

---

9. her] *Q1–2; not in Q3.*   11. to] *Qq;* on *S.MS.*   13. that] *Q1–2; not in Q3.*   plenished] *W–P;* perisht *Qq;* flourish'd *Delius;* nourished *conj. Tyrrell.*   14. methink] *Qq;* methinks *S.MS., Jacob.*   21. S.H.] *Q2* (Franc.), *Q3* (Frank.); Farn. *Q1.*

---

12. *reprehension*] censure, rebuke.

13. *Hydra's head that plenished by decay*] referring to the monstrous water-snake of the marshes of Lerna whose many heads *replenished* themselves when any of them were cut off (*by decay* = by decapitation [?]). The slaying of the Hydra was the second labour of Hercules (see i. 116, n.).

plenished] See L. Kellner, *Restoring Shakespeare* (1925), p. 91, for the misprinting of *p* for *pl*, and p. 96, for the misprinting of *r* for *n* in Elizabethan dramatic texts.

17. *trenchèd*] gashed, cut.

19. *heart's grief*] Cf. i. 258, and n. Watson's Sonnet 43 from *The Tears of Fancie* (see iii. 13–15, n.) contains the expression 'To end my harts griefe'.

21.] Cf. Peele's *Edward I*, 58 (ed. F. S. Hook, in *The Dramatic Works of George Peele*, II [1961]): 'Take comfort madam, leave these sad laments.'
leave] leave off; cease.

22–6.] Crawford compares *Sp.T.*, III. xiii. 14–19:
> If destinie thy miseries doe ease,
> Then hast thou health, and happy shalt thou be:
> If destinie denie thee life, *Hieronimo,*
> Yet shalt thou be assured of a tombe:
> If neither, yet let this thy comfort be,
> Heauen couereth him that hath no buriall.

If neither of these two do haply fall,
Yet let your comfort be that others bear   25
Your woes twice doubled all with patience.

Arden. My house is irksome; there I cannot rest.

Franklin. Then stay with me in London; go not home.

Arden. Then that base Mosby doth usurp my room
And makes his triumph of my being thence.   30
At home or not at home, where'er I be,
Here, here it lies [*He points to his heart.*], ah,
    Franklin, here it lies
That will not out till wretched Arden dies.

Here enters MICHAEL.

Franklin. Forget your griefs awhile. Here comes your man.

Arden. What o'clock is't, sirrah?

Michael.   Almost ten.   35

Arden. See, see, how runs away the weary time!
Come, Master Franklin, shall we go to bed?

Franklin. I pray you, go before; I'll follow you.—

Exeunt ARDEN *and* MICHAEL. *Manet* FRANKLIN.

Ah, what a hell is fretful jealousy!
What pity-moving words, what deep-fetched sighs,   40

24. haply] *S.MS.* (happly), *Delius;* happely *Q1–2;* happily *Q3.*   27. rest]
Qq; be *S.MS.*   32. S.D.] *B-H-N, after Hugo; not in Qq.*   38.1.] *so*
Hopkinson (2); after l. 37 Qq.   40. -moving] *Q2–3* (mouing); moning *Q1.*

---

24. *fall*] befall.

26. *patience*] trisyllabic.

28. *Then . . . London*] Cf. i. 51.

29. *room*] place.

30. *thence*] absent.

35.] Cf. *Con.*, II. iv. 1–2 ('*Humph.* Sirrha, whats a clocke? / *Seruing.*
Almost ten my Lord'; cf. *2H6*, II. iv. 5: 'Sirs, what's o'clock? / *Serv.* Ten,
my lord.').

39. *fretful jealousy*] Cf. *Corn.*, v. 387 ('Opposing of thy freatfull ielosie').
Sykes (p. 74) observes that the phrase is Kyd's translation of Garnier's
indignement ialouse and comments: 'the identity of phrase is the more
remarkable in that there is nothing in Garnier to suggest the word "fretful" '.

40. *deep-fetched sighs*] Cf. *The True Tragedy of Richard the Third*, 1774–5
('from the priuie sentire of his heart, / There comes such deepe fetch

What grievous groans and overlading woes
Accompanies this gentle gentleman!
Now will he shake his care-oppressèd head,
Then fix his sad eyes on the sullen earth,
Ashamed to gaze upon the open world;   45
Now will he cast his eyes up towards the heavens,
Looking that ways for redress of wrong.
Sometimes he seeketh to beguile his grief
And tells a story with his careful tongue;
Then comes his wife's dishonour in his thoughts   50
And in the middle cutteth off his tale,
Pouring fresh sorrow on his weary limbs.
So woe-begone, so inly charged with woe,
Was never any lived and bare it so.

Here enters MICHAEL.

Michael. My master would desire you come to bed.   55
Franklin. Is he himself already in his bed?
Michael. He is and fain would have the light away.—

Exit FRANKLIN. *Manet* MICHAEL.

Conflicting thoughts encampèd in my breast
Awake me with the echo of their strokes;
And I, a judge to censure either side,   60
Can give to neither wishèd victory.

---

41. overlading woes] *Qq;* Everlasting Sights *S.MS.*   42. Accompanies]
Qq; Accompany *Jacob.*   47. ways] *Qq;* way *Tyrrell.*   53. woe-begone]
Qq; woe opprest *S.MS.*   57.1.] *so Hugo; after l.* 56 *Qq.*

---

sighes and fearefull cries'), and *2H6*, II. iv. 33 ('To see my tears and hear my
deep-fet groans'; not in *Con.*).
    44.] Cf. *2H6*, I. ii. 5 ('Why are thine eyes fix'd to the sullen earth'; not in
Con.). Warnke and Proescholdt also compare *Sonn.*, XXIX. 11–12 ('Like to
the lark at break of day arising / From sullen earth . . .').
    48. *beguile*] 'divert attention in some pleasant way from' (*O.E.D.*, 5).
    49. *careful*] full of care.
    54. *Was*] i.e., there was (see Abbott 404 for ellipsis of *There* in Eliza-
bethan English).
    58 ff.] See viii. 1 ff., n. Cf. Holinshed, App. II, pp. 151–2. Michael's
qualm of conscience is the playwright's invention.
    60. *censure*] pass judgement on, pronounce sentence upon.

My master's kindness pleads to me for life
With just demand, and I must grant it him;
My mistress she hath forced me with an oath
For Susan's sake, the which I may not break,   65
For that is nearer than a master's love;
That grim-faced fellow, pitiless Black Will,
And Shakebag, stern in bloody stratagem—
Two rougher ruffians never lived in Kent—
Have sworn my death if I infringe my vow,   70
A dreadful thing to be considered of.
Methinks I see them with their bolstered hair,
Staring and grinning in thy gentle face,
And in their ruthless hands their daggers drawn,
Insulting o'er thee with a peck of oaths   75
Whilst thou, submissive, pleading for relief,
Art mangled by their ireful instruments.
Methinks I hear them ask where Michael is,
And pitiless Black Will cries, 'Stab the slave!
The peasant will detect the tragedy.'   80
The wrinkles in his foul, death-threat'ning face
Gapes open wide, like graves to swallow men.
My death to him is but a merriment,

---

72. bolstered] *Qq* (bolstred)*;* boltered *Sturgess.*   74. ruthless] *Qq;*
bloody *S.MS.*   75. thee] *Q3;* there *Q1–2.*   76. Whilst] *Qq* (Whilest).
relief] *Qq;* release *Tyrrell.*   81. in] *Q1–2;* of *Q3.*   82. Gapes] *Qq;*
Gape *Tyrrell.*

---

72. *bolstered*] stiff, rigid, bristly (so Brooke, *Apocrypha*, from *bolster*,
O.E.D., *v.*, †2: to support, to prop up). Hopkinson (3) observes, 'It is a
moot point as to whether this word should not be changed for *boltered*
[matted, tangled], an expression commonly used at one time in Warwick-
shire.' In support of the latter reading, *Mac.*, IV. i. 123 ('blood-bolter'd
Banquo') is usually cited.

73. *thy*] i.e., Arden's.

75. *Insulting*] exulting. Cf. *3H6*, I. iii. 14 ('And so he walks insulting o'er
his prey').

peck] heap.

76. *relief*] Tyrrell's reading is probably a misreading of Qq's long 'S'.

79. *pitiless Black Will*] Cf. l. 67 above.

80. *detect*] disclose, reveal.

And he will murder me to make him sport.
He comes, he comes! Ah, Master Franklin, help!   85
Call up the neighbours, or we are but dead!

Here enters FRANKLIN *and* ARDEN.

Franklin. What dismal outcry calls me from my rest?
Arden. What hath occasioned such a fearful cry?
Speak, Michael! Hath any injured thee?
Michael. Nothing, sir; but, as I fell asleep   90
Upon the threshold, leaning to the stairs,
I had a fearful dream that troubled me,
And in my slumber thought I was beset
With murderer thieves that came to rifle me.
My trembling joints witness my inward fear.   95
I crave your pardons for disturbing you.
Arden. So great a cry for nothing I ne'er heard.
What, are the doors fast locked and all things safe?
Michael. I cannot tell; I think I locked the doors.
Arden. I like not this, but I'll go see myself. [*He tries the doors.*]
Ne'er trust me but the doors were all unlocked.   101

---

86. are but dead] *Qq;* shall all be Killed *S.MS.*   87. S.H.] Fran. *Q2–3;*
Eran. *Q1.*   91. leaning] *Qq;* leading *Tyrrell.*   95. fear] *Qq;* parts
S.MS.   100. S.D.] *Oliphant; not in Qq.*   101. were] *Q1;* are *Q2–3;*
be not *S.MS.*

87–8.] Cf. *Sp.T.*, II. v. 1–2 ('What out-cries pluck me from my naked
bed, / And chill my throbbing hart with trembling feare'), and IV. iv. 108–9
('. . . I heare / His dismall out-cry eccho in the aire').

91. *leaning to*] leaning against (McIlwraith). The phrase makes sense in
reference to Michael (see Abbott 419a for the transposition of adjectival
phrases in Elizabethan English). Tyrrell's emendation is acceptable, of
course, in light of iii. 183–4: 'The stairs / That *leads* . . . to my master's
chamber' (italics added).

94. *rifle*] rob.

95. *trembling joints*] Cf. vi. 20.

98–100.] See App. I.

101. *were . . . unlocked*] Arden speaks this line as he returns to stage
centre after trying the doors at the back of the stage. The emendation to
are . . . locked by Q2–3, in view of other corrections in this signature (E) and
its verso, may reflect a slight difference in staging: Arden utters the line
just as he finishes trying the doors and is beginning to walk back.

This negligence not half contenteth me.
Get you to bed; and, if you love my favour,
Let me have no more such pranks as these.—
Come, Master Franklin, let us go to bed.   105
Franklin. Ay, by my faith; the air is very cold.—
Michael, farewell; I pray thee dream no more.   *Exeunt.*

[Sc. v]
    Here enters WILL, GREENE, *and* SHAKEBAG.

Shakebag. Black night hath hid the pleasures of the day,
And sheeting darkness overhangs the earth
And with the black fold of her cloudy robe
Obscures us from the eyesight of the world,
In which sweet silence such as we triumph.   5
The lazy minutes linger on their time,
Loath to give due audit to the hour,
Till in the watch our purpose be complete

104. pranks] *Qq;* doings *S.MS.*   106. by] *Q2–3;* be *Q1.*   107. S.D.]
so *Q2–3; after l. 106 Q1.*

Sc. v] *Hugo; not in Qq;* ACT III. SCENE II. *Outside* Franklin's *House.*
Tyrrell.   0.1.] so *Q2–3 (Enter Gre. Wil. and Shakebag.); after l. 1 Q1.*
1. pleasures] *Qq;* pleasure *Jacob.*   2. sheeting] *Qq* (sheting).   4.
Obscures] *Q2–3;* Obscure *Q1.*   7. Loath] *Qq* (Loth); As loth *S.MS.,
Jacob.*

---

   v. 1–5.] Conflicting schools of authorship attribution have compared the
opening lines to *1 Tamb.,* 2071 ff. ('O highest Lamp of euerliuing *Ioue*',
etc.), *2 Tamb.,* 2969 ff. ('Blacke is the beauty of the brightest day', etc.),
Faustus, 235–9 ('Now that the gloomy shadow of the earth', etc.), and *Sp.T.,*
II. iv. 1–3, 17–19 ('Now that the night begins with sable wings', etc.). The
opening line of *1H6* might be cited ('Hung be the heavens with black,
yield day to night!'), as well as of *R3,* I. ii. 131 ('Black night o'ershade thy
day') and of the anonymous *Woodstock,* IV. ii. 66 ('The lights of heaven are
shut in pitchy clouds'). Plays dating about the time of *Arden,* including
those by Shakespeare, can hardly escape the Marlovian influence. Cf. also
F.Q., III. xii. 1.1–4.
   2. *sheeting*] enfolding, covering. Cf. 'when snow the pasture sheets'
(*Ant.,* I. iv. 65).
   8. *watch*] Editors usually gloss as 'time division of the night' (see *O.E.D.,*
sb., 4); probably, more simply, the act of watching for Arden by the
murderers.

And Arden sent to everlasting night.

Greene, get you gone and linger here about,   10

And at some hour hence come to us again,

Where we will give you instance of his death.

Greene. Speed to my wish whose will soe'er says no;

And so I'll leave you for an hour or two.   *Exit* GREENE.

Will. I tell thee, Shakebag, would this thing were done;   15

I am so heavy that I can scarce go.

This drowsiness in me bodes little good.

Shakebag. How now, Will, become a Precisian?

Nay, then, let's go sleep when bugs and fears

Shall kill our courages with their fancy's work.   20

Will. Why, Shakebag, thou mistakes me much

And wrongs me too in telling me of fear.

Were't not a serious thing we go about,

It should be slipped till I had fought with thee

To let thee know I am no coward, I.   25

I tell thee, Shakebag, thou abusest me.

Shakebag. Why, thy speech bewrayed an inly kind of fear

---

19. then] *Q1–2; not in Q3.*   20. courages] *Qq;* courage *S.MS., Tyrrell.*
fancy's] *Tyrrell;* fancies *Qq;* fancies' *Delius.*   work] *Qq; omitted S.MS.*
21. mistakes] *Q3;* mistakest *Delius.*   22. wrongs] *Q1–2;*
wrongst *Q3;* wronge *S.MS., Tyrrell.*   me too in telling] *Q1;* me in the
telling *Q2–3.*   23. Were't] *Qq* (Wert).   27. bewrayed] *Qq;* betrayed
S.MS., Tyrrell.

---

12. *instance*] proof, evidence.

13. *Speed*] success.

whose will . . . no] 'no matter who wills the contrary' (Baskervill).

17. Cf. *E2*, 1911–12:

Looke vp my lord. *Baldock*, this drowsines
Betides no good, here euen we are betraied.

18. *Precisian*] Puritan (because the Puritans were believed to be so
exactingly precise in religious observances).

19. *bugs*] bugbears; terrors.

20. *courages*] 'formerly also in *plural* in reference to a number of persons'
(*O.E.D., courage, sb.,* 4.†b.).

fancy's work] workings upon the imagination.

22. *telling me of*] 'taxing me with' (Sturgess).

24. *slipped*] overlooked and deferred.

27. *bewrayed*] betrayed, revealed (unintentionally).

And savoured of a weak, relenting spirit.
Go forward now in that we have begun,
And afterwards attempt me when thou darest.   30

Will. And if I do not, heaven cut me off!
But let that pass, and show me to this house,
Where thou shalt see I'll do as much as Shakebag.

Shakebag. This is the door [*He tries it.*]—but soft, methinks
'tis shut.
The villain Michael hath deceivèd us.   35

Will. Soft, let me see. Shakebag, 'tis shut indeed.
Knock with thy sword; perhaps the slave will hear.

Shakebag. It will not be; the white-livered peasant
Is gone to bed and laughs us both to scorn.

Will. And he shall buy his merriment as dear   40
As ever coistrel bought so little sport.
Ne'er let this sword assist me when I need,
But rust and canker after I have sworn,
If I, the next time that I meet the hind,
Lop not away his leg, his arm, or both.   45

Shakebag. And let me never draw a sword again,
Nor prosper in the twilight, cockshut light,

---

31. off] *Qq;* Short *S.MS.*   34. S.D.] *This ed., after Oliphant; not in Qq.*
36. shut] *Qq; so S.MS.*   38–9.] *so Delius; divided in Qq at* bed / And.
40. buy] *Q2–3, S.MS.;* by *Q1;* 'by *Schelling.*

---

30. *attempt*] engage with, attack.

31. *And if*] if.

38. *white-livered*] cowardly (because, the Elizabethans believed, of deficiency of bile in the liver). Cf. description of Bardolph in *H5*, III. ii. 31–2 ('he is white-livered and red-faced; by the means whereof a' faces it out, but fights not').

40.] Cf. *Brewen*, p. 291, ll. 28–9 ('shee should . . . haue bought her merrement deerely'). Cf. also what Michael says about Will at iv. 83.

buy] Schelling footnotes his reading of '*by* (Q1 *by*) as *abide*. Cf. *Err.*, IV. i. 81–2 ('But, sirrah, you shall buy this sport as dear / As . . .').

41. *coistrel*] knave, base fellow (literally, a horse-groom).

44. *hind*] fellow.

47. *cockshut light*] evening time when (a) poultry are shut up for the night or, more appropriately, (b) woodcocks (i.e., gulls) 'shoot' or fly through the woods and are caught in nets. (See *O.E.D.*, with example from *R3*, v. iii. 70.)

L

When I would fleece the wealthy passenger,
But lie and languish in a loathsome den,
Hated and spit at by the goers-by,   50
And in that death may die unpitièd
If I, the next time that I meet the slave,
Cut not the nose from off the coward's face
And trample on it for this villainy.

Will.   Come, let's go seek out Greene; I know he'll swear.   55

Shakebag.   He were a villain and he would not swear.
'Twould make a peasant swear amongst his boys,
That ne'er durst say before but 'yea' and 'no',
To be thus flouted of a coisterel.

Will.   Shakebag, let's seek out Greene, and in the morning   60
At the alehouse 'butting Arden's house
Watch the outcoming of that prick-eared cur,
And then let me alone to handle him.   *Exeunt.*

---

53. off] *Q1–2; not in Q3.*   54. this] *Q1;* his *Q2–3, S.MS.*   56. and]
Qq; if *S.MS.*   57. peasant] *Qq;* pedant *conj. Sturgess.*   59. coisterel]
Q1–2 (coysterel)*;* coistrell *Q3.*   62. the] *Q2–3;* thee *Q1.*

---

48. *passenger*] passer-by, traveller. Cf. *2H6*, III. i. 129 ('Or foul felonious
thief that fleeced poor passengers').

56. *and*] if.

57. *'Twould . . . boys*] Sturgess in a note plausibly suggests, because 'the
line seems feeble', the reading of '"pedant" (=schoolteacher) for
"peasant" (Qq read "pesant")'.

59. *coisterel*] See note to l. 41 above; here, an interesting spelling variant
for metrical purposes.

61. *'butting*] abutting on.

62. *prick-eared*] having pointed or erect ears. Cf. *H5*, II. i. 40 ('thou
prick-ear'd cur of Iceland!').

63.] Hart, *S.S.C.*, parallels the identically worded line in *E2*, 2164.
let me alone] trust me (McIlwraith).

[Sc. vi]

Here enters ARDEN, FRANKLIN, *and* MICHAEL.

Arden [*to Michael*]. Sirrah, get you back to Billingsgate
And learn what time the tide will serve our turn.
Come to us in Paul's. First go make the bed,
And afterwards go hearken for the flood.—   *Exit* MICHAEL.
Come, Master Franklin, you shall go with me.   5
This night I dreamed that, being in a park,
A toil was pitched to overthrow the deer,
And I upon a little rising hill
Stood whistly watching for the herd's approach.
Even there, methoughts, a gentle slumber took me   10
And summoned all my parts to sweet repose.
But in the pleasure of this golden rest
An ill-thewed foster had removed the toil
And rounded me with that beguiling home
Which late, methought, was pitched to cast the deer.   15

Sc. vi] *Hugo; not in Qq;* ACT III. SCENE III. *Room in* Franklin's *House, as
before. Tyrrell.*   1. *to Michael*] *This ed., after Hugo; not in Qq.*   2. our
turn] *Qq; omitted S.MS.*   9. Stood whistly] *Qq;* had plac't my self
S.MS.   10. methoughts] *Q1;* me thought *Q2–3.*   13. -thewed] *Qq;*
lookt *S.MS.*   foster] *Qq;* forester *S.MS., Tyrrell.*

vi. 1. *Billingsgate*] the famous fish-market near the city gate by that name;
important at this time as 'a usual landing-place for travellers, from abroad
or from the lower reaches of the Thames. . . . A barge plied daily between
Billingsgate and Gravesend; the fare was twopence' (Sugden).
     2. *tide*] flood-tide.
     7.] The image occurs frequently in Elizabethan drama, e.g., *LLL.*, IV.
iii. 1–2; *Mas.P.*, 208–9; *Woodstock*, II. ii. 30.
     toil] net, trap.
     pitched] spread, fastened into place.
     9. *whistly*] silently.
     10. *methoughts*] Cf. *methought*, l. 15 below, the more usual form; but
Q1's reading here is not unknown, recurring several times in Shakespeare,
for instance, as in *R3*, I. iv. 9 (first example in *O.E.D.*; see note to l. 20 ff.
below), and *Wint.*, I. ii. 154.
     13. *ill-thewed foster*] rude, evil-natured forester. Cf. *F.Q.*, II. vi. 26.3
('Yet would not seeme so rude, and thewed ill').
     14. *rounded*] surrounded, encircled.
     beguiling home] i.e., the toil.
     15. *late*] but now.   *cast*] overthrow.

With that he blew an evil-sounding horn;
And at the noise another herdman came
With falchion drawn, and bent it at my breast,
Crying aloud, 'Thou art the game we seek.'
With this I waked and trembled every joint,   20
Like one obscurèd in a little bush
That sees a lion foraging about,
And, when the dreadful forest king is gone,
He pries about with timorous suspect
Throughout the thorny casements of the brake,   25
And will not think his person dangerless
But quakes and shivers though the cause be gone.
So, trust me, Franklin, when I did awake,
I stood in doubt whether I waked or no,
Such great impression took this fond surprise.   30
God grant this vision bedeem me any good!
Franklin. This fantasy doth rise from Michael's fear,
Who being awakèd with the noise he made,
His troubled senses yet could take no rest;
And this, I warrant you, procured your dream.   35
Arden. It may be so; God frame it to the best!

---

18. falchion] *Qq* (Fauchon).   20. waked] *Qq* (wakt); awaked *S.MS.*
21. obscurèd] *Q2–3;* oscured *Q1.*   22. sees] *Qq;* Seeks *S.MS.*   24.
pries] *Qq;* prest *S.MS.*   25. Throughout] *Q1–2;* Thorowout *Q3* (*et
passim*).   27. shivers] *Q3, S.MS.;* shewers *Q1–2.*   28. Franklin] *Qq;*
Arden *S.MS.*   30. fond] *Qq;* sudden *S.MS.*   31. bedeem] *Qq;* bodes
S.MS.; deemed *Jacob.*

---

18. *falchion*] a broad sword, somewhat curved; Qq's spelling reflects
Elizabethan pronunciation.
20 ff.] Clark compares Clarence's dream in *R3*, I. iv. 21 ff., and also *Tit.*,
II. iii. 212 ('A chilling sweat o'er-runs my trembling joints'). See iv. 95
above.
24. *suspect*] suspicion.
30. *took this fond surprise*] 'this foolish terror gave me' (Sturgess). See
App. I.
31. *bedeem me any good*] i.e., forebodes no evil for me. See App. I.
32–5.] Cf. Mercutio on the begetting of dreams in *Rom.*, I. iv. 96–8—
'Begot of nothing but vain fantasy [imagination, hallucination]'. Cf. also
Tilley, D587 ('Dreams are lies').
36. *frame*] cause, bring about.

But oftentimes my dreams presage too true.

Franklin. To such as note their nightly fantasies,
   Some one in twenty may incur belief.
   But use it not; 'tis but a mockery.   40

Arden. Come, Master Franklin, we'll now walk in Paul's,
   And dine together at the ordinary,
   And by my man's direction draw to the quay,
   And with the tide go down to Faversham.
   Say, Master Franklin, shall it not be so?   45

Franklin. At your good pleasure, sir; I'll bear you company.

Exeunt.

[Sc. vii]

   Here enters MICHAEL *at one door. Here enters* GREENE,
         WILL, *and* SHAKEBAG *at another door.*

Will. Draw, Shakebag, for here's that villain Michael.

Greene. First, Will, let's hear what he can say.

Will. Speak, milksop slave, and never after speak!

Michael. For God's sake, sirs, let me excuse myself;
   For here I swear, by heaven and earth and all,   5
   I did perform the outmost of my task
   And left the doors unbolted and unlocked.

---

38. fantasies] *Qq;* fancys *S.MS.*   46.] *so W-P; two lines in Qq, divided*
at sir, / Ile.

Sc. vii] *Hugo; not in Qq;* ACT III. SCENE IV. Aldersgate. *Tyrrell.*   2. Will]
Q1-2; not in Q3.   3. milksop slave] *Qq;* Milk sope, Slave *S.MS.,*
Delius.   5.] *Qq; omitted S.MS.*   6. outmost] *Qq;* utmost *S.MS.,*
Tyrrell.

---

   40. *use it not*] i.e., do not continue to 'note [your] nightly fantasies'.
   41.] Cf. iii. 33.
   43. *the quay*] the wharf at Billingsgate; see l. 1, n., above.
   46. *company*] probably dissyllabic ('comp'ny'); otherwise, the line can
be considered an alexandrine.

   vii. 1 ff.] Cf. Holinshed, App. II, p. 152.
   1.] Cf. iii. 52 ('Draw, Shakebag, draw'): the repetition of 'draw' here
would make the line metrically smooth.
   3. *milksop*] cowardly.
   6. *outmost*] utmost.

But see the chance: Franklin and my master
Were very late conferring in the porch,
And Franklin left his napkin where he sat,   10
With certain gold knit in it, as he said.
Being in bed, he did bethink himself,
And coming down he found the doors unshut.
He locked the gates and brought away the keys,
For which offence my master rated me.   15
But now I am going to see what flood it is;
For with the tide my master will away,
Where you may front him well on Rainham Down,
A place well fitting such a stratagem.

Will. Your excuse hath somewhat mollified my choler.—   20
Why now, Greene, 'tis better now nor e'er it was.

Greene. But, Michael, is this true?

Michael. As true as I report it to be true.

Shakebag. Then, Michael, this shall be your penance:
To feast us all at the Salutation,   25
Where we will plot our purpose thoroughly.

11. With . . . it] *Qq;* some Gold tyed in a Napkin *S.MS.*   16. flood it is]
Qq; time yᵉ tide will serve *S.MS.*   18. front] *Q3;* frons *Q1–2;* meet
S.MS.   19. stratagem] *Qq;* tragedy *S.MS.*   20. hath somewhat] *Qq;*
have a little *S.MS.*   21. nor] *Qq;* then *S.MS., Jacob.*   22. this] *Q1–2;*
it *Q3.*   25. Salutation] *Qq;* Salutation tavern *S.MS.*   26. plot] *S.MS.,*
Tyrrell; plat *Qq.*   thoroughly] *Q3* (thorowly); throughly *Q1–2.*

---

8. *chance*] i.e., mischance, mishap.

10. *napkin*] handkerchief.

11. *knit*] tied up.

15. *rated*] berated, reproved.

17–19.] Michael does not give this information in Holinshed (see App. II,
p. 152): 'Arden being redie to go homewards [from London], his maid
came to Greene & said; This night will my maister go downe. Whervpon
it was agreed that blacke Will should kill him on Reinam downe.'

18. *front*] confront, meet to oppose.

Rainham Down] the countryside surrounding Rainham, a 'village in
Kent, on the road from Rochester to Faversham, about 5 miles from the
former' (Sugden).

21. *nor*] than (dialectical).

25. *Salutation*] a Billingsgate tavern; its sign, writes Sugden, 'probably
represented the meeting between Gabriel and the Virgin Mary'.

26. *plot*] Qq's spelling (*plat*) is a collateral form at this time.

Greene. And, Michael, you shall bear no news of this tide
Because they two may be in Rainham Down
Before your master.
Michael. Why, I'll agree to anything you'll have me,   30
So you will except of my company.   *Exeunt.*

[Sc. viii]

Here enters MOSBY.

Mosby. Disturbèd thoughts drives me from company
And dries my marrow with their watchfulness.
Continual trouble of my moody brain

27–31. And . . . company.] *Qq;* and fix the place / where we may Chine him
at one blow / and send his dareing Soul, / downe to the Shades below,
S.MS.   28–9.] *so Delius; one line in Qq.*   31. except] *Q1–2;* accept
Q3.

Sc. viii] *Hugo; not in Qq;* ACT IV. SCENE I. Arden's *House at* Feversham.
Tyrrell; ACT III. SCENE V. *Delius.*   1. drives] *Qq;* drive *Jacob.*   2.
dries] *Qq;* drie *Jacob.*   3. moody] *Qq;* muddy *S.MS.*

---

31. *except*] one of the most ambiguous readings in the text, accepted here
primarily on the strength of the first two quartos and iii. 186, where
Michael, always so fearful of the two cutthroats, says, 'Now it were good
we parted company.' Baskervill glosses *except of my company* as 'excuse me
from accompanying you'. On the other hand, Oliphant and other editors
adopt Q3's reading, especially since the *O.E.D.* cites an example (rather
late—1635—but close to Q3's publication date) of *except* mistakenly used
for *accept* (also Epilogue to S.MS.: 'Except [i.e., Accept] of [this country
fare], & we'll be thankfull now'). The line, of course, would make equally
good sense with this reading: Michael, after his role in the recently
aborted attempt on Arden's life, is relieved not to be 'slaughtered' by Black
Will and therefore is willing to agree to anything just to be 'accepted'; he
can hardly, at this juncture, turn down the 'penance' of feasting them at
the Salutation that the conspirators impose upon him.

viii. 1.] Cairncross (see Intro., p. xlvi, n. 1) compares *Rom.,* I. i. 118 ('A
troubled mind drave me to walk abroad') with its counterpart in the 'bad'
quarto of the play (1597), l. 642 ('A troubled thought drew me from
companie') and the beginning of Mosby's soliloquy. Cf. also Michael's
soliloquy at iv. 58; *TRKJ,* pt II, 110 ff. ('Disturbed thoughts, foredoomers
of mine ill, . . . Confound my wits, and dull my senses so'); and Lodge's
Wounds of Civil War (ed. H. Hart for the Malone Society, 1910), l. 298
('Driueth confused thoughts through Scillas minde').

Feebles my body by excess of drink
And nips me as the bitter northeast wind   5
Doth check the tender blossoms in the spring.
Well fares the man, howe'er his cates do taste,
That tables not with foul suspicion;
And he but pines amongst his delicates
Whose troubled mind is stuffed with discontent.   10
My golden time was when I had no gold;
Though then I wanted, yet I slept secure;
My daily toil begat me night's repose;
My night's repose made daylight fresh to me.
But, since I climbed the top bough of the tree   15
And sought to build my nest among the clouds,
Each gentle starry gale doth shake my bed

4. by] *Qq;* like *S.MS., Oliphant.*   7. cates do taste] *Qq;* Case *S.MS.*
9. And he but] *Qq;* Better than He that *S.MS.*   11. time] *Qq;* days
S.MS.   12. Though] *Q2–3;* Thought *Q1.*   16. sought] *Qq;* think
S.MS.   17. gentle] *Qq;* gentlest *Sturgess, conj. McElwaine.*   starry]
Jacob, Tyrrell; stary *Qq;* Steary *S.MS.;* stirry *Delius, Bayne;* stirring
Hopkinson (2), *conj. Collier;* airy *Sturgess, conj. McElwaine.*   gale] *Qq*
(gaile).

---

4. *Feebles*] enfeebles.
drink] Bayne suggests a reading of *think*, but as a substantive the word is
not recorded in the *O.E.D.* before the mid-nineteenth century. The image
is simply the excessive drinking of trouble (cf. *R2,* IV. i. 189: 'Drinking my
griefs').
5–6.] Many parallels have been cited; but the image is commonplace in
Elizabethan drama, e.g., *Sp.T.,* I. i. 12–13, and III. xiii. 147–8; *LLL.,* I. i.
100–1; *2H6,* III. i. 89; *TRKJ,* pt 1, 485; *Leir,* 227; and Greene's *James the
Fourth* (ed. N. Sanders, 1970, for the Revels Plays), v. iv. 63–4.
7–18.] a frequent note in Seneca that is echoed often in Elizabethan
drama (cf. King Henry on the shepherd's life in *3H6,* II. v. 47–54). J. W.
Cunliffe, *The Influence of Seneca on Elizabethan Tragedy* (1893), p. 88,
compares this passage to *Hippolytus,* 1135–40.
7. *cates*] choice food, delicacies.
8. *tables*] dines.
suspicion] tetrasyllabic.
9. *delicates*] dainty foods, delicacies.
17. *gentle starry gale*] 'A *stary* gale is nonsense', wrote J. P. Collier (*The
History of English Dramatic Poetry* [1879], II, 444–5), who suggested
emending Qq's reading to *straying.* Tyrrell retained Jacob's emendation to
starry, but explained that it meant *stirring.* A compelling proposal, adopted
by Sturgess, is P. A. McElwaine's *gentlest airy gale* (in '*Arden of Feversham*',

And makes me dread my downfall to the earth.
But whither doth contemplation carry me ?
The way I seek to find where pleasure dwells   20
Is hedged behind me that I cannot back
But needs must on although to danger's gate.
Then, Arden, perish thou by that decree,
For Greene doth ear the land and weed thee up
To make my harvest nothing but pure corn.   25
And for his pains I'll heave him up awhile

20. pleasure] *Qq;* pleasures *S.MS.*   21. hedged] *Qq;* hid *S.MS.*
behind] *Qq;* beneath *Bullen.*   24. ear] *Q1* (erre), *Q2* (eyre), *Q3* (heyre)*;*
hire *S.MS.;* err *Tyrrell.*   land] *Qq;* lands *S.MS.*   weed] *Qq;* weed to
Eat *S.MS.*   26. heave] *Qq;* hive *Delius.*

N. & Q., 11th ser., II [1910], 226): "'Each gentlest" is not un-Elizabethan,
and whether the *i* in "gaile" is a compositor's misplacement of the *i* in
"airy" or not, would not much matter. A loose orthography might spell
"airy" as "ary". . . . "Gale" does not necessarily imply violent wind . . . .
just means a zephyr. "Airy" would emphasize the gentleness of the gale
which disturbs one "Whose troubled mind is stuffed with discontent".' (Cf.
translators who have almost intuitively accepted the idea of 'a gentle airy
gale': Tieck's *jeder leichte Wind* and Hugo's *la plus légère brise du ciel*.) But
Jacob's simple insertion of another r into Qq's *stary* alters the text least, and
it also makes perfectly good sense, as R. D. Cornelius explains ('Mosbie's
"Stary Gaile"', *P.Q.*, IX [1930], 72): 'Mosbie is lamenting that since he has
sought to build his nest in the clouds he is in constant fear of a rude downfall to the earth. What sort of gale, then, could be more appropriate than a
starry gale, that is, a gale blowing among the stars ? True, the clouds are not
quite so high as the stars, but it is not usual to press a poetic figure to
scientific accuracy.'
    19. *whither*] possibly monosyllabic.
    20–2.] Cf. *Mac.*, III. iv. 136–8:

                                    I am in blood
        Stepp'd in so far that, should I wade no more,
        Returning were as tedious as go o'er;

and also *R3*, IV. ii. 65–7:

                                    But I am in
        So far in blood that sin will pluck on sin:
        Tear-falling pity dwells not in this eye.

    24. *ear*] plough. Qq spellings are Elizabethan variants; Bullen was the
first editor actually to print *ear*.
    25. *nothing but pure corn*] i.e., unalloyed pleasure with Arden out of the
way.
    26. *heave him up*] extol, make him feel important. Clark, accepting
Delius's emendation to 'hive', compares *2H4*, IV. v. 78–9 ('We bring it to

And, after, smother him to have his wax;
Such bees as Greene must never live to sting.
Then is there Michael and the painter too,
Chief actors to Arden's overthrow,   30
Who, when they shall see me sit in Arden's seat,
They will insult upon me for my meed
Or fright me by detecting of his end.
I'll none of that, for I can cast a bone
To make these curs pluck out each other's throat;   35
And then am I sole ruler of mine own.
Yet Mistress Arden lives; but she's myself,
And holy church rites makes us two but one.
But what for that I may not trust you, Alice ?
You have supplanted Arden for my sake   40
And will extirpen me to plant another.
'Tis fearful sleeping in a serpent's bed,
And I will cleanly rid my hands of her.

---

30. actors to] *Qq;* actors unto *S.MS.;* actors both to *conj. Elze.*   31. shall]
Q1; not in Q2–3, S.MS.   32. meed] *Qq* (mede)*;* meat *S.MS.;* mead
Delius.   38. makes] *Qq;* make *Jacob.*   39. that] *Q1;* that, *Q2–3;* that ?
Delius.   41. And] *Qq;* You *Brooke.*   43. cleanly] *Qq;* clearly *S.MS.*

---

the hive; and, like the bees, / Are murder'd for our pains'); see the following
note.

27. *smother . . . wax*] referring to the practice of smoking out bees to
reach their honey and wax.

30.] See K. Elze, *Notes on Elizabethan Dramatists* (1880; new ed., 1889),
p. 1. Schelling notes: 'Perhaps *too* has fallen out here.'

32. *insult upon*] scornfully assail or abuse.

meed] reward (with implication that it is corruptly earned).

33. *detecting of*] disclosing, revealing.

34–5.] Cf. ix. 30 and n. The idea is proverbial: 'He has cast a bone
between them' (Tilley, B518) and 'The devil has cast a bone to set strife'
(Tilley, D237).

34. *a bone*] i.e., Susan (Mosby's sister). (Sturgess).

39. *what for that*] what about the fact that (Sturgess). This reading has
the advantage of keeping Q1's original punctuation; a question mark after
that is understandable, however: 'But what about the church rites ?' The
original reading is the stronger one, however: 'Even though the church
may make us one, what does it help if (or what about the fact that) I cannot
trust you, Alice ?'

41. *extirpen*] extirpate, root out.

43. *cleanly*] completely.

Here enters ALICE [*holding a prayerbook*].

But here she comes, and I must flatter her.—
How now, Alice! What, sad and passionate ?   45
Make me partaker of thy pensiveness;
Fire divided burns with lesser force.

Alice. But I will dam that fire in my breast
Till by the force thereof my part consume.
[*Sighing.*] Ah, Mosby!   50

Mosby. Such deep pathaires, like to a cannon's burst
Discharged against a ruinated wall,
Breaks my relenting heart in thousand pieces.
Ungentle Alice, thy sorrow is my sore;

43.1. *holding a prayerbook*] *Sturgess.*   46. partaker] *Qq;* partake *Tyrrell.*
48. dam] *Qq* (damne)*; damp S.MS.*   in] *Qq;* within *Jacob.*   49–50.] *so
Delius; one line in Qq.*   49.] *Qq;* untill my own part, be Consumed thereby *S.MS.*   part] *Qq;* hart (=heart) *conj. T. W. Craik (privately).*
50. S.D.] *This ed.; not in Qq.*   51. deep pathaires] *Qq;* deep-fet airs
Delius; depe-fet sighs *W-P.*   53. Breaks] *Qq;* Break *Jacob.*

43.1. holding a prayerbook] See l. 116 below.

45. *passionate*] sorrowfull, full of deep emotion.

46. *partaker*] Tyrrell's 'emendation' mistakenly follows the text of
Jacob, who corrects this error in his errata list.

47. *Fire*] dissyllabic.

48–9.] The sense is: 'I will suppress the passion that I have for you [*my
part*] until by the force of its own violence it consumes itself and disappears.
Cf. i. 207–8. The S.MS. is somewhat clearer in meaning. T. W. Craik
defends his suggested emendation of *part* to *heart* by noting (privately)
that '*heart* gives better sense, and an error of *part* for *hart*—so spelled three
lines later [in Q1–2]—is probable'. The compositor might also have been
influenced by *partaker* in l. 46 above.

51–2.] Cf. *TRKJ*, pt 1, 1514–15 ('As is the eccho of a Cannons crack /
Dischargd against the battlements of heaven').

51. *deep pathaires*] deeply-moving sighs or passionate outbursts. In citing
a parallel in W. Smith's *The Hector of Germanie* (1615; sig. B4ᵛ)—
    And I as little estimate a Father
    In these Pathaires, as he esteems my griefe—
P. Simpson (*M.L.R.*, I [1905–6], 326–7) seems to have effectively proved
the authenticity of this strange word (although Jackson, p. 55, thinks it
possible that Smith might have seen Q1 of *Arden* and have taken over a
compositor's error for *pathaines*, a word first suggested by W. Headlam in
The Athenaeum [26 December 1903]). H. Littledale (*M.L.R.*, I [1906], 233)
thought that the word should be *suspires*.

52. *ruinated*] about to be ruined or destroyed.

Thou know'st it well, and 'tis thy policy   55
To forge distressful looks to wound a breast
Where lies a heart that dies when thou art sad.
It is not love that loves to anger love.

Alice. It is not love that loves to murder love.

Mosby. How mean you that?   60

Alice. Thou knowest how dearly Arden lovèd me.

Mosby. And then?

Alice. And then—conceal the rest, for 'tis too bad,
Lest that my words be carried with the wind
And published in the world to both our shames.   65
I pray thee, Mosby, let our springtime wither;
Our harvest else will yield but loathsome weeds.
Forget, I pray thee, what hath passed betwixt us,
For now I blush and tremble at the thoughts.

Mosby. What, are you changed?   70

Alice. Ay, to my former happy life again,
From title of an odious strumpet's name
To honest Arden's wife, not Arden's honest wife.
Ha, Mosby, 'tis thou hast rifled me of that
And made me sland'rous to all my kin.   75
Even in my forehead is thy name engraven,
A mean artificer, that low-born name.

---

57. when] *Q2–3, S.MS.;* where *Q1.*   61. knowest] *Qq;* know *S.MS.;*
know'st *Delius.*   68. hath] *Q1–2;* hast *Q3;* have *S.MS.*   betwixt]
Q2–3; betwix *Q1.*   69. thoughts] *Qq;* thought *Tyrrell.*   73. honest
Arden's] *Qq;* Arden's honest *Oliphant.*   Arden's honest] *Qq;* honest
Arden's *Oliphant.*   75. sland'rous] *Q1* (slaundrous)*;* slanderous *Q2–3.*

---

56. *forge*] contrive.

57. *when*] On *Q1*'s *where*, see Kellner, p. 96, for the misprinting of *r* for *n*
in Elizabethan dramatic texts.

66.] Cf. ll. 5–6 above (Alice unwittingly carries on the metaphor).

73. *Arden's honest wife*] i.e., chaste wife. Oliphant's reversal of the
phrases seems plausible at first reading, but l. 74 makes it clear that Qq are
not in error: the *not* should be understood as 'even if no longer'. Cf.
Ieronimo, II. iii. 45–7:

> *Ier.* 'Yet hees an honest dukes son.'
> *Hor.* 'Yet hees an'—
> *Ier.* 'But not the honest son of a Duke.'

77. *artificer*] See i. 311.

I was bewitched. Woe worth the hapless hour
And all the causes that enchanted me!

Mosby. Nay, if thou ban, let me breathe curses forth;   80
And, if you stand so nicely at your fame,
Let me repent the credit I have lost.
I have neglected matters of import
That would have stated me above thy state,
Forslowed advantages, and spurned at time.   85
Ay, Fortune's right hand Mosby hath forsook
To take a wanton giglot by the left.
I left the marriage of an honest maid
Whose dowry would have weighed down all thy wealth,
Whose beauty and demeanour far exceeded thee.   90
This certain good I lost for changing bad,
And wrapped my credit in thy company.
I was bewitched—that is no theme of thine!—
And thou unhallowed hast enchanted me.
But I will break thy spells and exorcisms   95
And put another sight upon these eyes
That showed my heart a raven for a dove.

78. worth] *Qq;* was *S.MS.*   80. thou ban] *Qq;* you Can *S.MS.*   87.
left] *Qq;* hand *S.MS.*   90. demeanour] *Q1* (demianor).   92. wrapped]
Qq; Creckt *S.MS.*   95. exorcisms] *Q1–2* (excirsimes), *Q3* (exorcismes).
97. dove] *Q2* (Doue), *Q3* (Dove); dowe *Q1, B-H-N* (dow).

78. *I was bewitched*] Cf. i. 199–200.
Woe worth] a curse upon. (See *O.E.D., Worth, v.*¹, B.1.c.).
hapless] unfortunate, unlucky.
80. *ban*] curse.
81. *stand so nicely at*] scruple so fastidiously at.
fame] reputation, 'character'.
84. *stated . . . state*] placed (or raised) me above thy rank.
85. *Forslowed*] put off, wasted, lost by sloth.
87. *giglot*] or *giglet:* lewd, worthless woman.
88. *honest*] chaste.
92. *wrapped*] involved, so as to disguise; compromised.
93. *I was bewitched*] See l. 78 above.
94. *unhallowed*] i.e., like a witch.
95. *exorcisms*] conjurations.
97. *a raven for a dove*] a not unusual comparison, but frequent in Shakespeare, as in *2H6*, III. i. 75–6; *MND.*, II. ii. 114; and *Tw.N.*, v. i. 125.

Thou art not fair—I viewed thee not till now;
Thou art not kind—till now I knew thee not.
And now the rain hath beaten off thy gilt 100
Thy worthless copper shows thee counterfeit.
It grieves me not to see how foul thou art
But mads me that ever I thought thee fair.
Go, get thee gone, a copesmate for thy hinds!
I am too good to be thy favourite. 105

Alice. Ay, now I see, and too soon find it true,
Which often hath been told me by my friends,
That Mosby loves me not but for my wealth,
Which, too incredulous, I ne'er believed.
Nay, hear me speak, Mosby, a word or two; 110
I'll bite my tongue if it speak bitterly.
Look on me, Mosby, or I'll kill myself;
Nothing shall hide me from thy stormy look.
If thou cry war, there is no peace for me;
I will do penance for offending thee 115
And burn this prayerbook, where I here use
The holy word that had converted me.
See, Mosby, I will tear away the leaves,
And all the leaves, and in this golden cover
Shall thy sweet phrases and thy letters dwell; 120
And thereon will I chiefly meditate

---

99. thee] *Q2–3;* the *Q1.* 103. ever I] *Qq;* I ever *S.MS., Jacob.*
thought] *Q2–3;* chought *Q1.* 104. copesmate] *Q1ᵘ(M);* copesmate
Q1ᶜ(D, H). 107. me] *Q1, S.M.; not in Q2–3.* 112. or I'll] *Q1–2;*
or else I'll *Q3.* 116. where . . . use] *Qq;* wherein I use *S.MS.* 117.
had] *Q1–2;* hath *Q3.* 118. leaves] *Qq;* leaf *conj. T. W. Craik (privately).*
119. And . . . in] *Qq;* and in their place within *S.MS.* And all] *Qq;* Ay,
al *conj. W-P.* 121. chiefly] *Qq;* omitted *S.MS.*

---

101. *copper*] considered a base, worthless metal.
103. *mads*] maddens.
104. *copesmate*] companion (in contemptuous sense); paramour (Mc-Ilwraith). Cf. *Lucr.,* 925 ('Mis-shapen Time, copesmate of ugly Night').
hinds] servants.
116. *where*] wherein.
use] pursue, follow, comply with.

And hold no other sect but such devotion.
Wilt thou not look ? Is all thy love overwhelmed ?
Wilt thou not hear ? What malice stops thine ears ?
Why speaks thou not ? What silence ties thy tongue ?   125
Thou hast been sighted as the eagle is,
And heard as quickly as the fearful hare,
And spoke as smoothly as an orator,
When I have bid thee hear or see or speak.
And art thou sensible in none of these ?   130
Weigh all thy good turns with this little fault
And I deserve not Mosby's muddy looks.
A fount once troubled is not thickened still;

123. thou not] *Qq;* not thou *Jacob.*   overwhelmed] *Qq;* orewhelm'd
S.MS., Jacob.   125. speaks] *Q1–2;* speakest *Q3;* speak'st *Tyrrell.*
126. sighted] *Qq;* Slighted *S.MS.*   131. thy] *Qq;* my *Jacob.*   turns]
Qq; terms *W-P.*   133. fount once troubled] *Schelling* (font), *conj.*
Headlam; fence of trouble *Qq;* sense of trouble *Tyrrell.*

---

122. *hold . . . sect*] 'keep no other religious faith' (Sturgess).
126.] References to the royal eagle endowed with unusual sight occur
frequently in medieval and Elizabethan literature; cf. the proverbs: 'Only
the eagle can gaze at the sun' (Tilley, E3) and 'To have an eagle's eye'
(Tilley, E6).
sighted] endowed with sight (Baskervill).
127. *heard*] endowed with hearing.
quickly] sharply.
the fearful hare] proverbial ('As fearful as a hare', Tilley, H147), but
Clark compares *3H6*, II. v. 130 ('Having the fearful flying hare in sight').
128. *spoke*] endowed with speech.
130. *sensible*] conscious; capable of feeling or perceiving.
131. *thy good turns*] i.e., the good turns (deeds, services) that I have done
to you (Bayne).
133. *fount once troubled*] Despite ingenious interpretations of Qq's reading of 'fence of trouble' (Warnke and Proescholdt, for instance: 'The
quarrel which arose between us, has not yet thickened to so impenetrable
a fence as to separate us for ever'), only W. Headlam's suggested emendation (see note to l. 51 above), adopted by Schelling and Sturgess, is entirely
convincing and even anticipates questions that may have been unintentionally raised against it (see K. P. Wentersdorf, 'The "Fence of Trouble"
Crux in *Arden of Faversham*', *N. & Q.*, CCII [1957], 160–1). Headlam's
conviction is that 'the text arose from writing or printing "A fonce
troubled" instead of "A fon[t on]ce troubled"' and that 'what we find now
[in Qq] was an attempt to make some sense and metre of it.' In a follow-up
note in the same publication (*The Athenaeum*, 12 March 1904), I. Gollancz

Be clear again, I'll ne'er more trouble thee.

Mosby. O, no, I am a base artificer;   135
My wings are feathered for a lowly flight.
Mosby? Fie, no! not for a thousand pound.
Make love to you? Why, 'tis unpardonable;
We beggars must not breathe where gentles are.

Alice. Sweet Mosby is as gentle as a king,   140
And I too blind to judge him otherwise.
Flowers do sometimes spring in fallow lands,
Weeds in gardens, roses grow on thorns;
So, whatsoe'er my Mosby's father was,
Himself is valued gentle by his worth.   145

Mosby. Ah, how you women can insinuate
And clear a trespass with your sweet-set tongue!
I will forget this quarrel, gentle Alice,
Provided I'll be tempted so no more.

---

135. O, no] *Q1–2;* O, fie no *Q3.*   136. flight] *Q1ᶜ(D, H);* flght *Q1ᵘ(M).*
139. gentles] *Tyrrell;* gentiles *Qq;* Gentry *S.MS.*   142. do] *Q1–2; not in
Q3.*   143. Weeds] *Qq;* And weeds *Jacob.*   145. is] *S.MS., Jacob;
not in Qq.*

---

confirmed Headlam's emendation by observing that ' "fonce" = L. *fontes*
. . . is quite common; "fons doloris", a fount of trouble'. Cf. *TRKJ*, pt 1,
899–900 ('I trouble now the fountaine of thy youth, / And make it moodie
[pun: 'muddy'?] with my doles discourse'); curiously enough, the speaker
of these lines says a few lines earlier in the same passage: 'To fence thy
right'. Since both *TRKJ* and *Arden* suffer from memorial contamination,
it is also possible that the same actor in the latter hopelessly confused the
passage; both speeches belong to a woman's part. See also App. I.

136.] i.e., the opposite to what Alice suggested in l. 126 above.

137. *not . . . pound*] Cf. Symonds (pp. 446–7): 'The touch of *not for a
thousand pound* is rare. Alice never for a moment thought of money. It is the
churl, who expresses the extreme of scorn by hyperboles of cash.'

139. *gentles*] people of gentle birth or rank; gentlefolk.

140. *gentle*] well born.

143.] possibly a truncated foot.

roses . . . thorns] Cf. proverb: 'No rose without a thorn' (Tilley, R182).

145.] Cf. proverb: 'He is a gentleman that hath gentle conditions"
(Tilley, G71).

146–7.] Cf. proverb: 'A woman's weapon is her tongue' (Tilley, W675).

147.] Cf. *E2*, 118 ('trespasse of their tongues').

clear a trespass] acquit (themselves of) an offence.

Here enters BRADSHAW.

Alice. Then with thy lips seal up this new-made match.   150
                                               [*They kiss.*]

Mosby. Soft, Alice, for here comes somebody.

Alice. How now, Bradshaw, what's the news with you ?

Bradshaw. I have little news, but here's a letter
   That Master Greene importuned me to give you.

Alice. Go in, Bradshaw; call for a cup of beer.   155
   'Tis almost supper time; thou shalt stay with us.

                                    Exit [BRADSHAW].
                                    Then she reads the letter.

   'We have missed of our purpose at London, but shall
   perform it by the way. We thank our neighbour Bradshaw.

                         Yours,   160
                         Richard Greene.'

   How likes my love the tenor of this letter ?

Mosby. Well, were his date complete and expired!

Alice. Ah, would it were! Then comes my happy hour.
   Till then my bliss is mixed with bitter gall.   165
   Come, let us in to shun suspicion.

Mosby. Ay, to the gates of death to follow thee.   *Exeunt.*

149.1.] *so Qq; after l. 150 Hugo, l. 151 Tyrrell.*   150.1.] *This ed.; not in Qq.*
151. for] *Qq; omitted W-P.*   156.1.] *Q2–3; after l. 155 Q1.*   163.
complete] *Qq; completed Jacob.*   164.] *so Delius; two lines in Qq, divided
at* were, / Then.   167. S.H.] *Q3;* Ales. *Q1;* Alce. *Q2;* Alice *S.MS.*
Ay] *Qq;* I'll *S.MS.*

152.] See i. 107, n.
157–9.] The letter is, in fact, in Holinshed (see App. II, p. 151); but the
text is here confused: in scene ii (ll. 74–7), Greene entrusts the letter to
Bradshaw *before* he himself goes on to London and *before* the first attempt
on Arden's life. The Wardmote Book of Faversham implicates Bradshaw in
the murder whereas the chronicle account does not (see App. III, p. 160).
166. *suspicion*] tetrasyllabic.

M

[Sc. ix]

Here enters GREENE, WILL, *and* SHAKEBAG.

Shakebag. Come, Will, see thy tools be in a readiness.
            Is not thy powder dank, or will thy flint strike fire?
Will. Then ask me if my nose be on my face,
            Or whether my tongue be frozen in my mouth.
            Zounds, here's a coil!   5
            You were best swear me on the intergatories
            How many pistols I have took in hand,
            Or whether I love the smell of gunpowder,
            Or dare abide the noise the dag will make,
            Or will not wink at flashing of the fire.   10
            I pray thee, Shakebag, let this answer thee,
            That I have took more purses in this Down
            Than e'er thou handledst pistols in thy life.
Shakebag. Ay, haply thou hast picked more in a throng;
            But, should I brag what booties I have took,   15
            I think the overplus that's more than thine
            Would mount to a greater sum of money
            Than either thou or all thy kin are worth.

Sc. ix] *Hugo; not in Qq;* ACT IV. SCENE II. *Country near* Rochester.
Tyrrell; ACT III. SCENE VI. *Delius.*   1–2.] *so Qq (verse); prose Bullen.*
2.] *so Delius; two lines in Qq, divided at* dancke, / Or.   dank] *Qq;* damp
S.MS.   5–7.] *so Delius; two lines in Qq, divided at* the / intergatories
[Interrogatories *Q3*].   6. best swear] *Q1–2;* best to swear *Q3, S.MS.*
intergatories] *Q1–2, S.MS.;* Interrogatories *Q3.*   12. took] *Qq;* taken
S.MS.   13. handledst] *Qq;* handlest *S.MS.*   14. haply] *S.MS.,*
Tyrrell; happely *Q1;* happily *Q2–3.*   17. mount] *Qq;* amount *Hopkinson*
(*2*).

---

ix. 5. *coil*] stir, fuss.
6. *intergatories*] (syncopated form of) interrogatories: questions answer-
able under oath. Shakespeare has both forms of the word (see *Mer.V.*,
v. i. 298; *All's W.*, IV. iii. 171—syncopated form in a prose passage; *John*,
III. i. 147; and *Cym.*, v. v. 392).
9. *dag*] pistol.
10. *wink*] close (one's) eyes.
13. *handledst*] = hast handled.
17. *mount*] amount (*O.E.D., v.,* †6).

Zounds, I hate them as I hate a toad
That carry a muscado in their tongue   20
And scarce a hurting weapon in their hand.

Will. O Greene, intolerable!
It is not for mine honour to bear this.—
Why, Shakebag, I did serve the king at Boulogne,
And thou canst brag of nothing that thou hast done.   25

Shakebag. Why, so can Jack of Faversham,
That sounded for a fillip on the nose,
When he that gave it him holloed in his ear,
And he supposed a cannon-bullet hit him.   *Then they fight.*

Greene [*separating them*]. I pray you, sirs, list to Æsop's talk: 30
Whilst two stout dogs were striving for a bone,
There comes a cur and stole it from them both;
So, while you stand striving on these terms of manhood,
Arden escapes us and deceives us all.

---

20. tongue] *Qq*; tongues *Hopkinson* (2).   25. that] *Q1*; *not in Q2–3*.
26. can] *Qq*; did *S.MS.*   27. sounded] *Q1–2*; swounded *Q3*; swooned
Jacob.   on] *Qq*; of *McIlwraith*.   28. holloed] *Qq* (hollowed)*; hollaed
Delius.   30. S.D.] *This ed., after Hugo* (les séparant); *not in Qq.*   list]
Qq; listen *S.MS., Delius.*   34. escapes] *Q1–2*; escape *Q3, S.MS.*
us] *Qq*; you *S.MS.*   deceives] *Q2*; deceaue *Q1, 3, S.MS.*

19–21.] Cf. Shakebag's similar conviction at iii. 108.
    19.] a commonplace comparison; see, for instance, *Troil.*, II. iii. 154–5,
and *S. & P.*, III. ii. 27.
    20. *muscado*] weapon (?—cited by *O.E.D.*; Bullen suggests 'gadfly'
[Spanish *moscarda*], and along these lines Hopkinson [2] suggests 'a stinging speech'; perhaps a corruption of *mosca*, a mosquito'; Warnke and
Proescholdt note Italian *moschetto*).
    26. *Jack of Faversham*] Jack Fitten of ii. 68 ?
    27. *sounded*] swooned.
    fillip] blow (with the fist).
    28. *holloed*] shouted.
    30. *list*] listen.
    Æsop's talk] fable from any number of the collections attributed by
tradition to the Greek slave whom Herodotus claimed lived in the middle
of the sixth century B.C. Cf. viii. 34–5, and n. Elizabethan drama contains many allusions to Æsop.
    31. *stout*] fierce, valiant.
    33. *striving*] Repetition of l. 31 above ? Omission would create a penta-
meter line.

Shakebag. Why, he begun.

Will.   And thou shalt find I'll end.   35
     I do but slip it until better time.

     But, if I do forget—   *Then he kneels down and holds*
                                       up his hands to heaven.

Greene. Well, take your fittest standings, and once more
     Lime your twigs to catch this weary bird.

     I'll leave you, and at your dag's discharge   40
     Make towards, like the longing water-dog
     That coucheth till the fowling-piece be off,
     Then seizeth on the prey with eager mood.

     Ah, might I see him stretching forth his limbs
     As I have seen them beat their wings ere now.   45

Shakebag. Why, that thou shalt see if he come this way.

Greene. Yes, that he doth, Shakebag, I warrant thee.

     But brawl not when I am gone in any case,
     But, sirs, be sure to speed him when he comes;   49
     And in that hope I'll leave you for an hour.   *Exit* GREENE.
                 [BLACK WILL *and* SHAKEBAG *withdraw*
                               behind a stage pillar.]

---

36. until better] *Qq;* till a fitter *S.MS.*   39. Lime your] *Qq;* Lime well
your *Jacob.*   weary] *Qq;* wary *Jacob.*   40. dag's] *Jacob;* dags *Qq;*
dags' *B-H-N.*   46. come] *Qq;* Comes *S.MS.,Jacob.*   50.1-2.] *This ed.,*
after Hugo and Oliphant; not in Qq.

---

36. *slip*] postpone.

38. *fittest standings*] See iii. 39, n.

39. *Lime . . . bird*] i.e., set your trap; referring to the practice of smearing
(or *liming*) twigs with a sticky substance known as bird-lime to catch birds.
The image is a common one in the drama of the period.

     weary] wearisome or irksome (because Arden is proving such 'to catch';
he is not in the least 'wary').

40-3.] Clark compares *R3,* IV. iv. 49-50 ('That dog, that had his teeth
before his eyes, / To worry lambs and lap their gentle blood').

41. *water-dog*] 'one trained to retrieve waterfowl' (*O.E.D.,* I. a.).

42. *coucheth*] crouches, lies down.

     fowling-piece] 'light gun for shooting wild fowl' (*O.E.D.,* citing 1596 as
the first example).

45. *them*] i.e., the waterfowl.

48. *in any case*] See i. 111, n.

Here enters ARDEN, FRANKLIN, *and* MICHAEL.

Michael. 'Twere best that I went back to Rochester.
    The horse halts downright; it were not good
    He travelled in such pain to Faversham.
    Removing of a shoe may haply help it.

Arden. Well, get you back to Rochester; but, sirrah, see   55
    Ye overtake us ere we come to Rainham Down,
    For it will be very late ere we get home.

Michael. [*Aside*] Ay, God he knows, and so doth Will and
    Shakebag,

50.3.] *so Qq; Oliphant adds:* 'on horseback from the other side.'   52.
downright; it] *Qq;* downright, [and] it *Oliphant.*   54. haply] *S.MS.,*
Delius; happely *Q1;* happily *Q2–3.*   55–6.] *so Delius; as prose Q1–2,*
verse Q3, with all Qq divided at ye | overtake [Over-take *Q3*]; *divided in*
Hopkinson (2) at sirrah, | See.   57. For it will] *Qq;* For't will *Hopkinson*
(2).   58. *Aside*] *Tyrrell; not in Qq.*   he] *Qq; omitted S.MS., Tyrrell.*

50.3.] The ensuing dialogue would seem to justify, at first, Oliphant's
addition (*on horseback*) to Qq's original stage direction; but the introduction
of animals on to the Elizabethan stage was an extremely rare occurrence
and most deftly avoided. Dialogue and possibly even equestrian accoutre-
ments were all that were necessary to suggest the situation. In *Mac.,* III. iii.
8, the murderers 'hear horses', and then the stage direction follows: '*Enter*
BANQUO, *and* FLEANCE *with a torch*'. (See correspondence of W. J. Lawrence
in *T.L.S.,* 5 June 1919, p. 312.) In this particular scene of *Arden,* with the
addition later of Lord Cheyne and his men, the likelihood of at least five or
six horses milling about on the planked platform (with spectators possibly
sitting on the sides) is extremely small because the circumstances would be
highly impracticable. In fact, Lord Cheyne's command at l. 116 below furnishes clear evidence that he is not on horseback and that the horse is not
on the stage. Note, too, xiii. 59–60, where Arden emphasizes to Franklin
that their horses 'are gone home before'.

   51 ff.] Cf. Holinshed, App. II, p. 152.

   52. *halts downright*] limps badly.

   55.] Jackson (pp. 23–4) suggests that 'the line (to resort to mere guess-
work) may once have been:
      Well get you back sirra, but see that ye . . .'
The phrase 'back to Rochester' may be merely repeating l. 51 above.

   56.] The basic neutrality of the Elizabethan stage gave rise to the con-
vention of indicating locale and distance by dialogue, 'by specifying a place
at large but not a particular section of it' (B. Beckerman, *Shakespeare at the*
Globe, 1599–1609 [1962], p. 66). This line suggests that, although the conspirators are already there, Arden and Franklin are still some way from
Rainham Down; by l. 91 they are 'almost' there, and we may assume that
the rest of the scene does take place there.

That thou shalt never go further than that Down;
And therefore have I pricked the horse on purpose 60
Because I would not view the massacre.   *Exit* MICHAEL.

Arden. Come, Master Franklin, onwards with your tale.

Franklin. I assure you, sir, you task me much.
A heavy blood is gathered at my heart,
And on the sudden is my wind so short 65
As hindereth the passage of my speech.
So fierce a qualm yet ne'er assailèd me.

Arden. Come, Master Franklin, let us go on softly.
The annoyance of the dust or else some meat
You ate at dinner cannot brook with you. 70
I have been often so and soon amended.

Franklin. Do you remember where my tale did leave?

Arden. Ay, where the gentleman did check his wife.

Franklin. She being reprehended for the fact,
Witness produced that took her with the deed, 75
Her glove brought in which there she left behind,

---

62. onwards] *Qq;* onward *Jacob.*   67. fierce] *Q3;* ferse *Q1-2.*   70. ate]
Q3; eat *Q1-2, S.MS.*   brook with you] *Q2-3, S.MS.;* brooke you *Q1.*
74. fact,] *Q1ᶜ(D, H);* fact *Q1ᵘ(M).*

---

60. *pricked the horse*] pierced the foot of the horse (to cause lameness
[*O.E.D.*, *prick*, *v.*, 1. c, citing as an example Greene's *Blacke Booke's
Messenger*, 1592: 'His horse . . . halted right downe: . . . I wondred at it,
and thought he was prickt']).

64. *heavy*] oppressive.

67. *qualm*] fit of illness (*transfiguratively*, misgiving). See xiv. 301-2, n.
Taylor believes that this particular passage derives from Greene's *James
the Fourth*, v. i. 65-6 ('a sudden qualm / Assails my heart').

68. *softly*] gently.

70. *ate*] Q3's spelling is not actually an emendation since *eat* was pronounced *ate* at this time (see H. Kökeritz, *Shakespeare's Pronunciation*
[1953], pp. 20, 175, 198; and cf. *Paradise Lost*, IX. 781: 'she plucked, she
eat').

brook with] in the sense of *put up with*, anticipates the *O.E.D.* first
example of 1658 (*Brook*, *v.*, 3.†b. *intr.*).

72. *leave*] i.e., leave off or break off.

73. *check*] reprove.

74. *fact*] (criminal or evil) deed.

75. *took her with*] caught her in.

And many other assurèd arguments,

Her husband asked her whether it were not so.

Arden. Her answer then? I wonder how she looked,

Having forsworn it with such vehement oaths,   80

And at the instant so approved upon her.

Franklin. First did she cast her eyes down to the earth,

Watching the drops that fell amain from thence;

Then softly draws she forth her handkercher,

And modestly she wipes her tear-stained face;   85

Then hemmed she out, to clear her voice should seem,

And with a majesty addressed herself

To encounter all their accusations.—

Pardon me, Master Arden, I can no more;

This fighting at my heart makes short my wind.   90

Arden. Come, we are almost now at Rainham Down.

Your pretty tale beguiles the weary way;

I would you were in state to tell it out.

Shakebag. [*Aside*] Stand close, Will; I hear them coming.

Here enters LORD CHEYNE *with his* Men.

78. Her] *Q1ᶜ(D, H);* He *Q1ᵘ(M).*   whether] *Qq;* if *S.MS.*   80. oaths]
Qq; lyes *S.MS.*   81. approved] *Qq;* proved *S.MS.*   84. handkercher]
Qq; handkerchief *S.MS., Tyrrell.*   86. voice should] *Qq;* voice't should
Oliphant.   90. fighting] *Qq;* Sighing *S.MS.*   93. state] *Q1–2;* case *Q3.*
94, 95. Aside] *Hugo; not in Qq.*

77. *arguments*] proofs.

81. *approved upon*] proved against.

83. *amain*] with full force.

86. *voice should*] See Abbott 404 on ellipsis of *it* in Elizabethan English.

90.] Hopkinson (3) compares *Ham.*, v. ii. 4–5 ('Sir, in my heart there was
a kind of fighting, / That would not let me sleep').

93. *state*] condition.

94.1.] At this point the playwright condenses the narrative in Holinshed,
who has Arden, after Michael leaves him, 'ouertooke' by 'diuerse gentlemen of his acquaintance, who kept him companie: so that blacke Will mist
here also of his purpose'. When he arrives home, Alice plots with a servant
to have Arden go visit Lord Cheyne.

LORD CHEYNE] (1485 ?–1558); never actually Lord Cheyne, but Sir
Thomas Cheyne (first spelling in *D.N.B.*); his son was raised to the Peerage.
There is probably some confusion here with his titles of Lord Warden of
the Cinque Ports and Lord Lieutenant of Kent. The *D.N.B.* records that

Will. [*Aside*] Stand to it, Shakebag, and be resolute.   95
Lord Cheyne. Is it so near night as it seems,
　　Or will this black-faced evening have a shower ?—
　　What, Master Arden ? You are well met.
　　I have longed this fortnight's day to speak with you.
　　You are a stranger, man, in the Isle of Sheppey.   100
Arden. Your honour's always ! Bound to do you service !
Lord Cheyne. Come you from London and ne'er a man with you ?
Arden. My man's coming after,
　　But here's my honest friend that came along with me.
Lord Cheyne [*to Franklin*]. My Lord Protector's man, I take
　　you to be.   105
Franklin. Ay, my good lord, and highly bound to you.
Lord Cheyne. You and your friend come home and sup with me.
Arden. I beseech your honour pardon me ;
　　I have made a promise to a gentleman,
　　My honest friend, to meet him at my house.   110
　　The occasion is great, or else would I wait on you.
Lord Cheyne. Will you come tomorrow and dine with me,
　　And bring your honest friend with you ?
　　I have divers matters to talk with you about.
Arden. Tomorrow we'll wait upon your honour.   115
Lord Cheyne. One of you stay my horse at the top of the hill.—
　　[*Seeing Black Will.*] What, Black Will ! For whose purse
　　wait you ?
　　Thou wilt be hanged in Kent when all is done.
Will. Not hanged, God save your honour.

---

99. speak with] *Qq; see S.MS.*   100. stranger, man, in] *Jacob;* stranger
man in *Q1–2;* stranger man, in *Q3.*   Sheppey] *Q1ᶜ(D, H)* (Sheppy)*;*
Shepny *Q1ᵘ(M).*   101. always ! Bound] *Qq* (alwayes bound)*;* alwayes :
bound *W-P.*   103–4.] *so Qq; divided in W-P at* here's | My*; prose this ed.
conj.*   105. S.D.] *This ed.; not in Qq.*   110. honest] *Qq; omitted S.MS.*
115. we'll] *Qq;* I would *S.MS.;* we will *Tyrrell.*   117. S.D.] *Sturgess,
after* Hugo ('Apercevant Blackwill')*; not in Qq.*

---

he entertained King Henry VIII and Anne Boleyn at Shurland Castle on
the Isle of Sheppey in 1532 and that he was one who 'profited largely by the
dissolution of the monasteries in Kent'. See i. 2–5, n.
　113. *your honest friend*] i.e., Franklin.

I am your beadsman, bound to pray for you.   120
Lord Cheyne. I think thou ne'er saidest prayer in all thy life.—
    One of you give him a crown.—
    And, sirrah, leave this kind of life.
    If thou beest 'tainted for a penny matter
    And come in question, surely thou wilt truss.—   125
    Come, Master Arden, let us be going;
    Your way and mine lies four mile together.   *Exeunt.*
                    Manet BLACK WILL *and* SHAKEBAG.
Will. The devil break all your necks at four miles' end!
    Zounds, I could kill myself for very anger!
    His lordship chops me in even when   130
    My dag was levelled at his heart.
    I would his crown were molten down his throat.
Shakebag. Arden, thou hast wondrous holy luck.
    Did ever man escape as thou hast done?
    Well, I'll discharge my pistol at the sky,   135
    For by this bullet Arden might not die. [*He fires.*]

                Here enters GREENE.

Greene. What, is he down? Is he dispatched?
Shakebag. Ay, in health towards Faversham to shame us all.
Greene. The devil he is! Why, sirs, how escaped he?
Shakebag. When we were ready to shoot,   140
    Comes my Lord Cheyne to prevent his death.
Greene. The Lord of Heaven hath preservèd him.

---

121. saidest] *Q1;* saydst *Q2;* saidst *Q3.*   124. beest] *Q1–2;* best *Q3;*
be'st *Delius;* art *Tyrrell.*   a] *Q1–2;* one *Q3.*   127. mile] *Q1–2;* miles
Q3, S.MS.   130–1.] *so Qq; divided in Delius at* in, / Even.   130. even]
Qq; E'en *Hopkinson* (2).   132. were molten] *Qq;* was melting *S.MS.*
136. S.D.] *This ed., after Hugo; not in Qq.*   138. Ay, in] *Qq;* I home in
S.MS.   139. escaped] *Qq;* 'scaped *Tyrrell.*   140. were ready] *Qq;*
were Just ready *S.MS.*

---

120. *beadsman*] one paid to pray for others (*O.E.D.*, 2). L. 122 suggests
that Lord Cheyne must protect Will.
    124–5. *If . . . truss.*] i.e., If you are caught and accused of even the most
trivial offence and come to trial, you will surely hang.
    130. *chops me in*] suddenly interrupts.

Will. The Lord of Heaven a fig! The Lord Cheyne hath
     preservèd him
     And bids him to a feast to his house at Shorlow.
     But by the way once more I'll meet with him;   145
     And if all the Cheynes in the world say no,
     I'll have a bullet in his breast tomorrow.
     Therefore come, Greene, and let us to Faversham.
Greene. Ay, and excuse ourselves to Mistress Arden.
     O, how she'll chafe when she hears of this!   150
Shakebag. Why, I'll warrant you she'll think we dare not do it.
Will. Why, then let us go, and tell her all the matter,
     And plot the news to cut him off tomorrow.   *Exeunt.*

---

143. The Lord of Heaven a fig!] *Sturgess, conj. Jackson;* Preserued, a figge,
Qq; Preserved? a fig! *Delius.*   144. to (2)] *Qq;* at *S.MS., Tyrrell.*
Shorlow] *Qq;* Shurland *Jacob;* Shorland *Hopkinson* (2).   148. let us] *Qq;*
let's go *Hopkinson* (3).   152. let us] *Qq;* let's *Hopkinson* (2).   153. plot]
Q3; plat *Q1–2, S.MS.*

---

143. *The Lord . . . a fig !*] Jackson (p. 28) argues thus for the emendation:
'Will's denial that Arden has been preserved ("Preserued, a figge") is con-
tradictory. He should speak some such line as:
     The Lord of Heaven a fig! Lord Cheiny hath,
the quibble being upon the two different kinds of "Lord". It is surprising
that the play should have been edited so many times without anyone's
having recognized that the text is pointless as it stands.'
     144. *bids*] invites.
     Shorlow] i.e., Shurland, 'the residence of Lord [Cheyne], in Kent, not
far from Faversham', on the Isle of Sheppey (Sugden).
     146. *And if*] i.e., and even if.
     151–2.] The repetition of *Why* is feeble and suspect.
     153. *plot the news*] plot a new means (Schelling).
     cut him off] kill him.

[Sc. x]

Here enters ARDEN *and his* Wife,
FRANKLIN, *and* MICHAEL.

Arden. See how the Hours, the guardant of heaven's gate,
        Have by their toil removed the darksome clouds,
        That Sol may well discern the trampled pace
        Wherein he wont to guide his golden car.
        The season fits. Come, Franklin, let's away.   5

Alice. I thought you did pretend some special hunt
        That made you thus cut short the time of rest.

Arden. It was no chase that made me rise so early
        But, as I told thee yesternight, to go
        To the Isle of Sheppey, there to dine with my Lord
            Cheyne;
        For so his honour late commanded me.   11

Alice. Ay, such kind husbands seldom want excuses;
        Home is a wild cat to a wand'ring wit.
        The time hath been—would God it were not past!—

Sc. x] *so Hugo; not in Qq;* ACT IV. SCENE III. Arden's *House at* Feversham.
Tyrrell; ACT IV. SCENE I. *Delius.* 1. the (2)] *Qq; omitted Tyrrell.*
guardant] *Q1* (gardeant); gardeat *Q2;* gaurd at *Q3;* Gardent *S.MS.;*
guardeants *Jacob;* guardians *Tyrrell.* 3. discern] *Q3* (discerne), *Q2*
(deserne); deserue *Q1.*   pace] *Qq;* path *W-P.*   9–10.] *so W-P;*
divided in Qq at Sheppy: / There; *divided in Delius at* yesternight, / To
and dine / With.   13. wand'ring] *Qq;* wandering *Tyrrell.*

---

x. 1–4.] See App. I.
      1. *the Hours . . . gate*] referring to the traditional classical image of the
daughters of Jupiter and Themis who also presided over the changes of the
seasons.
      guardant] guardian, keeper, protector.
      3. *Sol*] the sun (personified). See Ovid's *Metamorphoses*, II. 116–21,
where the Hours yoke Titan's (Sol's) steeds.
      pace] path, passage.
      5. *The season fits.*] The weather is suitable.
      6. *pretend*] intend.
      10. *the Isle of*] if omitted, an iambic pentameter line.
      11. *late*] recently, lately.
      12. *want*] lack, are without.
      14. *The time hath been*] Cf. passage beginning 'The time was once' in
Err., II. ii. 112 ff., in which Adriana berates her 'husband'.

That honour's title nor a lord's command 15
Could once have drawn you from these arms of mine.
But my deserts or your desires decay,
Or both; yet if true love may seem desert,
I merit still to have thy company.

Franklin. Why, I pray you, sir, let her go along with us. 20
I am sure his honour will welcome her
And us the more for bringing her along.

Arden. Content.—[*To Michael.*] Sirrah, saddle your mistress' nag.

Alice. No, begged favour merits little thanks.
If I should go, our house would run away 25
Or else be stol'n; therefore I'll stay behind.

Arden. Nay, see how mistaking you are. I pray thee, go.

Alice. No, no, not now.

Arden. Then let me leave thee satisfied in this,
That time nor place nor persons alter me 30
But that I hold thee dearer than my life.

Alice. That will be seen by your quick return.

Arden. And that shall be ere night and if I live.
Farewell, sweet Alice; we mind to sup with thee. *Exit* ALICE.

Franklin. Come, Michael, are our horses ready? 35

Michael. Ay, your horse are ready, but I am not ready, for I

---

15. honour's title] *Qq* (honors tytle)*;* honours, title *Jacob.* 17. desires]
W-P; deserues *Q1;* desernes *Q2;* deserves *Q3;* deserts *S.MS.* 23. S.D.]
Sturgess, after Hugo (*A Michel*)*; not in Qq.* 26. stol'n] *Qq* (stolne);
stolen *S.MS.*, *Tyrrell.* behind] *Qq;* at home *S.MS.* 27.] so *W-P;*
two lines in Qq, divided at are, / I. 31. dearer] *Q1ᶜ(D, H);* de rer *Q1ᵘ(M).*
32. seen by] *Qq;* seen soon by *Tyrrell.* 33. be] *Q1–2; not in Q3.*
36–8.] *so Delius; as verse in Qq, lines ending* ready, / purse, / in it, / Nagge.
36. horse] *Q1–2;* horses *Q3, S.MS.*

---

17. *deserts*] merits.
18. *desert*] i.e., desertful; deserving.
21.] Jackson (p. 23) suggests that the line probably was intended to read:
'His honour, I am sure, will welcome her.' As it stands, the line suggests a
reporter's poor ear for verse.
31.] Cf. i. 39.
33. *and if*] if.
36–41.] Cf. Holinshed, App. II, p. 153.
36. *horse are*] See i. 363, n.

      have lost my purse with six-and-thirty shillings in it, with
      taking up of my master's nag.
Franklin. Why, I pray you, let us go before
      Whilst he stays behind to seek his purse.   40
Arden. Go to, sirrah! See you follow us to the Isle of Sheppey,
      To my Lord Cheyne's, where we mean to dine.

            Exeunt ARDEN *and* FRANKLIN. *Manet* MICHAEL.

Michael. So, fair weather after you; for before you lies Black
      Will and Shakebag in the broom close, too close for you.
      They'll be your ferrymen to long home.   45

        Here enters the Painter [CLARKE].

      But who is this? The painter, my corrival, that would
      needs win Mistress Susan.
Clarke. How now, Michael? How doth my mistress and all at
      home?

38. of] *Q1–2; not in Q3.*   master's] *W-P;* M. *Q1–2;* mistres *Q3;*
Mistrises *S.MS.*   41. See you] *Q1–2;* see that you *Q3.*   43–7.]
so W-P; as verse in Qq, lines ending you, / Shakebag, / you, / home, /
[S.D.] / corrival, / Susan; *as prose in Delius to* 'long home', *then as Qq.*
43. weather] *Q1c(D, H);* whether *Q1u(M).*   you lies] *Q1c(D, H)*
(you, lyes), *Q1u(M)* (you lyes,).   44. too] *Q1c(D, H);* to *Q1u(M).*
45. to long home] *Qq;* to yʳ long-home *S.MS.;* to a long home *Tyrrell.*
45.1. CLARKE] *Tyrrell; not in Qq.*   48–9.] *so W-P; as verse in Qq,
divided at* Mistresse, / And.

---

   38. *taking up of*] ? catching (Sturgess); making gambol (Baskervill);
possibly, to get moving, to urge on (see *O.E.D., Take,* v., 90. †*q*).
   44. *broom close*] enclosed field of shrubs. Holinshed writes that Black
Will (as well as Shakebag) 'was willed in anie wise to be vp earlie in the
morning, to lie in wait for maister Arden in a certeine broome close,
betwixt Feuersham & the ferrie (which close he must needs passe) there to
doo his feat' (see App. II, p. 153).
   45. *ferrymen*] Cf. *R3,* I. iv. 46 ('that grim [sour] ferryman which poets
write of'—i.e., Charon, who conveyed the dead souls over the River Styx
to Hades).
   to long home] to (your) last home, i.e., the grave. Cf. *Ecclesiastes,* xii. 5
('because man goeth to his long home, and the mourners go about the
streets'), and the proverb, 'He is gone to his long (last) home' (Tilley,
H533). Jackson (p. 175) writes: 'There is a quibble on "holme", meaning
a little island in the river. Arden is about to take the ferry to the Isle of
Sheppy; Michael says that the two murder[er]s will act as his Charon-like
ferrymen to a home/holme of a different kind.'

Michael. Who ? Susan Mosby ? She is your mistress, too ?   50
Clarke. Ay, how doth she and all the rest ?
Michael. All's well but Susan; she is sick.
Clarke. Sick ? Of what disease ?
Michael. Of a great fear.
Clarke. A fear of what ?   55
Michael. A great fever.
Clarke. A fever ? God forbid!
Michael. Yes, faith, and of a lurdan, too, as big as yourself.
Clarke. O Michael, the spleen prickles you. Go to; you carry
    an eye over Mistress Susan.   60
Michael. Ay, faith, to keep her from the painter.
Clarke. Why more from a painter than from a serving-
    creature like yourself?
Michael. Because you painters make but a painting-table of a
    pretty wench and spoil her beauty with blotting.   65
Clarke. What mean you by that ?

---

54. fear] *Qq;* fever *Delius;* fe'er *McIlwraith.*   56. A great] *Q1–2;* Of a
great *Q3.*   58.] *so Delius; as verse in Qq, divided at* too, / As.   lurdan]
Qq (lordaine)*;* logershead *S.MS.*   59–60.] *so Delius; as verse in Qq,
divided at* you. / Go.   59. prickles] *Q1;* pricks *Q2–3, S.MS.*   61. Ay,
faith] *Qq* (I faith)*;* I'faith *Delius.*   62–3.] *so Q1–2; as verse Q3, divided
at* serving / Creature *(same lineation as Q1–2).*   62. a (1)] *Qq;* the *Jacob.*
65. with blotting] *Q1–2;* with a blotting *Q3.*

---

54. *fear*] In support of fe'er, McIlwraith writes: '*Apparently Michael
mumbles the word* fever, *but the point is obscure.*'
58. *lurdan*] 'loafer' (with word-play on *Fever-lurden*: the disease of
laziness [*O.E.D.*]).
59. *spleen*] peevish temper.
prickles] goads.
59–60. *carry an eye over*] have an eye on, i.e., have designs on.
64–5.] Cf. *Con.,* IV. vii. 11–13 ('Why ist not a miserable thing, that of the
skin of an innocent lamb should parchment be made, & then with a litle
blotting ouer with inke, a man should vndo himselfe'—spoken by Jack
Cade; cf. *2H6.* IV. ii. 74–7: 'Is not this a lamentable thing, that of the skin
of an innocent lamb should be made parchment ? that parchment, being
scribbled o'er, should undo a man ?').
64. *painting-table*] 'a board or other flat surface on which a picture is
painted; hence, the picture itself' (see *O.E.D., Table, sb.,* †3); palette
(Schelling).

Michael. Why, that you painters paint lambs in the lining of
    wenches' petticoats, and we servingmen put horns to
    them to make them become sheep.

Clarke. Such another word will cost you a cuff or a knock.   70

Michael. What, with a dagger made of a pencil? Faith, 'tis too
    weak, and therefore thou too weak to win Susan.

Clarke. Would Susan's love lay upon this stroke!

                    Then he breaks Michael's head.

      Here enters MOSBY, GREENE, *and* ALICE.

Alice. I'll lay my life, this is for Susan's love.—
    [*To Michael.*] Stayed you behind your master to this end?   75
    Have you no other time to brabble in
    But now when serious matters are in hand?—
    Say, Clarke, hast thou done the thing thou promised?

Clarke. Ay, here it is; the very touch is death.

Alice. Then this, I hope, if all the rest do fail,   80
    Will catch Master Arden
    And make him wise in death that lived a fool.
    Why should he thrust his sickle in our corn,
    Or what hath he to do with thee, my love,
    Or govern me that am to rule myself?   85
    Forsooth, for credit sake, I must leave thee!

67–9.] *so Delius; as verse in Qq, divided at* peticots / And.   67. lining]
Qq; linings *Tyrrell.*   70. cuff] *Qq;* kick *S.MS.*   71–2.] *so Delius; as
verse in Qq, lines ending* pensell? / weake, / Susan.   75. S.D.] *This ed.,
after Hugo; not in Qq.*   76. brabble] *Qq;* brangle *S.MS.*   77.] *so Qq;
Oliphant adds:* 'Exit MICHAEL.'   78. promised?] *Q1–2;* promisedst? *Q3.*
83. corn] *Qq;* Comepany *S.MS.*

68–9. *put horns . . . sheep*] proverbial allusion to the horns of the cuckold.

70. *cuff*] blow.

73.1. breaks] See iii. 51.2, n.

74. *lay*] wager.

76. *brabble*] brawl, quarrel noisily (see iii. 56, n.).

78. *done the thing thou promised?*] See i. 609 ff., concerning the poisoned
crucifix that Clarke had promised to make for Alice and Mosby.

83.] Cf. proverb: 'Put not thy sickle in another man's corn' (Tilley,
S420).

86. *Forsooth*] in truth, certainly.

Nay, he must leave to live that we may love,
May live, may love; for what is life but love ?
And love shall last as long as life remains,
And life shall end before my love depart.   90

Mosby. Why, what's love without true constancy ?
Like to a pillar built of many stones,
Yet neither with good mortar well compact
Nor cement to fasten it in the joints
But that it shakes with every blast of wind   95
And, being touched, straight falls unto the earth
And buries all his haughty pride in dust.
No, let our love be rocks of adamant,
Which time nor place nor tempest can asunder.

Greene. Mosby, leave protestations now,   100
And let us bethink us what we have to do.
Black Will and Shakebag I have placed
In the broom close, watching Arden's coming.
Let's to them and see what they have done.   *Exeunt.*

---

90. depart] *Qq;* Change *S.MS.*   91. what's] *Qq;* what is *S.MS., Jacob;*
Why, is love *Hopkinson* (3).   94. cement] *Q3;* semell *Q1-2, S.MS.*
101. let us] *Qq;* let's *Jacob.*   102-4.] *so Qq; lines ending in Delius at*
broom, / them, / done.

87-90.] Cf. Symonds (p. 457): 'Could the selfishness of passion, identi-
fying itself with existence, brushing away the life that stands between
anticipation and fruition like a fly, be more condensed than in these
monosyllables ?'

91-4.] Crawford compares *Euphues and His England* (ed. E. Arber,
[1868], p. 417, ll. 14-17): '—in no other manner standeth it with love, for to
be secreate and not constant, or constant and not secret, were to builde a
house of morter without stones, or a wall of stones without morter' (note
ll. 98-9 below). Cf. also *Woodstock*, II. ii. 166-7 ('If once the pillars and
supporters quail / How can the strongest castle choose but fail ?').

93. *compact*] composed.

94. *cement*] Q1's spelling *semell* is probably a compositor's error for
original variant spelling of *sement* (see *O.E.D.*).

97. *his*] its.

99. *asunder*] put asunder, part.

100. *leave*] leave off.

[Sc. xi]

Here enters ARDEN *and* FRANKLIN.

Arden. O ferryman, where art thou?

Here enters the Ferryman.

Ferryman. Here, here! Go before to the boat, and I will follow
you.

Arden. We have great haste; I pray thee come away.

Ferryman. Fie, what a mist is here!   5

Arden. This mist, my friend, is mystical,
Like to a good companion's smoky brain,
That was half-drowned with new ale overnight.

Ferryman. 'Twere pity but his skull were opened to make
more chimney room.   10

Franklin. Friend, what's thy opinion of this mist?

Ferryman. I think 'tis like to a curst wife in a little house, that
never leaves her husband till she have driven him out at
doors with a wet pair of eyes. Then looks he as if his house
were afire, or some of his friends dead.   15

Arden. Speaks thou this of thine own experience?

Ferryman. Perhaps ay, perhaps no; for my wife is as other
women are, that is to say, governed by the moon.

___

Sc. xi] *Hugo; not in Qq;* ACT IV. SCENE IV. *The Kentish Coast opposite the
Isle of Sheppey. Tyrrell;* ACT IV. SCENE II. *Delius.*   2–3.] *so W-P; as
verse in Qq, divided at* boat. / And.   4. have] *Qq;* are in *S.MS.*   9–10.]
so W-P; as verse in Qq, divided at opened, / To.   11. what's] *Q1, 3;*
what *Q2.*   12–15.] *so Delius; as verse in Qq, lines ending at* house, / him /
eyes, / fire, / dead.   12. to] *Q1; not in Q2–3.*   13. she have driven] *Q1;*
she driue *Q2–3;* she drivs *S.MS.*   at] *Q1–2;* of *Q3, S.MS.*   16.
Speaks] *Q1–2;* Speakest *Q3;* Speak'st *Jacob.*   17–18.] *so Q1–2; as
verse in Q3, divided at* other / Women (*same lineation as Q1–2*).   18. are]
Qq; omitted Tyrrell.

___

Sc. xi] This scene and the next are the playwright's invention.

7. *good*] i.e., good-drinking.

9. *but*] unless, if . . . not.

12. *curst*] shrewish, cantankerous.

13. *at*] of.

18. *governed by the moon*] Cf. proverb: 'As changeful (inconstant) as the
moon' (Tilley, M1111). Cf. also *R3*, II. ii. 69 (Queen Elizabeth speaking):

N

Franklin. By the moon ? How, I pray thee ?

Ferryman. Nay, thereby lies a bargain, and you shall not have   20
it fresh and fasting.

Arden. Yes, I pray thee, good ferryman.

Ferryman. Then for this once: let it be midsummer moon, but
yet my wife has another moon.

Franklin. Another moon ?   25

Ferryman. Ay, and it hath influences and eclipses.

Arden. Why, then, by this reckoning you sometimes play the
man in the moon.

Ferryman. Ay, but you had not best to meddle with that moon
lest I scratch you by the face with my bramble-bush.   30

Arden. I am almost stifled with this fog. Come, let's away.

Franklin. And, sirrah, as we go, let us have some more of your
bold yeomanry.

Ferryman. Nay, by my troth, sir, but flat knavery.   *Exeunt.*

20–1.] *so Delius; as verse in Qq, divided at* bargane. / And.   20. Nay] *Q3;*
Na *Q1–2.*   23–4.] *so Delius; as verse in Qq, divided at* Moone, / But.
23. once: let] *Q1* (once, let); once let *Q2–3.*   24. has] *Q3;* as *Q1–2;*
is as *S.MS.*   27–8.] *so Delius; as verse in Qq, divided at* sometimes / Play
[play *Q2*].   29–30.] *so Delius; as verse in Qq, divided at* moone / Least.
29. not best] *Qq;* best not *W-P.*   32–3.] *so Q1–2; as verse in Q3, divided
at* your / Bold (*same lineation as Q1–2*).

'I, being govern'd by the watery moon'), and *End.*, I. ii. 27 ('*Cynthia* [the
Moon] gouerneth all things'). 'Perhaps an allusion to the menstrual cycle'
(Jackson, p. 77).

21. *fresh and fasting*] 'before eating; in your eagerness; for nothing (?)'
(Baskervill).

23. *midsummer moon*] 'The lunar month in which Midsummer Day
[24 June] comes; sometimes alluded to as a time when lunacy is supposed
to be prevalent' (*O.E.D.*, citing *Tw.N.*, III. iv. 53: 'Why, this is very midsummer madness').

26. *influences and eclipses*] obvious sexual allusion. Cf. *End.*, I. ii. 31
('her [Cynthia's] influence both comforteth all things'), and see note to
l. 18 above.

28. *man in the moon*] See Intro., p. xliv; and cf. *MND.*, v. i. 237–8 ('This
lanthorn doth the horned moon present; / Myself the man i' the moon do
seem to be'; *horned* = cuckolded).

30. *bramble-bush*] Cf. again *MND.*, v. i. 250–2 ('All that I have to say, is,
to tell you that the lanthorn is the moon; I, the man i' the moon; this thorn-
bush, my thorn-bush; and this dog, my dog').

33. *yeomanry*] honest, homely speech of the yeoman class.

[Sc. xii]

Here enters WILL *at one door and* SHAKEBAG
at another.

Shakebag. O, Will, where art thou?

Will. Here, Shakebag, almost in hell's mouth, where I cannot
see my way for smoke.

Shakebag. I pray thee speak still that we may meet by the
sound, for I shall fall into some ditch or other unless my   5
feet see better than my eyes.

Will. Didst thou ever see better weather to run away with
another man's wife or play with a wench at potfinger?

Shakebag. No; this were a fine world for chandlers if this
weather would last, for then a man should never dine nor   10
sup without candlelight. But, sirrah Will, what horses are
those that passed?

Will. Why, didst thou hear any?

Shakebag. Ay, that I did.

Will. My life for thine, 'twas Arden and his companion, and   15
then all our labour's lost.

Shakebag. Nay, say not so; for, if it be they, they may haply
lose their way as we have done, and then we may chance
meet with them.

Sc. xii] *Hugo; not in Qq;* ACT IV. SCENE III. *Delius (no new scene in Tyrrell);
Another place on the Coast. W-P.*   2–3.] *so Delius; as verse in Qq, divided
at* mouth, / Where.   5. for] *Q1–2; or Q3.*   7. Didst] *Q2; Did'st Q3;
Didest Q1.*   9–12.] *so Delius; as verse in Qq, lines ending* chandlers, /
man / candle light, / past?   13. thou] *Q1–2; not in Q3.*   15–16.] *so
Q2; as verse in Q1, 3, divided at* companion, / And *(same lineation as Q2).*
15. 'twas] *Qq;* it was *Jacob.*   17–19.] *so Delius, as uncertain prose/verse in
Qq, lines ending* happely / done / them.   17. haply] *Q3;* happely *Q1;*
happily *Q2.*

---

xii. 4–6.] By and large Q1–2 tend to print prose while Q3 sets up their
prose lineation as verse throughout scene.

4. *speak still*] go on speaking.

5. *sound*] the stretch of water between Faversham and the Isle of
Sheppey.

8. *at potfinger*] sexual allusion (passage cited by *O.E.D.*, which also
quotes Withals *Dictionary* [1666]: 'A potte made in the mouthe, with one
finger, as children vse to do').

Will.   Come, let us go like a couple of blind pilgrims.   20

  Then SHAKEBAG *falls into a ditch.*

Shakebag.   Help, Will, help! I am almost drowned.

Here enters the Ferryman.

Ferryman.   Who's that that calls for help?

Will.   'Twas none here; 'twas thou thyself.

Ferryman.   I came to help him that called for help. Why, how
  now? Who is this that's in the ditch? [*He helps Shakebag*   25
  out.] You are well enough served to go without a guide
  such weather as this!

Will.   Sirrah, what companies hath passed your ferry this
  morning?

Ferryman.   None but a couple of gentlemen that went to dine   30
  at my Lord Cheyne's.

Will.   Shakebag, did not I tell thee as much?

Ferryman.   Why, sir, will you have any letters carried to them?

Will.   No, sir; get you gone.

Ferryman.   Did you ever see such a mist as this?   35

Will.   No, nor such a fool as will rather be houghed than get his
  way.

Ferryman.   Why, sir, this is no Hough Monday; you are
  deceived.—What's his name, I pray you, sir?

---

20. let us] *Q1;* lets *Q2;* let's *Q3.*   24–7.] *so Delius; as verse in Qq, lines
ending in Q1–2* help, / ditch? / this; *in Q3* helpe. / ditch? / guide / this.
25. that's in] *Q1–2;* that lies in *Q3.*   25–6. S.D.] *Oliphant, after Hugo;
not in Qq.*   28–9.] *so Tyrrell; as one line verse in Qq.*   28. companies]
Q1 (companyes); companions *Q2–3;* Company *S.MS., Jacob.*   hath]
Q1–2; have *Q3, S.MS.*   32. not I] *Qq;* I not *Tyrrell.*   36. houghed]
Qq (hought); hocked *Delius.*   38–9.] *so Delius; as verse in Qq, divided
at* deceiud / Whats.

20.1. a ditch] i.e., through trap-door of stage.
26. *to go*] for going (Sturgess).
28. *companies*] groups of people, as in *Cym.*, IV. ii. 69–70 ('search / What
companies are near').
36. *houghed*] hocked or hamstrung. Cf. *Con.*, IV. vii. 83 ('Hough him for
running').
get] go (McIlwraith).
38. *Hough Monday*] or Hock Monday: a popular holiday the second

Shakebag. His name is Black Will.   40

Ferryman. I hope to see him one day hanged upon a hill.

                       Exit Ferryman.

Shakebag. See how the sun hath cleared the foggy mist,

   Now we have missed the mark of our intent.

      Here enters GREENE, MOSBY, *and* ALICE.

Mosby. Black Will and Shakebag, what make you here?

   What, is the deed done? Is Arden dead?   45

Will. What could a blinded man perform in arms?

   Saw you not how till now the sky was dark,

   That neither horse nor man could be discerned?

   Yet did we hear their horses as they passed.

Greene. Have they escaped you then and passed the ferry?   50

Shakebag. Ay, for a while; but here we two will stay

   And at their coming back meet with them once more.

   Zounds, I was ne'er so toiled in all my life

   In following so slight a task as this.

Mosby [*to Shakebag*]. How cam'st thou so berayed?   55

Will. With making false footing in the dark.

   He needs would follow them without a guide.

Alice [*giving money*]. Here's to pay for a fire and good cheer.

   Get you to Faversham to the Flower-de-Luce,

   And rest yourselves until some other time.   60

Greene. Let me alone; it most concerns my state.

---

52. with] *Qq;* omitted *S.MS.*   55. S.D.] *This ed., after Hugo; not in Qq.*
berayed] *Qq* (beraide); bewrayed *McIlwraith.*   58. S.D.] *Oliphant;
not in Qq.*

Monday after Easter during which women customarily compelled men to
pay a ransom by roping them in or otherwise restraining them (i.e., hocking
them). See *O.E.D.*: *Hocktide.*

   44. *make you*] are you doing.

   52. *meet with them*] Omitting *with* would make the line metrical. Jackson
(pp. 21–2) postulates that the reporter was influenced by l. 19 above and by
ix. 145.

   53. *toiled*] fatigued, wearied.

   55. *berayed*] spattered with mud, befouled.

   61. *Let me alone*] (1) Let me leave you and look after them (?); (2) Let
me alone take care of everything (because it most concerns my state) (?).

Will. Ay, Mistress Arden, this will serve the turn
    In case we fall into a second fog.

                    Exeunt GREENE, WILL, *and* SHAKEBAG.

Mosby. These knaves will never do it; let us give it over.

Alice. First tell me how you like my new device: 65
    Soon, when my husband is returning back,
    You and I both marching arm in arm,
    Like loving friends, we'll meet him on the way
    And boldly beard and brave him to his teeth.
    When words grow hot and blows begin to rise,   70
    I'll call those cutters forth your tenement,
    Who, in a manner to take up the fray,
    Shall wound my husband Hornsby to the death.

Mosby. Ah, fine device! Why, this deserves a kiss. [*He kisses her.*]
                                  Exeunt.

---

64. let us] *Qq;* let's *Sturgess.*   70. blows] *Q1–2;* words *Q3.*   73.
Hornsby] *Qq;* Hornbeast *W-P.*   the] *Q1–2; not in Q3.*   74. Ah, fine]
Qq; A fine *S.MS., Delius.*   74. S.D.] *This ed.; not in Qq.*

64.] Cf. xiv. 2.

65. *device*] stratagem, plot.

68.] Cf. xiii. 60, 91.

69. *beard*] defy. See App. I.

71. *cutters*] cutthroats.

forth] i.e., forth from.

tenement] dwelling-place. Holinshed writes that 'Mosbie had a sister that dwelt in a tenement of maister Ardens neere to his house in Feuersham: and on the faire eeuen, blacke Will was sent for to come thither' (see App. II, p. 154).

73. *Hornsby*] = the cuckold. Warnke and Proescholdt emend on the basis of xiii. 82.

74.] At this point in Holinshed, Mosby 'at the first would not agree to that cowardlie murthering of him, but in a furie floong awaie'.

[Sc. xiii]

Here enters DICK REEDE *and a* Sailor.

Sailor. Faith, Dick Reede, it is to little end.
    His conscience is too liberal and he too niggardly
    To part from anything may do thee good.
Reede. He is coming from Shorlow as I understand.
    Here I'll intercept him, for at his house   5
    He never will vouchsafe to speak with me.
    If prayers and fair entreaties will not serve
    Or make no batt'ry in his flinty breast,

Here enters FRANKLIN, ARDEN, *and* MICHAEL.

    I'll curse the carl and see what that will do.
    See where he comes to further my intent.—   10
    Master Arden, I am now bound to the sea.
    My coming to you was about the plot of ground
    Which wrongfully you detain from me.
    Although the rent of it be very small,
    Yet will it help my wife and children,   15

Sc. xiii] *Hugo; not in Qq;* ACT IV. SCENE V. *The Open Country. Tyrrell;*
ACT IV. SCENE IV. *Delius.*   2. liberal] *Qq;* large *S.MS.*   4. Shorlow]
Qq; Shurland *Jacob;* Shorland *Hopkinson* (2).   6. vouchsafe] *Q2–3;*
vouchafe *Q1.*   8. batt'ry] *Qq;* battery *Tyrrell.*   8.1.] *so Qq; after l. 9*
Delius, l. 10 Tyrrell.   12–13.] *Qq; divided by W-P at* plat / Of.   12.
plot] *Q3;* plat *Q1–2.*

Sc. xiii] Not in Holinshed; the playwright's invention, but see App. II,
p. 159.
    1. *Faith, Dick Reede*] Jackson (p. 17) regards this phrase as an actor's
interpolation and suggests that ll. 1–2 read:
            It is to little end. His conscience is
            Too liberal and he too niggardly . . .
The phrase, however, serves the important function of introducing Dick
Reede to the audience.
    2. *liberal*] easy, without restraint; hence, indifferent.
    4. *Shorlow*] See ix. 144, n.
    8.] Cf. i. 47 and n., and also *3H6,* III. i. 37 ('Her sighs will make a battery
in his breast').
    9. *carl*] villain; more specifically, churlish, miserly fellow.
    12. *plot*] See vii. 26, n., and note Qq's spelling *plot* in l. 32 below.
    15. *children*] probably trisyllabic ('childeren').

Which here I leave in Faversham, God knows,
Needy and bare. For Christ's sake, let them have it!
Arden. Franklin, hearest thou this fellow speak?
That which he craves I dearly bought of him
Although the rent of it was ever mine.—   20
Sirrah, you that ask these questions,
If with thy clamorous impeaching tongue
Thou rail on me, as I have heard thou dost,
I'll lay thee up so close a twelvemonth's day
As thou shalt neither see the sun nor moon.   25
Look to it; for, as surely as I live,
I'll banish pity if thou use me thus.
Reede. What, wilt thou do me wrong and threat me too?
Nay, then, I'll tempt thee, Arden, do thy worst.
God, I beseech thee, show some miracle   30
On thee or thine in plaguing thee for this.
That plot of ground which thou detains from me—
I speak it in an agony of spirit—
Be ruinous and fatal unto thee!
Either there be butchered by thy dearest friends,   35
Or else be brought for men to wonder at,
Or thou or thine miscarry in that place,
Or there run mad and end thy cursèd days.
Franklin. Fie, bitter knave, bridle thine envious tongue;
For curses are like arrows shot upright,   40

27. thou] *Q1–2;* you *Q3.*   28. threat] *Q1–2, S.MS.;* threaten *Q3.*
29. Arden, do] *Qq* (Arden doo)*;* Arden; do *B–H–N.*   31. plaguing] *Q2–3;*
plauging *Q1.*   32. detains] *Q1–2;* detainest *Q3;* detain'st *Delius.*

---

22. *impeaching*] censuring, accusing.
24. *lay thee up so close*] place you in such close confinement, i.e., send you
to prison.
25. *As*] that.
29. *tempt*] provoke (one) to (see Abbott 349 on the omission of the
infinitive in Elizabethan English).
32. *detains*] withholds.
37. *miscarry*] perish; come to harm.
39. *envious*] spiteful, malicious.
40–1.] Cf. proverbs: 'Curses return upon the heads of those that

Which, falling down, light on the shooter's head.

Reede. Light where they will! Were I upon the sea,

    As oft I have in many a bitter storm,

    And saw a dreadful southern flaw at hand,

    The pilot quaking at the doubtful storm,   45

    And all the sailors praying on their knees,

    Even in that fearful time would I fall down

    And ask of God, whate'er betide of me,

    Vengeance on Arden or some misevent

    To show the world what wrong the carl hath done.   50

    This charge I'll leave with my distressful wife;

    My children shall be taught such prayers as these.

    And thus I go but leave my curse with thee.

                      Exeunt REEDE *and* Sailor.

Arden. It is the railingest knave in Christendom,

    And oftentimes the villain will be mad.   55

    It greatly matters not what he says,

    But I assure you I ne'er did him wrong.

Franklin. I think so, Master Arden.

Arden. Now that our horses are gone home before,

    My wife may haply meet me on the way;   60

    For God knows she is grown passing kind of late

---

41. shooter's] *Q3;* sutors *Q1–2;* shuters *W–P.*   48. ask] *Qq;* beg *S.MS.*
51. my] *Q1* (wy).   54. railingest] *Q1–2;* railing'st *Q3, S.MS.*   56.
what] *Qq;* whatever *conj. W–P.*   60. haply] *Q3;* hapely *Q1;* happily *Q2.*
me] *Q1–2;* not in *Q3.*

---

curse' (Tilley, C924) and 'Oftentimes the arrow hits the shooter' (Tilley,
A324).

    44. *flaw*] sudden burst of wind; squall. Cf. *2H6,* III. i. 354 ('Do calm the
fury of this mad-bred flaw').

    45. *doubtful*] fearful, dreaded.

    47. *Even*] monosyllabic (*E'en*).

    49. *misevent*] mischance.

    59.] See ix. 50.3, n.

    60.] Cf. phrasing at xii. 68 and at l. 91 below.

    61. *passing*] very, exceedingly.

    61–4.] 'Here a collapse in the metre is heralded by the actors' tag "God
knowes" (found also at [i. 485, 487; xiv. 210; and l. 16 above]) and accompanied by the duplication of "ould" and the possible recollection or antici-

And greatly changèd from the old humour
Of her wonted frowardness,
And seeks by fair means to redeem old faults.

Franklin. Happy the change that alters for the best!   65
But see in any case you make no speech
Of the cheer we had at my Lord Cheyne's
Although most bounteous and liberal,
For that will make her think herself more wronged
In that we did not carry her along;   70
For sure she grieved that she was left behind.

Arden. Come, Franklin, let us strain to mend our pace
And take her unawares playing the cook;

Here enters ALICE *and* MOSBY [*arm in arm*].

For I believe she'll strive to mend our cheer.

Franklin. Why, there's no better creatures in the world   75
Than women are when they are in good humours.

Arden. Who is that? Mosby? What, so familiar?
Injurious strumpet and thou ribald knave,
Untwine those arms.

Alice. Ay, with a sugared kiss let them untwine.   80

[*She kisses Mosby.*]

Arden. Ah, Mosby! perjured beast! Bear this and all!

62–3.] *so Qq; divided in Delius at* from / The; *in Brooke at* old / Humor.
73. her] *Q1–2; not in Q3.*   playing] *Q1–2;* to play *Q3.*   73.1.] *so Qq;*
after l. 76 Hugo.   arm in arm] *Sturgess, after Hugo and Oliphant; not*
in Qq.   75. creatures] *Q1, S.MS.;* creature *Q2–3.*   80.1.] *This ed.;*
not in Qq.

---

pation of words in the immediate context, such as "humors" in [l. 76
below] and "greatly" in [l. 56 above]' (Jackson, p. 20).

62. *humour*] temperament, disposition.
63. *frowardness*] perversity.
67. *cheer*] hospitality, reception.
72. *mend*] better, improve.
78. *Injurious*] insulting.
ribald] scurrilous, offensive.
81. *perjured beast*] See i. 326–57 and 413.
Bear . . . all!] See Abbott 399, on the ellipsis of the nominative in
Elizabethan English.

Mosby. And yet no hornèd beast; the horns are thine.

Franklin. O monstrous! Nay, then, 'tis time to draw.

[ARDEN, FRANKLIN, *and* MOSBY *draw.*]

Alice. Help! help! They murder my husband.

Here enters WILL *and* SHAKEBAG.

Shakebag. Zounds, who injures Master Mosby?   85

[*They fight.* FRANKLIN *wounds Shakebag;*
ARDEN *wounds Mosby.*]

—Help, Will! I am hurt.

Mosby. I may thank you, Mistress Arden, for this wound.

Exeunt MOSBY, WILL, *and* SHAKEBAG.

Alice. Ah, Arden, what folly blinded thee?

Ah, jealous harebrain man, what hast thou done?

When we, to welcome thee, intended sport,   90

Came lovingly to meet thee on thy way,

Thou drew'st thy sword, enraged with jealousy,

And hurt thy friend whose thoughts were free from harm—

All for a worthless kiss and joining arms,

Both done but merrily to try thy patience.   95

82.] *so Q2–3; two lines in Q1, divided at* beast, / The.   hornèd beast]
Q1–2; horne-beast *Q3.*   83.1.] *B-H-N, after Hugo; not in Qq.*
85.1–2.] *This ed., after Hugo; not in Qq.*   89. jealous] *Q3;* Jelious *Q1;*
iealious *Q2.*   harebrain] *Qq;* hair brain'd *S.MS., Tyrrell.*   done?]
Tyrrell; don, *Qq;* done! *Thorndike.*   90. thee, intended] *B-H-N;* thy
intended *Qq;* thee with intended *W-P;* thee intending *Schelling.*   92.
drew'st] *Qq;* drewest *S.MS., Tyrrell.*   93.] *so Delius; two lines in Qq,
divided at* freende, / Whose.   friend] *Qq;* friends *Sturgess.*   95.
merrily] *Q2–3;* mirrely *Q1;* merely *Sturgess, conj. W-P.*

82. *hornèd beast*] i.e., cuckold. Cf. *Oth.,* IV. i. 62 ('A horned man is a
monster and a beast'). See Intro., p. xlii.

85.1–2. S.D.] after Black Will's description, xiv. 54–67.

89. *harebrain*] For this form of the adjective, see *O.E.D.*

90. *thee*] Qq's *thy* may have resulted from the compositor's dropping his
glance to *thy* in the next line.

intended] pretended.

95. *merrily*] in jest. Alice's next line would lend support to this reading,
but there may be orthographical grounds for Warnke and Proescholdt's
suggested reading of *merely*: cf. Q1's *happely* and Q2–3's *happily* for *haply*
(i. 602 and generally throughout the text), Q1–2's *cherely* for *cheerly* (i.
585). The present reading fits the metre better.

And me unhappy that devised the jest,
Which, though begun in sport, yet ends in blood!

Franklin. Marry, God defend me from such a jest!

Alice. Couldst thou not see us friendly smile on thee
   When we joined arms and when I kissed his cheek ?   100
   Hast thou not lately found me overkind ?
   Didst thou not hear me cry they murder thee ?
   Called I not help to set my husband free ?
   No, ears and all were 'witched. Ah me accursed,
   To link in liking with a frantic man!   105
   Henceforth I'll be thy slave, no more thy wife;
   For with that name I never shall content thee.
   If I be merry, thou straightways thinks me light;
   If sad, thou sayest the sullens trouble me;
   If well attired, thou thinks I will be gadding;   110
   If homely, I seem sluttish in thine eye.
   Thus am I still, and shall be while I die,
   Poor wench abused by thy misgovernment.

Arden. But is it for truth that neither thou nor he
   Intendedst malice in your misdemeanour ?   115

Alice. The heavens can witness of our harmless thoughts.

---

96. And me] *Qq;* Aye me *Delius;* Ah me *conj. Sturgess.* 99. thee] *Qq;*
this *Jacob.* 108. thinks] *Q1–2;* thinkst *Q3;* think *Tyrrell;* think'st *Delius.*
109. sayest] *Q1–2;* sai'st *Q3;* sayst *Delius.* 110. thinks] *Q1–2;* thinkst
Q3; thinkest *S.MS.;* think'st *Delius.* 112. while] *Q2–3;* whill *Q1;* till
S.MS., Brooke. die] *Qq;* live *Tyrrell.* 113. wench abused] *Qq;*
wretch abused *S.MS.;* wench, abused *Jacob.* 114. is it] *Qq;* is't *Delius.*
neither] *Q1ᶜ(D, M);* neitheir *Q1ᵘ(H).* 115. Intendedst] *Q1* (Enten-
dedst)*; Entendest *Q2–3;* Intended *S.MS.*

---

104. *'witched*] bewitched (cf. viii. 78).
106–7.] Rubow compares Kyd's *Hovsholders Philos.*, p. 254, ll. 21–2 ('he
hath not taken her for a slaue or seruaunt, but for a fellow and companion
of his life').
109. *sullens*] gloomy disposition, sulks.
111. *homely*] plainly attired.
sluttish] untidy.
112. *still*] always.
while] until (*O.E.D.*, B. *conj.*, 3).
113. *misgovernment*] misconduct.

Arden. Then pardon me, sweet Alice, and forgive this fault.
    Forget but this and never see the like.
    Impose me penance, and I will perform it;
    For in thy discontent I find a death,   120
    A death tormenting more than death itself.

Alice. Nay, hadst thou loved me as thou dost pretend,
    Thou wouldst have marked the speeches of thy friend,
    Who going wounded from the place, he said
    His skin was pierced only through my device.   125
    And if sad sorrow taint thee for this fault,
    Thou wouldst have followed him, and seen him dressed,
    And cried him mercy whom thou hast misdone;
    Ne'er shall my heart be eased till this be done.

Arden. Content thee, sweet Alice, thou shalt have thy will,   130
    Whate'er it be. For that I injured thee
    And wronged my friend, shame scourgeth my offence.
    Come thou thyself, and go along with me,
    And be a mediator 'twixt us two.

Franklin. Why, Master Arden, know you what you do?   135
    Will you follow him that hath dishonoured you?

Alice. Why, canst thou prove I have been disloyal?

Franklin. Why, Mosby taunts your husband with the horn.

Alice. Ay, after he had reviled him
    By the injurious name of perjured beast.   140
    He knew no wrong could spite a jealous man
    More than the hateful naming of the horn.

Franklin. Suppose 'tis true, yet is it dangerous
    To follow him whom he hath lately hurt.

Alice. A fault confessed is more than half amends,   145

117.] *so Tyrrell; two lines in Qq, divided at* Ales, / And.   125. pierced]
Q1ᶜ(D, M) (peirst); peirct *Q1ᵘ(H).*   130. sweet] *Q1ᶜ(D, M);* seete
Q1ᵘ(H).   138. taunts your] *Q3;* traunt you *Q1;* taunt you *Q2;* taunt
your *S.MS.;* traunt your *Jacob;* taunted your *Delius.*   141. a] *Q3;*
an *Q1–2.*   jealous] *Q3;* Jelious *Q1;* iealious *Q2.*   143. is it] *Qq;* it is
S.MS., Sturgess.

---

   127. *dressed*] treated (for wounds).
   128. *misdone*] harmed; wronged. Cf. iii. 195.
   131. *For that*] because (see Abbott 288).

But men of such ill spirit as yourself
Work crosses and debates 'twixt man and wife.
Arden. I pray thee, gentle Franklin, hold thy peace;
I know my wife counsels me for the best.
I'll seek out Mosby where his wound is dressed   150
And salve his hapless quarrel if I may.

Exeunt ARDEN *and* ALICE.

Franklin. He whom the devil drives must go perforce.
Poor gentleman, how soon he is bewitched!
And yet, because his wife is the instrument,
His friends must not be lavish in their speech.   155

Exit FRANKLIN.

[Sc. xiv]

Here enters WILL, SHAKEBAG, *and* GREENE.

Will. Sirrah Greene, when was I so long in killing a man?
Greene. I think we shall never do it; let us give it over.
Shakebag. Nay, zounds! We'll kill him though we be hanged
at his door for our labour.
Will. Thou knowest, Greene, that I have lived in London this   5
twelve years, where I have made some go upon wooden

---

147. debates 'twixt] *Q1–2, S.MS.;* debate betwixt *Q3.*   148. thee] *Q2–3;*
the *Q1.*   149. me] *Q1–2; not in Q3.*   150.] *Q1 repeats S.H.* Ard.
151. his] *Qq;* this *S.MS.,Jacob.*   may] *Qq;* Can *S.MS.*   152. perforce
Qq; by force *S.MS.*   154. wife is] *Qq;* wife's *Tyrrell.*

Sc. xiv] *Hugo; not in Qq;* ACT V. SCENE I. *A street in* Feversham. *Tyrrell.*
0.1. SHAKEBAG] *Q1* (shakabage).   1.] *so Q1–2; as verse in Q3, divided at*
so / Long.   2.] *so Delius; as verse in Qq, divided at* it. / Let [let *Q2*].
3–4.] *so Delius; as verse in Qq, divided at* him. / Though [though *Q2*].
5–9.] *so Delius; as verse in Qq, lines ending in* / yeers. / legges, / me, / saying, /
blackwill. / blades, / Nutes.   5. this] *Qq;* these *Jacob.*

---

151. *hapless*] unfortunate.
152.] Cf. proverb: 'He must needs go that the devil drives' (Tilley,
D278).
perforce] of necessity.

Sc. xiv] See Intro., p. xxxv.
2.] Cf. xii. 64.

legs for taking the wall on me; divers with silver noses for
saying, 'There goes Black Will.' I have cracked as many
blades as thou hast done nuts.

Greene. O monstrous lie!   10

Will. Faith, in a manner I have. The bawdy-houses have paid
me tribute; there durst not a whore set up unless she have
agreed with me first for op'ning her shop windows. For a
cross word of a tapster I have pierced one barrel after
another with my dagger and held him by the ears till all   15
his beer hath run out. In Thames Street a brewer's cart
was like to have run over me; I made no more ado but
went to the clerk and cut all the notches off his tallies and
beat them about his head. I and my company have taken
the constable from his watch and carried him about the   20
fields on a coltstaff. I have broken a sergeant's head with

---

7. on] *Q1;* of *Q2–3.*   11–29.] *so Delius; as verse in Qq, lines ending* haue. /
tribute, / aggreed / windowes. / Tapster, / dager, / out, / runne / clark /
tales, / head. / watch, / coltstaffe. / mace, / buckler. / morning, / hand, /
drinke: / his / night / this, / Miracle.   13. op'ning] *Q1;* opening *Q2–3.*
15. by] *Q2–3;* be *Q1.*   16. beer] *Q2–3* (beere); beare *Q1.*   18. clerk]
Q3; clark *Q1–2.*   cut all the] *Q1, S.MS.;* cut of all the *Q2;* cut off the
Q3.   notches] *Qq* (natches).   tallies] *S.MS.* (tally's), *Jacob;* tales *Qq.*
20. him] *Q1–2; not in Q3.*

---

7. *taking the wall on me*] taking the side next to the wall, i.e., the cleaner
and safer side, and thus forcing me into the street.

silver noses] i.e., false noses.

11–13. *The bawdy-houses . . . windows*] Bayne compares *2H6,* IV. vii. 113–
16, where Jack Cade (see x. 64–5, n.) says: 'The proudest peer in the realm
shall not wear a head on his shoulders, unless he pay me tribute; there
shall not a maid be married, but she shall pay to me her maidenhead ere
they have it' (cf. *Con.,* IV. vii. 62–5).

12. *set up*] establish a business.

18. *notches*] Qq's spelling (*natches*) is a variant. Since Black Will is the
speaker here, one might observe that the habit of unrounding Middle
English short *o* to *a* was 'current among the inferior orders of the metro-
polis [London]' during this period, according to H. C. Wyld, *A History of
Modern Colloquial English,* 3rd ed. (1956), p. 240. See also collation and
commentary at vii. 26 and collation at iii. 156.

tallies] sticks on which notches were made to record accounts. (Note
Qq's spelling *tales* and see *O.E.D., Tale, sb.,* †8: an account.)

19. *company*] crew of followers.

21. *coltstaff*] (or cowl-staff): 'a pole or staff used to carry burdens, sup-

his own mace, and bailed whom I list with my sword and
buckler. All the tenpenny alehouses would stand every
morning with a quart pot in their hand, saying, 'Will it
please your worship drink?' He that had not done so had   25
been sure to have had his sign pulled down and his lattice
borne away the next night. To conclude, what have I not
done? Yet cannot do this; doubtless, he is preserved by
miracle.

Here enters ALICE *and* MICHAEL.

Greene. Hence, Will! Here comes Mistress Arden.   30
Alice. Ah, gentle Michael, art thou sure they're friends?
Michael. Why, I saw them when they both shook hands.
When Mosby bled, he even wept for sorrow
And railed on Franklin that was cause of all.
No sooner came the surgeon in at doors,   35
But my master took to his purse and gave him money,
And, to conclude, sent me to bring you word
That Mosby, Franklin, Bradshaw, Adam Fowle,
With divers of his neighbours and his friends,

---

23. alehouses] *Qq;* alehouse men *Jacob;* alehouses men *W-P.*   24. their]
Q2–3; his *Q1.*   hand] *Qq;* hands *Jacob.*   26. sign] *Q2–3* (Signe)*;*
Singne *Q1.*   29.1.] *so Qq; after l. 30 Hopkinson (2).*   32. shook] *Q1*
(shoke).   36. to] *Q1–2; not in Q3.*

---

ported on the shoulders of two bearers. . . . It was formerly a familiar
household requisite and a ready weapon' (*O.E.D.*). Falstaff, it will be
recalled, was carried out in a basket on a coltstaff (*Wiv.*, III. iii. 129 ff.).
    21–2. *I . . . mace*] Taylor compares *Con.*, IV. vii. 84, where it is said of the
captive sergeant: 'Braue [Brane? = Brain] him with his owne mace' (not
in *2H6*).
    21. *sergeant's*] referring to the officer who arrested offenders or sum-
moned them to court.
    22. *mace*] staff of office.
    list] pleased, desired.
    23. *tenpenny alehouses*] i.e., keepers of the alehouses where ale was sold
at tenpence a quart.
    26. *sign pulled down*] Cf. Will at iii. 63–4.
    lattice] An alehouse was recognized by its red- (see *2H4*, II. ii. 76–7) or
green-painted (see Jonson's *Every Man in His Humor*, III. iii. 62–3 [quarto
of 1601, ed. Herford and Simpson, vol. III, 1927]) lattice.

Will come and sup with you at our house this night.   40
Alice. Ah, gentle Michael, run thou back again;
And, when my husband walks into the fair,
Bid Mosby steal from him and come to me;
And this night shall thou and Susan be made sure.
Michael. I'll go tell him.   45
Alice. And, as thou goest, tell John cook of our guests,
And bid him lay it on; spare for no cost.   *Exit* MICHAEL.
Will. Nay, and there be such cheer, we will bid ourselves.—
Mistress Arden, Dick Greene and I do mean to sup with
you.
Alice. And welcome shall you be. Ah, gentlemen,   50
How missed you of your purpose yesternight?
Greene. 'Twas long of Shakebag, that unlucky villain.
Shakebag. Thou dost me wrong; I did as much as any.
Will. Nay then, Mistress Alice, I'll tell you how it was. When
he should have locked with both his hilts, he in a bravery   55

---

44. shall] *Q1;* shalt *Q2–3.*   46. goest] *Qq;* go'st *Hopkinson (2).*   cook]
Q1–2 (cooke)*;* Cooke *Q3.*   47. cost] *Q2–3;* coast *Q1.*   48–9.] *so Qq;
divided in Tyrrell at* ourselves. / Mistress Arden, / Dick.   48. we will]
Q1; wele *Q2,* S.MS.*;* wee'll *Q3.*   54–67.] *so Sturgess; as verse in Qq,
lines ending* was, / hilts, / head. / lustely / away, / feete, / costerd. / out /
lyfe. / fence / warde, / hand, / castell. / it. / faint. / sword, / tryce; *prose l.* 57
('away') *to l.* 65 ('tried it') *Delius; lineation as Qq in W-P except lines ending*
foole / danger. / come, / fence, / it; / castell.   54. Alice] *Qq;* Arden *W-P.*

---

42. *the fair*] i.e. of St Valentine; see Intro., p. lxviii and n. 1.
46. *John cook*] i.e., John the cook (for construction, cf. *2H4,* v. i. 9–10
and 27).
47. *lay it on*] same as 'spare for no cost' (see remainder of sentence); be
lavish in expense.
48. *and*] if.
bid] invite.
51. *missed you*] did you fail.
52. *'Twas long of*] it was on account of.
54–67.] A current of blank verse is, perhaps, perceptible in these lines
(particularly at the end, beginning with 'Mosby, perceiving this', etc.), but
in general a prose rhythm predominates; the thought itself does not call for
setting forth in verse.
55. *locked*] crossed (swords with an opponent).
hilts] sword (often used in the plural, although Sturgess suggests that
here it may refer to both 'sword and dagger').
in a bravery] with bravado.

O

flourished over his head. With that comes Franklin at him
lustily and hurts the slave; with that he slinks away. Now
his way had been to have come in hand and feet, one and
two round at his costard. He like a fool bears his sword-
point half a yard out of danger. I lie here for my life. [*He*   60
takes a position of defence.] If the devil come and he have
no more strength than fence, he shall never beat me from
this ward. I'll stand to it, a buckler in a skilful hand is as
good as a castle; nay, 'tis better than a sconce, for I have
tried it. Mosby, perceiving this, began to faint. With that   65
comes Arden with his arming-sword and thrust him
through the shoulder in a trice.

Alice. Ay, but I wonder why you both stood still.

Will. Faith, I was so amazed I could not strike.

Alice. Ah, sirs, had he yesternight been slain,   70
        For every drop of his detested blood

---

56. over] *Qq;* o'er *Delius.*   58. to have come] *Q1;* to come *Q2–3, S.MS.*
in] *This ed.; not in Qq.*   feet] *Qq;* foote *S.MS.*   60–1. S.D.] *B-H-N,*
after Hugo; not in Qq.   62. than fence] *Qq;* then I *S.MS.;* than I have
fence *W-P.*   63. ward. I'll . . . it,] *Jacob;* warde, Ile . . . it, *Qq.*   ward]
Qq; gaurd [*sic*] *S.MS.*

---

57. *lustily*] vigorously.

58. *come in*] 'to make a pass or home-thrust, to get within the opponent's
guard' in fencing (*O.E.D.*, Come, *v.* 59. †e, which cites as an example
Falstaff's 'but I followed me close, came in foot and hand' in *1H4*, II. iv.
209–10).

59. *round*] roundly; swinging.

costard] head (actually, a large apple but humorously applied to the
head).

60. *I . . . life.*] 'I take up this fencing attitude to defend my life'
(Schelling).

62. *fence*] fencing skill; the art of fencing.

63. *ward*] defensive posture; position of guard.

I'll stand to it] 'I'll maintain that.' If Tyrrell's punctuation is accepted for
Qq's ambiguous punctuation so that the phrase is part of the preceding
sentence, the meaning is: 'I'll fight doggedly to maintain it.'

64. *sconce*] small fort.

65. *this*] i.e., Shakebag's wound (Sturgess).

faint] lose courage.

66. *arming-sword*] sword with which he is armed (McIlwraith); cf. verbal
substantive *sword-armed*.

I would have crammed in angels in thy fist,
And kissed thee, too, and hugged thee in my arms.
Will. Patient yourself; we cannot help it now.
Greene and we two will dog him through the fair,   75
And stab him in the crowd, and steal away.

Here enters MOSBY [, *his arm bandaged*].

Alice. It is unpossible. But here comes he
That will, I hope, invent some surer means.—
Sweet Mosby, hide thy arm; it kills my heart.
Mosby. Ay, Mistress Arden, this is your favour.   80
Alice. Ah, say not so; for, when I saw thee hurt,
I could have took the weapon thou lett'st fall
And run at Arden, for I have sworn
That these mine eyes, offended with his sight,
Shall never close till Arden's be shut up.   85
This night I rose and walked about the chamber,
And twice or thrice I thought to have murdered him.
Mosby. What, in the night? Then had we been undone!
Alice. Why, how long shall he live?
Mosby. Faith, Alice, no longer than this night.—   90
Black Will and Shakebag, will you two
Perform the complot that I have laid?
Will. Ay, or else think me as a villain.

72. have crammed in angels] *Q3;* cramme in Angels *Q1;* have camd in angels *Q2;* have Cramed Angles into *S.MS.;* have cramm'd an angel *conj.* T. W. Craik *(privately).*   73. my] *Q1;* mine *Q2–3.*   76.1.] *so Qq; after* l. 78 *Oliphant.*   *his arm bandaged*] *Sturgess, after Hugo, Oliphant; not in Qq.*   77. unpossible] *Qq;* impossible, *S.MS., Tyrrell.*   82. took] *Qq;* taken *S.MS.*   88. had we] *Qq;* we had *Sturgess.*   91–2.] *so Qq; divided in W-P at* performe / The.   93. me as a] *Q1;* me a *Q2–3, S.MS.*

72. *angels*] coins (see ii. 86, n.).
74. *Patient yourself*] calm yourself.
80. *favour*] gift given 'to a lover . . . to be worn conspicuously as a token of affection' (*O.E.D., sb.,* 7; cf. i. 187).
84. *his sight*] i.e., the sight of him (see Abbott 218).
86. *This night*] i.e., last night.
92. *complot*] plot.
93. *as*] also (Abbott 106).

Greene. And rather than you shall want, I'll help myself.

Mosby. You, Master Greene, shall single Franklin forth   95
    And hold him with a long tale of strange news,
    That he may not come home till supper time.
    I'll fetch Master Arden home; and we, like friends,
    Will play a game or two at tables here.

Alice. But what of all this ? How shall he be slain ?   100

Mosby. Why, Black Will and Shakebag, locked within the
    countinghouse,
    Shall, at a certain watchword given, rush forth.

Will. What shall the watchword be ?

Mosby. 'Now I take you'—that shall be the word.
    But come not forth before in any case.   105

Will. I warrant you. But who shall lock me in ?

Alice. That will I do; thou'st keep the key thyself.

Mosby. Come, Master Greene, go you along with me.—
    See all things ready, Alice, against we come.

94.] *so Delius; two lines in Qq, divided at* want, / Ile.   100.] *so Tyrrell;*
two lines in Qq, divided at this ? / How.   101.] *so Qq; two lines in Delius,*
divided at Why— / Black Will.   104. 'Now . . . you'] *Qq;* Now Mr Arden
I Can take you *S.MS.*   107. do] *Q1; not in Q2–3.*   thou'st] *Q1–2;*
thou'lt *Q3.*

---

94. *want*] fail (*O.E.D., v.* 1. †d).

99. *tables*] backgammon.

101–2.] Jackson (pp. 20–1) argues as follows for emendation: 'Something should probably be eliminated. Since this is the first mention of the
scheme, the fact that it is the "countinghouse" in which Will and Shakebag
are to hide is a necessary piece of information. So "countinghouse"cannot
be the superfluous word. But "lockt within" could be dispensed with. The
phrase may anticipate "who shall lock me in" at [l. 106] and "Black Will is
lockt within" at [l. 160], following upon reference to "the countinghouse
doore" at [l. 158]. The ejaculation "Why" is extrametrical. Perhaps the
author's original read:

        Black Will and Shakebag, in the countinghouse
        Shall at a certain watchword given, rush forth.'

101. *countinghouse*] private chamber used as a business office.

104. '*Now I take you*'] i.e., to put the opponent out of the game by cap-
turing all his pieces; here, with the double meaning of *taking* Arden's life.
With S.MS.'s addition of *Can*, which regularizes the metre of the line,
cf. l. 232 below.

109. *against*] by the time that.

Alice. Take no care for that; send you him home.   110
        And, if he e'er go forth again, blame me.—

                            Exeunt MOSBY *and* GREENE.

        Come, Black Will, that in mine eyes art fair;
        Next unto Mosby do I honour thee.
        Instead of fair words and large promises
        My hands shall play you golden harmony.   115
        How like you this? Say, will you do it, sirs?

Will. Ay, and that bravely, too. Mark my device:
        Place Mosby, being a stranger, in a chair,
        And let your husband sit upon a stool,
        That I may come behind him cunningly   120
        And with a towel pull him to the ground,
        Then stab him till his flesh be as a sieve.
        That done, bear him behind the Abbey,
        That those that find him murdered may suppose
        Some slave or other killed him for his gold.   125

Alice. A fine device! You shall have twenty pound,
        And, when he is dead, you shall have forty more;
        And, lest you might be suspected staying here,
        Michael shall saddle you two lusty geldings.
        Ride whither you will, to Scotland or to Wales,   130

111.1.] *so Hugo; after l. 110 Qq.*   112. mine] *Q1–2;* my *Q3.*   122. stab
him till] *Qq;* stab him fine till *Bullen.*   as] *Qq;* like *S.MS.*   sieve] *Q2*
(siue), *Q3* (sive); sine *Q1.*

---

110. *Take . . . for*] do not worry about.

115. *My . . . harmony*] i.e., I'll give you money.

117. *bravely*] splendidly.

118–19.] an interesting commentary, so it seems, on the sparse furnish-
ings of even a well-to-do Elizabethan gentleman's household. In *English
Decoration and Furniture of the Early Renaissance (1500–1650)* (1924), p.
241, M. Jourdain observes: 'This scarcity of chairs is due to their rarity
during the early Renaissance. Stools and forms outnumbered the chairs in
hall and parlour until the Restoration. . . . In domestic use the chair was the
rightful seat of the master of the house, only given up by courtesy.'

122. *sieve*] Sturgess suggests that *seine* (Q1's *sine*), a fishing-net, 'is
marginally possible'. (*O.E.D.* notes 1623 Folio spelling of *All's W.,* I. iii.
193: 'Yet in this captious, and intemible [intenible: unretentive] Siue'.)

126. *A fine device!*] Cf. xii. 74.

126–7. *You . . . more;*] Cf. i. 522–3, 568–9; ii. 103–4.

I'll see you shall not lack where'er you be.

Will. Such words would make one kill a thousand men!
Give me the key. Which is the countinghouse?

Alice. Here would I stay and still encourage you,
But that I know how resolute you are.   135

Shakebag. Tush! You are too faint-hearted; we must do it.

Alice. But Mosby will be there, whose very looks
Will add unwonted courage to my thought
And make me the first that shall adventure on him.

Will. Tush, get you gone! 'Tis we must do the deed.   140
When this door opens next, look for his death.

        [*Exeunt* WILL *and* SHAKEBAG.]

Alice. Ah, would he now were here, that it might open!
I shall no more be closed in Arden's arms,
That like the snakes of black Tisiphone
Sting me with their embracings. Mosby's arms   145

---

132. a thousand] *Q3;* 1000. *Q1–2.* 141.1] *W-P; not in Qq; Exeunt* WILL
and SHAKEBAG *into the countinghouse. Oliphant (after Hugo);* Will *and*
Shakebag *retire. McIlwraith.* 145. embracings] *Q2–3;* enbraceings *Q1;*
Imbracing *S.MS.*

---

139. *adventure*] i.e., venture.

141.1.] The preceding line, as well as l. 160 below, makes it clear that
Will and Shakebag leave through one of the stage doors which serves as the
entrance to the countinghouse and behind which presumably they listen to
the ensuing dialogue until they reappear at the start of the game of 'tables'
at ll. 225.1–2. Mrs Diane Davidson, author of the novel *Feversham* (1969),
observes, in private correspondence with the editor, that if the playwright
actually knew Faversham or Arden's House he would have made use of the
trap door because local tradition, as well as some odd wording in the
Harley MSS. ('Than they toke hym and caried hym away to lay hym in the
countynge howse and w^t ye beringe of hym downe'; see Intro., pp. xli–xliii)
that could be interpreted differently from Holinshed, places the countinghouse in the *cellar* of Arden's House. Instead of *laying* 'the body in the
countinghouse' (l. 248.1), a much more melodramatic effect could have
been achieved by lowering the body!

144. *Tisiphone*] One of the Furies or avengers of crime, especially crime
against kin, she was represented with a whip in her hand, a serpent in her
hair, and snakes encircling her arms. Anticipating as it does the final
moments of the play, it is an extremely ironic image for Alice Arden to use
since the *embracings* of Tisiphone's snakes awakened remorse by *stinging*
the conscience. Cf. *E2*, 2031–2 ('Or like the snakie wreathe of *Tisiphon,* /
Engirt the temples of his hatefull head').

Shall compass me; and, were I made a star,
I would have none other spheres but those.
There is no nectar but in Mosby's lips!
Had chaste Diana kissed him, she like me
Would grow lovesick and from her wat'ry bower   150
Fling down Endymion and snatch him up.
Then blame not me that slay a silly man
Not half so lovely as Endymion.

Here enters MICHAEL.

Michael. Mistress, my master is coming hard by.
Alice. Who comes with him?   155
Michael. Nobody but Mosby.
Alice. That's well, Michael. Fetch in the tables; and, when
        thou hast done, stand before the countinghouse door.
Michael. Why so?
Alice. Black Will is locked within to do the deed.   160
Michael. What? Shall he die tonight?
Alice. Ay, Michael.
Michael. But shall not Susan know it?
Alice. Yes, for she'll be as secret as ourselves.
Michael. That's brave! I'll go fetch the tables.   165

150. wat'ry] *Qq*; watery *S.MS., Tyrrell.*   151. snatch] *Q2-3*; snath *Q1.*
153.1.] *Qq*; ACT V. SCENE II. *A Room in* Arden's *House. Enter* Michael *and*
Alice. *Tyrrell.*   157-8.] *so Delius; as verse in Qq, divided at* tables, / And;
lines ending in Sturgess at tables, / done, / door.   161. Shall] *Q1* (shull).

149-53.] An extravagant comparison of Mosby, described by Holinshed
as 'a blacke swart man', to Endymion, the most beautiful of men who was
so passionately loved by Diana, the moon-goddess, that she descended from
her 'wat'ry bower' (i.e., the moon, cradled—it was believed—in the ocean)
every night to embrace him as he slept naked on Mount Latmos. The myth
was the subject of Lyly's play of 1585-8, *Endimion, The Man in Moone*
(pub. 1591), for the Children of Paul's. In the same passage from Marlowe's
translation of Ovid quoted in i. 60-4, n., we read the following (ll. 43-4):
        The Moone sleepes with *Endymion* euery day,
        Thou art as faire as she, then kisse and play.
152. *silly*] foolish.
154. *hard by*] 'close at hand in time' (*O.E.D.*).
157. *tables*] the dice-board for backgammon.
165. *brave*] splendid.

Alice. But, Michael, hark to me a word or two:
When my husband is come in, lock the street door;
He shall be murdered or the guests come in.—

                                   Exit MICHAEL [*and re-enters shortly*
                                                  with the tables].

                   Here enters ARDEN *and* MOSBY.

Husband, what mean you to bring Mosby home?
Although I wished you to be reconciled,   170
'Twas more for fear of you than love of him.
Black Will and Greene are his companions,
And they are cutters and may cut you short;
Therefore, I thought it good to make you friends.
But wherefore do you bring him hither now?   175
You have given me my supper with his sight.

Mosby. Master Arden, methinks your wife would have me gone.

Arden. No, good Master Mosby, women will be prating.—
Alice, bid him welcome; he and I are friends.

Alice. You may enforce me to it if you will,   180
But I had rather die than bid him welcome.
His company hath purchased me ill friends,
And therefore will I ne'er frequent it more.

---

168. or] *Q1–2;* ere *Q3, S.MS.;* or e'er *Jacob;* or ere *Delius.*   168.1–2.
and . . . tables] *Sturgess; not in Qq.*   170. Although] *Q2–3;* Althought *Q1.*
178. prating] *Q1;* pratling *Q2;* prattling *Q3.*   180. will] *Qq;* please
S.MS.   181. than bid] *Q1–2;* than to bid *Q3.*

167–8.] The repetition of 'come in' in the second line is suspect.
168. *or*] before.
171. *of you*] for you.
172. *Greene*] Sturgess rightly observes that 'one would expect "Shakebag", not "Greene", at this point' since 'Greene is not a "cutter", and it
was Shakebag, not Greene, involved with Mosby and Black Will in the
scuffle of scene xiii.' But, as Sturgess goes on to point out, '"Greene"
better suits the rhythm of the line'.
     companions] tetrasyllabic.
174. *make you friends*] Cf. phrasing at l. 199 below.
176.] i.e., the mere sight of Mosby takes my appetite away.
180. *enforce*] compel.
182.] Cf. l. 209 below.

Mosby. [*Aside*] O, how cunningly she can dissemble!

Arden. Now he is here, you will not serve me so.   185

Alice. I pray you be not angry or displeased;
    I'll bid him welcome, seeing you'll have it so.—
    You are welcome, Master Mosby. Will you sit down?

      [MOSBY *sits down in chair facing the countinghouse door.*]

Mosby. I know I am welcome to your loving husband,
    But for yourself you speak not from your heart.   190

Alice. And if I do not, sir, think I have cause.

Mosby. Pardon me, Master Arden; I'll away.

Arden. No, good Master Mosby.

Alice. We shall have guests enough though you go hence.

Mosby. I pray you, Master Arden, let me go.   195

Arden. I pray thee, Mosby, let her prate her fill.

Alice. The doors are open, sir; you may be gone.

Michael. [*Aside*] Nay, that's a lie, for I have locked the doors.

Arden. Sirrah, fetch me a cup of wine; I'll make them friends.—

                        [*Exit* MICHAEL.]

    And, gentle Mistress Alice, seeing you are so stout,   200
    You shall begin. Frown not; I'll have it so.

Alice. I pray you meddle with that you have to do.

Arden. Why, Alice, how can I do too much for him
    Whose life I have endangered without cause?

      [*Re-enter* MICHAEL *with wine.*]

Alice. 'Tis true; and, seeing 'twas partly through my means,   205
    I am content to drink to him for this once.—
    Here, Master Mosby! And, I pray you, henceforth
    Be you as strange to me as I to you.

---

184. *Aside*] *Tyrrell; not in Qq.*   188.1.] *This ed., after Gassner; not in Qq.*
192. Master] *Jacob;* M. *Q1–2;* mistris *Q3;* Mʳ *S.MS.*   198. *Aside*]
Tyrrell; not in Qq.   199.] *so Delius; two lines in Qq, divided at* Wine. / Ile.
199.1.] *Gassner; not in Qq.*   204.1.] *Gassner; not in Qq;* Michel
apporte du vin. *Hugo (after l. 199).*   208. you (1)] *Q1; not in Q2–3,
S.MS.*

---

191. *And if*] if.
200. *stout*] stubborn, obstinate.
201. *shall begin*] i.e., the toasting by drinking to Mosby (cf. l. 206).

Frontispiece to the 1633 Quarto, illustrating the murder of Arden at the 'game of tables'

Your company hath purchased me ill friends,
And I for you, God knows, have undeserved   210
Been ill spoken of in every place;
Therefore, henceforth frequent my house no more.

Mosby. I'll see your husband in despite of you.—
Yet, Arden, I protest to thee by heaven,
Thou ne'er shalt see me more after this night.   215
I'll go to Rome rather than be forsworn.

Arden. Tush, I'll have no such vows made in my house.

Alice. Yes, I pray you, husband, let him swear;
And, on that condition, Mosby, pledge me here.

Mosby. Ay, as willingly as I mean to live.   [*He and* ALICE *drink.*]

Arden. Come, Alice, is our supper ready yet?   221

Alice. It will by then you have played a game at tables.

Arden. Come, Master Mosby, what shall we play for?

Mosby. Three games for a French crown, sir, and please you.

Arden. Content.   [*He sits down on stool opposite Mosby.*]
                            Then they play at the tables.

[*Re-enter* WILL *and* SHAKEBAG *from behind Arden.*]

Will. [*Aside*] Can he not take him yet? What a spite is that!   226

---

210. undeserved] *Qq;* undeservedly *S.MS.*   216. than be] *Q1–2;* then
to be *Q3.*   219. Mosby] *Q1; not in Q2–3.*   220. S.D.] *This ed.; not in
Qq.*   222. game at] *Qq;* Game or two at *S.MS.*   224.] *so Delius; two
lines in Qq, divided at* sir, / And.   225. S.D.] *This ed.; not in Qq.*
225.2.] *This ed., after W-P; not in Qq.*   226, 227, 228, 229. Aside] *Hugo,
W-P; not in Qq.*   226. he] *Qq;* we *Hopkinson* (3).

209.] See l. 182 above.
210. *undeserved*] undeservedly.
219. *pledge me*] (give me assurance by) drinking to me.
221–5.] Cf. Holinshed, App. II, p. 154.
222. *then*] by the time (that).
224. *French crown*] See iii. 73, n.
and please you] if it please you.
225.1. ff.] As they were playing, 'Michaell maister Ardens man', Holinshed writes, 'stood at his masters backe, holding a candle in his hand, to
shadow blacke Will, that Arden might by no meanes perceiue him comming
foorth' (App. II, p. 155).
226. *take*] See l. 104 above, and n.

Alice. [*Aside*] Not yet, Will. Take heed he see thee not.

Will. [*Aside*] I fear he will spy me as I am coming.

Michael. [*Aside*] To prevent that, creep betwixt my legs.

Mosby. One ace, or else I lose the game. [*He throws the dice.*] 230

Arden. Marry, sir, there's two for failing.

Mosby. Ah, Master Arden, 'Now I can take you.'

                    Then WILL *pulls him down with a towel.*

Arden. Mosby! Michael! Alice! What will you do ?

Will. Nothing but take you up, sir, nothing else.

Mosby. There's for the pressing iron you told me of.   235

                                   [*He stabs Arden.*]

Shakebag. And there's for the ten pound in my sleeve.

                                   [*He stabs him.*]

Alice. What, groans thou ?—Nay, then give me the weapon!—
Take this for hind'ring Mosby's love and mine.

                                   [*She stabs him.*]

---

230. S.D.] *Sturgess; not in Qq.*   232. Ah] *Qq;* Ay *Sturgess.*   235.1,
236.1, 238.1.] *Tyrrell; not in Qq.*   237. groans] *Q1–2;* gronest *Q3.*
238. hind'ring] *Qq;* hindering *S.MS., Tyrrell.*

227–32.1.] Cf. dialogue of the two murderers in the anonymous *Wood-stock*, v. i. 213–19:

    1st M. Creep close to his back, ye rogue, be ready with the towel, when
        I have knocked him down, to strangle him.
    2nd M. Do it quickly whilst his back is towards ye, ye damned villain:
        If thou lett'st him speak but a word, we shall not kill him.
    1st M. I'll watch him for that, down on your knees and creep, ye rascal.
    230. *ace*] i.e., on the dice.

231. *for failing*] i.e., if one is not enough (for you to win). (*For* = 'to prevent'.)

234. *take you up*] settle with you (playing on the catchword).

235.] See i. 313. The playwright does not seem to be following his source, which has Mosby attack Arden *with* his pressing iron (see Holinshed, App. II, p. 155, and also the Wardmote Book of Faversham, App.III, p. 161).

237. *groans thou ?*] '. . . as they were about to laie him downe, the pangs of death comming on him, he gaue a great grone' (Holinshed). Symonds (p. 458) compares Lady Macbeth: 'Infirm of purpose! / Give me the daggers' (*Mac.*, II. ii. 52–3).

238.1. She stabs him] Cf. Holinshed: 'After that blacke Will was gone, mistresse Arden came into the counting house, and with a knife gaue him seuen or eight p[r]icks into the brest.' The Wardmote Book records no such action.

Michael. O, mistress!   [ARDEN *dies.*]

Will. Ah, that villain will betray us all.   240

Mosby. Tush, fear him not; he will be secret.

Michael. Why, dost thou think I will betray myself?

Shakebag. In Southwark dwells a bonny northern lass,
The widow Chambley. I'll to her house now;
And, if she will not give me harborough,   245
I'll make booty of the quean even to her smock.

Will. Shift for yourselves; we two will leave you now.

Alice. First lay the body in the countinghouse.

> *Then they lay the body in the countinghouse.*

Will. We have our gold. Mistress Alice, adieu;
Mosby, farewell; and, Michael, farewell too.   250

> *Exeunt* [WILL *and* SHAKEBAG].

> *Enter* SUSAN.

Susan. Mistress, the guests are at the doors. [*Knocking.*]
Hearken! They knock. What, shall I let them in?

Alice. Mosby, go thou and bear them company.—   *Exit* MOSBY.
And, Susan, fetch water and wash away this blood.

> [*Exit* SUSAN, *returns with pail of water*
> *and begins washing the floor.*]

Susan. The blood cleaveth to the ground and will not out.   255

Alice. But with my nails I'll scrape away the blood.—

> [*She tries to scrape away the stain.*]

239. S.D.] *Hugo* (Arden *expire*); *not in Qq.*   245. And] *Q2–3;* Ind *Q1.*
harborough] *Qq;* harbour *S.MS., Tyrrell.*   246. I'll make] *Qq;* Ile to
her, and make *S.MS.*   250.1. WILL *and* SHAKEBAG] *Hugo; not in Qq.*
251. S.D.] *This ed.; not in Qq.*   252. Hearken! They] *This ed.;* Hearken,
they *Q3;* Hearken they *Q1–2.*   254. this] *Qq;* yᵉ *S.MS.;* the *Jacob.*
254.1–2.] *This ed., after Sturgess, Oliphant; not in Qq.*   255. cleaveth]
Qq; cleaves *Delius.*   256.1.] *This ed., after Oliphant; not in Qq.*

243. *Southwark*] 'a borough, formerly independent of the London city
government,' south of the Thames between Lambeth and Deptford in the
county of Surrey; 'the highway from London to the South was the Old
Kent Road and the Borough High Street' (Sugden).

245. *harborough*] harbour, shelter.

246. *quean*] strumpet, wench.

254–7.] Clark compares *Mac.,* II. ii. 60–1 ('Will all great Neptune's ocean
wash this blood / Clean from my hand?').

The more I strive, the more the blood appears!
Susan. What's the reason, Mistress, can you tell?
Alice. Because I blush not at my husband's death.

Here enters MOSBY.

Mosby. How now, what's the matter? Is all well?   260
Alice. Ay, well, if Arden were alive again!
      In vain we strive, for here his blood remains.
Mosby. Why, strew rushes on it, can you not?
      This wench doth nothing.—[*To Susan.*] Fall unto the work.
Alice. 'Twas thou that made me murder him.
Mosby.   What of that?   265
Alice. Nay, nothing, Mosby, so it be not known.
Mosby. Keep thou it close, and 'tis unpossible.
Alice. Ah, but I cannot. Was he not slain by me?
      My husband's death torments me at the heart.
Mosby. It shall not long torment thee, gentle Alice.   270
      I am thy husband; think no more of him.

Here enters ADAM FOWLE *and* BRADSHAW.

Bradshaw. How now, Mistress Arden? What ail you weep?
Mosby. Because her husband is abroad so late.
      A couple of ruffians threat'ned him yesternight,
      And she, poor soul, is afraid he should be hurt.   275
Adam. Is't nothing else? Tush, he'll be here anon.

Here enters GREENE.

Greene. Now, Mistress Arden, lack you any guests?

265. made] *Q1–2;* madest *Q3.*   267. unpossible] *Qq;* Impossible *S.MS.,*
Tyrrell.   272, 277, 353. Mistress] *Q1–2* (M.)*;* Mrs. *Q3.*   275. she,
poor soul,] *Qq* (she poore soule)*;* the poore soule *Bullen.*

---

263. *rushes*] 'Down to the seventeenth century green rushes were commonly employed for strewing on the floors' (*O.E.D.*). Cf. proverb: 'Strew
green rushes for the stranger' (Tilley, R213).
      267. *close*] secret.
      272. *What ail you weep?*] i.e., What ails you that you weep? Cf. l. 301
below.
      273. *abroad*] out, in public.

Alice. Ah, Master Greene, did you see my husband lately?

Greene. I saw him walking behind the Abbey even now.

Here enters FRANKLIN.

Alice. I do not like this being out so late.—   280

Master Franklin, where did you leave my husband?

Franklin. Believe me, I saw him not since morning.

Fear you not; he'll come anon. Meantime,

You may do well to bid his guests sit down.

Alice. Ay, so they shall.—Master Bradshaw, sit you there;   285

I pray you be content, I'll have my will.—

Master Mosby, sit you in my husband's seat.

[MOSBY *sits down on the chair, the guests on stools.*]

Michael. [*Aside*] Susan, shall thou and I wait on them?

Or, and thou say'st the word, let us sit down too.

Susan. [*Aside*] Peace, we have other matters now in hand.   290

I fear me, Michael, all will be bewrayed.

Michael. [*Aside*] Tush, so it be known that I shall marry thee

in the morning, I care not though I be hanged ere night.

But to prevent the worst I'll buy some ratsbane.

Susan. [*Aside*] Why, Michael, wilt thou poison thyself?   295

Michael. [*Aside*] No, but my mistress, for I fear she'll tell.

Susan. [*Aside*] Tush, Michael, fear not her; she's wise enough.

287.1.] *This ed.; not in Qq.*   288, 290, 292, 295, 296, 297. *Aside*] *Hugo,
W-P; not in Qq.*   289. say'st] *Qq* (saist); sayest *Tyrrell.*   291.
bewrayed] *Qq* (bewraied); betrayed *S.MS., Tyrrell.*   292–4.] *so Delius;
as verse in Qq, lines ending* the / night. / rats bane.   294. buy] *Q3*; by *Q1–2.*
some ratsbane] *Q1c(D, M)* (some rats bane); some, rats bane *Q1u(H).*

279. *behind the Abbey*] Cf. l. 123 above and l. 377 below.

280–3. *I . . . anon.*] Cf. Holinshed, App. II, p. 156: 'After supper, mistres
Arden caused hir daughter to plaie on the virginals, and they dansed, and
she with them, and so seemed to protract time as it were, till maister Arden
should come, and she said, I maruell where he is so long; well, he will come
anon I am sure.'

292–3. *Tush . . . night*] Cf. proverbs: 'Some laugh in the morning that
weep at night' (Tilley, M1176) and 'Wedding and hanging go by destiny'
(Tilley, W232).

291. *bewrayed*] revealed, betrayed, exposed.

294. *to prevent the worst*] Cf. i. 383.

ratsbane] rat-poison; arsenic.

Mosby. Sirrah Michael, give's a cup of beer.—
Mistress Arden, here's to your husband.

Alice. My husband!   300

Franklin. What ails you, woman, to cry so suddenly?

Alice. Ah, neighbours, a sudden qualm came over my heart;
My husband's being forth torments my mind.
I know something's amiss; he is not well,
Or else I should have heard of him ere now.   305

Mosby. [*Aside*] She will undo us through her foolishness.

Greene. Fear not, Mistress Arden; he's well enough.

Alice. Tell not me; I know he is not well.
He was not wont for to stay thus late.—
Good Master Franklin, go and seek him forth,   310
And, if you find him, send him home to me,
And tell him what a fear he hath put me in.

Franklin. [*Aside*] I like not this; I pray God all be well.—
I'll seek him out and find him if I can.

                    Exeunt FRANKLIN, MOSBY, *and* GREENE.

Alice. [*Aside*] Michael, how shall I do to rid the rest away?   315

Michael. [*Aside*] Leave that to my charge; let me alone.—
'Tis very late, Master Bradshaw,
And there are many false knaves abroad,
And you have many narrow lanes to pass.

Bradshaw. Faith, friend Michael, and thou sayest true.   320

---

298. give's] *Qq; give us Jacob.*   301. ails] *Q1ᶜ(D, M)* (ailes); Ales *Q1ᵘ(H).*
302. over] *Qq;* o'er *Tyrrell.*   303. husband's] *Q1–2;* husband *Q3.*
being] *Q3;* beeing *Q2;* deing *Q1.*   forth] *Qq;* out *S.MS.*   306. *Aside*]
S.MS., Hugo; not in Qq.   307. he's] *Qq;* he is *S.MS., Tyrrell.*   313.
Aside] *W-P; not in Qq.*   314.1.] *so Tyrrell; after l. 313 Qq.*   315, 316.
Aside] *Hugo; not in Qq.*   319. narrow] *Q1–2; not in Q3.*

301–2.] Crawford compares *S. & P.,* II. i. 49–50:
Lucina. What ailes you, madam, that your colour changes?
Perseda. A suddaine qualme, . . .
Taylor, however, compares *Con.,* I. i. 49–50:
King. How now vnkle, whats the matter that you stay so sodenly.
Humphrey. Pardon my Lord, a sodain qualme came ouer my hart.
(Cf. last line with *2H6,* I. i. 51: 'Some sudden qualm hath struck me at the
heart'.)

Therefore I pray thee light's forth and lend's a link.

Alice. Michael, bring them to the doors, but do not stay;
    You know I do not love to be alone.—

                    Exeunt BRADSHAW, ADAM, *and* MICHAEL.

Go, Susan, and bid thy brother come.

But wherefore should he come? Here is nought but fear.   325

Stay, Susan, stay, and help to counsel me.

Susan. Alas, I counsel! Fear frights away my wits.

                    Then they open the countinghouse door
                    and look upon Arden.

Alice. See, Susan, where thy quondam master lies,
    Sweet Arden, smeared in blood and filthy gore.

Susan. My brother, you, and I shall rue this deed.   330

Alice. Come, Susan, help to lift his body forth,
    And let our salt tears be his obsequies.

                    [*They bring forth his body.*]

                Here enters MOSBY *and* GREENE.

Mosby. How now, Alice, whither will you bear him?

Alice. Sweet Mosby, art thou come? Then weep that will;
    I have my wish in that I joy thy sight.   335

Greene. Well, it 'hoves us to be circumspect.

Mosby. Ay, for Franklin thinks that we have murdered him.

Alice. Ay, but he cannot prove it for his life.
    We'll spend this night in dalliance and in sport.

                Here enters MICHAEL.

323.1.] *so Hugo; after l. 321 Qq.*   325. Here is] *Q1–2;* here's *Q3, S.MS.*
329. filthy] *Q1; not in Q2–3, S.MS.*   332.1.] *This ed., after Sturgess; not*
in Qq.   334.] *so Delius; two lines in Qq, divided at* come? | Then.
336. 'hoves] *Qq;* behoves *S.MS., Delius.*   us to] *Qq;* us for to
Tyrrell.

---

321. *link*] torch.
326. *Stay . . . stay*] Cf. i. 121 and iii. 135; see Intro., pp. xxvii–xxviii.
328. *quondam*] former.
335.] Cf. identically worded line in *E2*, 151.
joy] enjoy, takes pleasure in.
336. *'hoves*] behoves.

P

Michael. O mistress, the mayor and all the watch   340
   Are coming towards our house with glaives and bills.
Alice. Make the door fast; let them not come in.
Mosby. Tell me, sweet Alice, how shall I escape?
Alice. Out at the back door, over the pile of wood,
   And for one night lie at the Flower-de-Luce.   345
Mosby. That is the next way to betray myself.
Greene. Alas, Mistress Arden, the watch will take me here
   And cause suspicion where else would be none.
Alice. Why, take that way that Master Mosby doth;
   But first convey the body to the fields.   350
      Then they [MOSBY, GREENE, SUSAN, *and* MICHAEL]
        bear the body into the fields [*and then return*].
Mosby. Until tomorrow, sweet Alice, now farewell;
   And see you confess nothing in any case.
Greene. Be resolute, Mistress Alice; betray us not,
   But cleave to us as we will stick to you.
                 Exeunt MOSBY *and* GREENE.

340. all] *Q1–2; not in Q3.*   341. glaives] *Qq;* Staves *S.MS.*   346. next]
Qq; first *S.MS.*   350.1–2. *additions to* S.D.] *Sturgess, after Hugo;*
Susan *and* Michael *carry out the body.* Oliphant.   354.1.] *Qq; Exeunt*
MOSBIE, GREENE, MICHAEL *and* SUSAN *bearing away the body. Hopkinson*
(2).

340–1. *the mayor ... coming*] Cf. difference in Holinshed (App. II, pp.
156–7): 'Then she began to make an outcrie, and said; Neuer woman had
such neighbors as I haue, and herewith wept: in somuch that hir neighbors
came in, and found hir making great lamentation, pretending to maruell
what was become of hir husband. Wherevpon, the maior and others came
to make search for him.'
341. *glaives and bills*] broadswords and halberds.
345. *lie*] lodge.
346. *next*] quickest, most direct.
350.1–2.] Holinshed writes (App. II, p. 156): 'Then they tooke the dead
bodie, and caried it out, to laie it in a field next to the church-yard, and
ioining to his garden wall, through the which he went to the church.' In the
Wardmote Book of Faversham, Cecily Pounder, Mosby's sister, after
having given Black Will his reward, 'went to thesaid Arderns / and did
help to beare the deade corps out into A medowe there comonly called
the Amery croft on the backside of thesaid Arderns Garden' (App. III,
p. 161). On the inexplicitness of the original stage direction, see Intro.,
p. xxx.

Alice. Now let the judge and juries do their worst;   355
    My house is clear, and now I fear them not.

Susan. As we went, it snowèd all the way,
    Which makes me fear our footsteps will be spied.

Alice. Peace, fool! The snow will cover them again.

Susan. But it had done before we came back again.   [*Knocking.*]

Alice. Hark, hark, they knock! Go, Michael, let them in.—   361
                          [MICHAEL *opens the door.*]

    Here enters the Mayor *and the* Watch.

How now, Master Mayor, have you brought my husband
    home?

Mayor. I saw him come into your house an hour ago.

Alice. You are deceived; it was a Londoner.

Mayor. Mistress Arden, know you not one that is called
    Black Will?   365

Alice. I know none such. What mean these questions?

Mayor. I have the Council's warrant to apprehend him.

Alice. [*Aside*] I am glad it is no worse.—
    Why, Master Mayor, think you I harbour any such?

Mayor. We are informed that here he is;   370
    And, therefore, pardon us, for we must search.

Alice. Ay, search, and spare you not, through every room.

---

360. S.D.] *This ed., after Hugo; not in Qq.*   361.] *so Delius; two lines in
Qq, divided at* knocke, / go.   361.1.] *This ed.; not in Qq.*   364. deceived
. . . was] *Qq;* Mistaken S^r twas *S.MS.*   365.] *so Delius; two lines in
Qq, divided at* one / That [That *Q3*].   368–9.] *so Qq; divided in Sturgess
at* Mayor, / Think.   368. *Aside*] *Tyrrell; not in Qq.*

355–60.] See Intro., pp. xlii–xliii.

357.] Cf. Holinshed, App. II, p. 156.

360. *done*] stopped.

362. *Master Mayor*] The mayor of Faversham at this time was one
William Marshall (Jacob, *History,* p. 121).

364. *a Londoner*] In Holinshed, after the murder takes place, Mistress
Arden 'sent for two Londoners to supper, the one named Prune, and the
other Cole, that were grosers' (App. II, pp. 155–6).

365. *that is called*] Jackson (p. 16) thinks this phrase may be a reporter's
interpolation.

366. *questions*] trisyllabic.

Were my husband at home, you would not offer this.—

Here enters FRANKLIN.

Master Franklin, what mean you come so sad ?
Franklin. Arden, thy husband and my friend, is slain.   375
Alice. Ah, by whom ? Master Franklin, can you tell ?
Franklin. I know not, but behind the Abbey
    There he lies murdered in most piteous case.
Mayor. But, Master Franklin, are you sure 'tis he ?
Franklin. I am too sure; would God I were deceived!   380
Alice. Find out the murderers; let them be known.
Franklin. Ay, so they shall. Come you along with us.
Alice. Wherefore ?
Franklin.   Know you this hand-towel and this knife ?
Susan. [*Aside*] Ah, Michael, through this thy negligence
    Thou hast betrayèd and undone us all.   385
Michael. [*Aside*] I was so afraid I knew not what I did.
    I thought I had thrown them both into the well.
Alice [*to Franklin*]. It is the pig's blood we had to supper.
    But wherefore stay you ? Find out the murderers.
Mayor. I fear me you'll prove one of them yourself.   390
Alice. I one of them ? What mean such questions ?
Franklin. I fear me he was murdered in this house
    And carried to the fields, for from that place
    Backwards and forwards may you see

379. you] *Q1–2; not in Q3.*   381, 389. murderers] *Q3;* murtherers *Q2;*
Murthrers *Q1.*   384, 386. Aside] *Tyrrell; not in Qq.*   388. S.D.]
This ed., after Hugo; not in Qq.   391. questions] *Q1ᶜ(D, M);* questiones
Q1ᵘ(H).   392, 399. murdered] *Q3;* murthered *Q2;* murthred *Q1.*
394. you see] *Qq;* you plainly see *S.MS.*   see] *Q1ᶜ(D, M)* (see,);* see.
Q1ᵘ(H).

373.] In Holinshed, the mayor and the watch, not Franklin, search for
and find the body and incriminating evidence.

378. *piteous case*] lamentable state.

383. *Know . . . knife ?*] The hand-towel ('clout' or cloth in the source) and
knife are mentioned in Holinshed, but the Wardmote Book omits these
details.

388. *to*] at, for.

389. *Find . . . murderers*] Jackson (p. 19) suggests omitting *out,* which
may have been recalled from l. 381 above.

    The print of many feet within the snow.   395
    And look about this chamber where we are,
    And you shall find part of his guiltless blood;
    For in his slipshoe did I find some rushes,
    Which argueth he was murdered in this room.

Mayor. Look in the place where he was wont to sit.—   400
    See, see! His blood! It is too manifest.

Alice. It is a cup of wine that Michael shed.

Michael. Ay, truly.

Franklin. It is his blood, which, strumpet, thou hast shed.
    But, if I live, thou and thy complices   405
    Which have conspired and wrought his death shall rue it.

Alice. Ah, Master Franklin, God and heaven can tell
    I loved him more than all the world beside.
    But bring me to him; let me see his body.

Franklin [*pointing to Michael and Susan*]. Bring that villain
       and Mosby's sister too;   410
    And one of you go to the Flower-de-Luce,
    And seek for Mosby, and apprehend him too.   *Exeunt.*

[Sc. xv]

       Here enters SHAKEBAG *solus.*

Shakebag. The widow Chambley in her husband's days I kept;
    And, now he's dead, she is grown so stout

396. this] *Qq;* the *Sturgess.*   chamber] *Q1ᶜ(D, M), Q3;* chambor
Q1ᵘ(H), Q2.   406.] *so Delius; two lines in Qq, divided at* death, / Shall.
410. S.D.] *This ed., after Hugo; not in Qq.*   412. too] *Qq; omitted
Jacob.*

Sc. xv] *Hugo; not in Qq;* ACT V. SCENE III. *An obscure street in* London.
Tyrrell; ACT V. SCENE II. *Delius;* Le faubourg de Southwark. *Hugo.*
1–2.] *so Qq; divided in Delius at* days / I.   2. he's] *Qq;* he is *S.MS.*
she is] *Qq;* she's *Delius;* she has *Tyrrell.*

    398. *slipshoe*] slipper.
    401.] Cf. both Holinshed, App. II, p. 157, and the Wardmote Book,
App. III, p. 161.
    405. *complices*] accomplices.

    xv. o.1. *solus*] alone.
    1. *The widow Chambley*] Cust (p. 126) thinks that there may be an 'in-

She will not know her old companions.
I came thither, thinking to have had
Harbour as I was wont,   5
And she was ready to thrust me out at doors.
But, whether she would or no, I got me up;
And, as she followed me, I spurned her down the stairs,
And broke her neck, and cut her tapster's throat;
And now I am going to fling them in the Thames.   10
I have the gold; what care I though it be known?
I'll cross the water and take sanctuary.   *Exit* SHAKEBAG.

[Sc. xvi]

> *Here enters the* Mayor, MOSBY, ALICE, FRANKLIN,
> MICHAEL, *and* SUSAN [, *guarded by the* Watch].

Mayor. See, Mistress Arden, where your husband lies.
Confess this foul fault and be penitent.

4–5.] *so Qq; divided in Delius at* harbour / As.   4. thither] *Qq;* hither
Sturgess.   7. got] *Q1–2;* goe *Q3.*   8. spurned] *Q1* (spurnd); spurd *Q2;*
spur'd *Q3.*   10. the] *Q1ᶜ(M);* ehe *Q1ᵘ(H).*

Sc. xvi] *Hugo; not in Qq;* ACT V. SCENE IV. Arden's *House at* Feversham.
Tyrrell; ACT V. SCENE III. *Delius;* Devant l'abbaye de Feversham. *Hugo.*
0.2. guarded . . . Watch] *This ed., after Hugo; not in Qq.*

---

joke' here; believing that 'Marlowe was in some way responsible for' the
play, he notes that 'among Marlowe's friends accused like him of dissemi-
nating irreligious doctrines was Richard Cholmley, who was eventually
arrested by order of the Privy Council. Wit in a circle of friends like
Marlowe's was not refined, but the similarity of names may be nothing but
coincidence.'
    kept] (1) frequented; (2) kept as a mistress.
    2. *stout*] proud, haughty.
    3. *companions*] tetrasyllabic.
    5. *Harbour*] shelter.
    8. *spurned*] kicked.
    12. *take sanctuary*] i.e., take refuge in one of the specially designated
areas of a church or royal palace where criminals, other than blasphemers
and traitors, were safe from arrest. The playwright seems to have erred
here in making it necessary for Shakebag to 'cross the water' (that is, the
Thames) since he is apparently already in Southwark (see xiv. 243 and n.),
where the Mint was designated a sanctuary and where he apparently
remains, according to the Epilogue (l. 3), until 'sent for out'. Cf. iii. 44–6,
and see iii. 45, n.

Alice [*leaning over the body*]. Arden, sweet husband, what
  shall I say ?
 The more I sound his name, the more he bleeds.
 This blood condemns me and in gushing forth   5
 Speaks as it falls and asks me why I did it.
 Forgive me, Arden; I repent me now;
 And, would my death save thine, thou shouldst not die.
 Rise up, sweet Arden, and enjoy thy love,
 And frown not on me when we meet in heaven;   10
 In heaven I love thee though on earth I did not.
Mayor. Say, Mosby, what made thee murder him ?
Franklin. Study not for an answer; look not down.
 His purse and girdle found at thy bed's head
 Witness sufficiently thou didst the deed.   15
 It bootless is to swear thou didst it not.
Mosby. I hired Black Will and Shakebag, ruffians both,
 And they and I have done this murd'rous deed.

3. S.D.] *This ed., after Hugo; not in Qq.* 5. gushing] *Qr*^c*(M);* guishing
Qr^u*(H).* 11. I (1)] *Qq;* I'll *Tyrrell.* 17–19.] *so Delius; lines ending in
Qq* Shakebagge, / both, / deed, / we ? / hence. 18. murd'rous] *Qr*
(murthrous)*;* murtherous *Q2;* murderous *Q3.*

4–6.] alluding to the popular superstition that the corpse of a mur-
dered man bled in the presence of his assassin (see under 'Bier Right' in
R. H. Robbins, *The Encyclopedia of Witchcraft and Demonology* [1960]).
Holinshed writes: 'hir selfe [Alice] beholding hir husbands bloud, said;
Oh the bloud of God helpe, for this bloud haue I shed.' Clark compares *R3*,
I. ii. 55–6 ('O, gentlemen, see, see! dead Henry's wounds / Open their
congeal'd mouths and bleed afresh'), and *Mac.*, v. i. 37–8 ('Yet who would
have thought the old man to have had so much blood in him ?') and 48
('Here's the smell of blood still'). In *Pre-Restoration Stage Studies* (1937),
p. 239, W. J. Lawrence argues that the corpse of Arden actually bleeds as
Alice speaks these lines.
 11. *I love*] The present tense, odd though it may sound here to the
modern ear, effectively conveys the impression that Alice is assured, in her
own mind at least, of the results of her repentance. Cf. parallel in *E2*, 1947
('In heauen we may, in earth neuer shall wee meete').
 13. *Study not*] do not cast about or search, i.e., do not invent.
 14–18.] Cf. Holinshed, App. II, p. 158.
 14. *girdle*] belt worn round the waist (to carry the purse) (*O.E.D.*).
 16. *bootless*] useless.
 17.] Greene did the actual hiring (ii. 82 ff.), as Sturgess reminds us; but,
whether 'Mosby's assumption of extra guilt here, is either an error of the

But wherefore stay we ? Come and bear me hence.

Franklin. Those ruffians shall not escape. I will up to London 20
And get the Council's warrant to apprehend them.   *Exeunt.*

[Sc. xvii]

Here enters WILL.

Will. Shakebag, I hear, hath taken sanctuary;
But I am so pursued with hues and cries
For petty robberies that I have done
That I can come unto no sanctuary.
Therefore must I in some oyster-boat   5
At last be fain to go aboard some hoy,
And so to Flushing. There is no staying here.
At Sittingburgh the watch was like to take me;

19. Come] *Qq;* Command *Jacob.*   20–1.] *so Delius; Q1–2 divided at*
escape, / I; *Q3 at* escape, / I *and* warrand / To.   20. escape] *Qq;*
'scape *Delius.*   up] *Q1–2; not in Q3.*

Sc. xvii] *Hugo; not in Qq;* ACT V. SCENE V. *The* Kentish *Coast. Tyrrell;*
ACT V. SCENE IV. *Delius.*   6. go aboard] *Qq;* get on board *S.MS.;* go on
board *Bayne.*   8. Sittingburgh] *Qq* (Sittinburgh); Sittingbourne *S.MS.,*
Jacob.

playwright or a device by the playwright to cover Greene's absence', the
point is not too troubling: Mosby's confession stems from a desperate
awareness that the game is up. L. 19 makes it obvious that he wants the
whole affair quickly over with.
    19. *But . . . we ?*] Cf. xiv. 389.
    Come . . . hence.] Cf. xviii. 35.
    21.] Cf. xiv. 367.

xvii. 5–7. *Therefore . . . Flushing*] Jacob, in his history of Faversham
(pp. 75–7), points out that the Kentish coast was famous for its oysters ('so
much esteemed by the Romans') and that 'amongst the different parts of
these general oyster grounds, that of Faversham is most regarded by the
industrious Hollanders, who have had, time immemorial, a constant traffic
here, they always giving the preference to our oysters, and never dealing
with others'.
    6. *fain*] obliged, content.
    hoy] small vessel generally 'employed in carrying passengers and goods,
particularly in short distances on the sea-coast' (*O.E.D.*). Cf. Jonson's
Volpone, IV. i. 60–1 (ed. Herford and Simpson, vol. v, 1937): 'Your hoigh /
Carries but three men in her, and a boy'.
    8. *like*] likely.

And, had I not with my buckler covered my head
And run full blank at all adventures,   10
I am sure I had ne'er gone further than that place,
For the constable had twenty warrants to apprehend me;
Besides that, I robbed him and his man once at Gadshill.
Farewell, England; I'll to Flushing now.   *Exit* WILL.

[Sc. xviii]

Here enters the Mayor, MOSBY, ALICE, MICHAEL,
      SUSAN, *and* BRADSHAW, [*led by the* Watch].

Mayor [*to the Watch*].   Come, make haste, and bring away the
      prisoners.
Bradshaw.   Mistress Arden, you are now going to God,
      And I am by the law condemned to die
      About a letter I brought from Master Greene.
      I pray you, Mistress Arden, speak the truth: 5

9–10.] *so Qq; divided in Hopkinson* (2) *at* covered / My.   9. I not] *Q1,
S.MS.;* not I *Q2–3.*   10. run] *Qq;* ran *S.MS., Jacob.*   12. twenty]
Q3; 20 *Q1–2.*   13.] *so Q1–2; divided in Q3 at* once / At.   14.] *so Qq;*
Now for flushing, I know tis me they seek / Let happen what will, I dare to
stay and speak / Being thus armed no danger Can I see / No Ile make
danger stand in fear of me. *S.MS.*   England; I'll to] *Qq;* England, for
I'll to *Tyrrell;* England; I'll go to *Thorndike.*

Sc. xviii] *Hugo; not in Qq;* ACT V. SCENE VI. *Justice Room at* Feversham.
Tyrrell. ACT V. SCENE V. *Delius.*   0.2. led . . . Watch] *This ed., after
Hugo; not in Qq.*   1. S.D.] *This ed., after Hugo; not in Qq.*   2.
Mistress] *Q3c* (mistres), *Tyrrell;* M. *Q1–2;* Master *Q3u;* Madam *S.MS.*

─────────────────────────────────────

10. *full . . . adventures*] completely without reserve whatever the consequences.

13. *Gadshill*] 'A hill on the road from London to Rochester, 2½ miles
from Rochester and about 27 from London. It was a well-known resort of
footpads and highwaymen' (Sugden). Also the scene of Falstaff's famous
non-robbery (*1H4*, II. ii).

Sc. xviii] The Wardmote Book of Faversham indicates that the sentencing took place 'in the Abbey Halle wch ye said Ardern p[ur]chased'—in
what is probably the guest hall of Arden's House today.

2ff.] The Wardmote Book implicates Bradshaw as one of 'thabettors and
councellors to thesaid murder', but Holinshed makes much of his innocence
(see App. II, p. 158).

4. *About*] because of.

Was I ever privy to your intent or no?

Alice. What should I say? You brought me such a letter,
But I dare swear thou knewest not the contents.
Leave now to trouble me with worldly things,
And let me meditate upon my Saviour Christ,   10
Whose blood must save me for the blood I shed.

Mosby. How long shall I live in this hell of grief?
Convey me from the presence of that strumpet.

Alice. Ah, but for thee I had never been strumpet.
What cannot oaths and protestations do   15
When men have opportunity to woo?
I was too young to sound thy villainies,
But now I find it and repent too late.

Susan [*to Mosby*]. Ah, gentle brother, wherefore should I die?
I knew not of it till the deed was done.   20

Mosby. For thee I mourn more than for myself,
But let it suffice I cannot save thee now.

Michael [*to Susan*]. And if your brother and my mistress
Had not promised me you in marriage,
I had ne'er given consent to this foul deed.   25

Mayor. Leave to accuse each other now,
And listen to the sentence I shall give:
Bear Mosby and his sister to London straight,

7.] *so Delius; two lines in Qq, divided at* say? / You.   should] *Qq;* shall
S.MS.   10. upon] *Qq;* on *S.MS.*   14. been strumpet] *Qq;* been a
strumpet *Jacob.*   15. cannot] *Qq;* will not *S.MS.*   19. S.D.] *This ed.,*
after Hugo; not in Qq.   22. But] *Qq;* omitted *Jacob.*   23. S.D.] *This ed.,*
after Hugo; not in Qq.   25. ne'er] *Q1* (nere)*; neuer *Q2;* never *Q3.*

---

6. *privy to*] familiar with, in on the secret of.

12–14.] In *Brewen* (p. 292, ll. 14–16), Parker, the lover, says, 'I would be
twice aduised how I did wed with such a strumpet as thy selfe', and then
reviles 'her most shamefully': 'Wherevnto shee answered shee had neuer
been strumpet but for him.'

17. *sound*] sound out, probe.

25. *given*] probably monosyllabic.

28. *straight*] straightway, directly.

28–32.] Holinshed and the Wardmote Book, as well as extracts from the
Privy Council book (see App. III), agree in essentials on the sentencing. In
her novel *Feversham*, Diane Davidson has Sir Thomas Cheyne investigate

Where they in Smithfield must be executed;
Bear Mistress Arden unto Canterbury,   30
Where her sentence is she must be burnt;
Michael and Bradshaw in Faversham must suffer death.

Alice. Let my death make amends for all my sins.

Mosby. Fie upon women!—this shall be my song.

But bear me hence, for I have lived too long.   35

Susan. Seeing no hope on earth, in heaven is my hope.

Michael. Faith, I care not, seeing I die with Susan.

Bradshaw. My blood be on his head that gave the sentence!

Mayor. To speedy execution with them all!   *Exeunt.*

[Epilogue]

Here enters FRANKLIN.

Franklin. Thus have you seen the truth of Arden's death.
As for the ruffians, Shakebag and Black Will,
The one took sanctuary and, being sent for out,
Was murdered in Southwark as he passed
To Greenwich, where the Lord Protector lay.   5

30. Mistress] *Q3;* M. *Q1–2.*   31. Where] *Qq;* Where as *Jacob.*
33. amends] *Qq* (a mends).   37. not, seeing] *Q1ᶜ(H);* not seeing
Q1ᵘ(M).   38. that] *Qq;* who *Jacob.*

Epilogue] *Hugo, Hopkinson (2); not in Qq;* ACT V. SCENE VI. *Delius.*

---

the murder as he most likely would have done as Lord Lieutenant of the
shire.

29. *Smithfield*] 'An open space, East of the Tower of London, just outside the city walls. It was a haunt of riverside thieves, and was often used as
the place for their execution' (Sugden).

35.] See App. I, and cf. Mosby's attitude to Macbeth's (v. iii. 22) as the
latter recognizes that 'I have lived long enough'; for both, 'vaulting
ambition' has brought only a life 'fall'n into the sear, the yellow leaf'.

38.] Bradshaw's death makes for a somewhat mixed ending; see Intro.,
p. lxxiv.

Ep. 1 ff.] Cf. Holinshed (App. II, pp. 158–9), the Wardmote Book, and
the extracts from the Privy Council book (App. III, pp. 161–2) on the disposition of the other conspirators in the murder. Black Will's demise
follows Holinshed.

3. *The one*] the former.

Black Will was burnt in Flushing on a stage;
Greene was hangèd at Osbridge in Kent;
The painter fled, and how he died we know not.
But this above the rest is to be noted:
Arden lay murdered in that plot of ground   10
Which he by force and violence held from Reede,
And in the grass his body's print was seen
Two years and more after the deed was done.
Gentlemen, we hope you'll pardon this naked tragedy
Wherein no filèd points are foisted in   15
To make it gracious to the ear or eye;
For simple truth is gracious enough
And needs no other points of glozing stuff.   [*Exit.*]

FINIS.

7. Osbridge] *Qq;* Ospringe *Jacob.*   18. glozing] *Q2–3;* glosing *Q1.*
S.D.] *W-P; not in Qq.*

---

6. *stage*] scaffold.
7. *Osbridge*] i.e., Ospringe, 'a village in Kent, on the old Pilgrims' Road
to Canterbury, a mile or so South-West of Faversham' (Sugden).
9–13.] Only Holinshed mentions this 'miracle' (the source of sc. xiii of
the play); see App. II, p. 159.
14. *naked*] i.e., for the reasons given in the next two lines.
15. *filèd points*] smoothly polished points of rhetoric (or rhetorical
figures). *Points* was also the name given to the tagged laces that attached
hose to the doublet, and hence the probable play on the idea that the
author was not adding adornments to his simple style.
16. *gracious*] favourable, attractive.
17–18.] Although the idea behind these lines is proverbial (see Tilley,
T561, 'As naked as truth'; T565: 'It is as true as truth itself'; T575: 'Truth
has no need of rhetoric [figures]'; T585: 'Truth needs no colors'; T589:
'The truth shows best being naked'; and T593: 'Truth's tale is simple'),
Clark observes the astounding frequency with which it recurs in Shakespeare, a few outstanding places being: *Gent.*, II. ii. 18; *Err.*, V. i. 223;
LLL., IV. iii. 366 and V. i. 14–16; *R2*, II. i. 5 ff.; *R3*, I. iii. 52 and IV. iv. 358;
Ham., II. ii. 95; and *Sonn.*, CI, l. 6. Cf. also *1H6*, IV. vii. 72: 'Here is a silly
stately style indeed!' *Arden* apparently set the fashion for such apologies at
the end of 'domestic' tragedies (see, for example, *A Warning for Fair
Women*).
18. *glozing*] specious, wordy, empty and flattering.

'Parallels' in *Arden of Faversham*

Since genuine parallels to passages in other contemporary plays definitely exist in *Arden of Faversham*, the temptation has been great to seek further 'parallels' even where they clearly do not exist or are dubious at best in the effort to determine authorship or date of composition. Thus the most trivial and commonplace words, phrases, rhetorical devices, and proverbial expressions have been brought forth as 'evidence' for *Arden's* being the work of a particular author or the collaborative effort of several or for its having been composed before or after another play. The process, unfortunately, tends to be deductive: a feeling about authorship often seems to precede the search for proof, and without a rigorous definition of what a 'parallel' actually is 'proof' is always easily forthcoming.[1] This objection holds true for the cases made for Kyd, Marlowe, Shakespeare, or any other writer or combination of writers. J. M. Robertson, for instance, found just on the basis of such 'parallels' enough evidence to uphold Kyd's claim, along with Greene's 'collaboration' and Marlowe's 'intervention' (*An Introduction to the Study of the Shakespeare Canon* [1924], pp. 403–4 *et passim*). And because the overwhelming number of 'parallels' usually cited refer not to *The Spanish Tragedy* but rather to *Soliman and Perseda*, an anonymous play to which Kyd's claim is seriously disputed, the case for Kyd becomes at once questionable. Even more disconcerting has been the failure to recognize the defectiveness of many of the dramatic quartos which have been 'quarried' for parallels (see Schoenbaum's fifth principle), especially those texts which betray considerable evidence of memorial contamination, as the plays in the 'Pembroke group' do to varying degrees (see Intro., pp. xxv–xxvi).

By themselves, parallels are never likely to prove authorship or to be of any help in dating when their priority cannot be safely estab-

---

[1] See the 'five "golden rules" for parallel-hunters' in M. S. C. Byrne, 'Bibliographical Clues in Collaborate Plays', *Libr.*, 4th ser., XIII (1933), 24–5, and also the eight 'first principles' set forth by S. Schoenbaum, *Internal Evidence and Elizabethan Dramatic Authorship*, pp. 162–83.

lished; this is certainly the case when they are to texts that have been
recognized as corrupt or, of course, to anonymous texts.[1] In *Arden*
parallels afford at best one more sign, along with others (see Intro.,
pp. xxvi–xxx), that the quarto of 1592 is, in part at least, a reconstruc-
tion. They also justify an *initial* impression that (1) the author or
authors were steeped in the vocabulary of Kyd, Marlowe, and early
Shakespeare or (2) reporters (actors ?) were. A corollary impression
is that the author (or authors) or reporters frequently resorted to
commonplaces.[2]

The reader who is interested in pursuing the matter of parallels
further and in seeing what has been offered in the way of 'proof' is
advised to consult the works by Crawford, Miksch, Sykes, Clark,
Taylor, Smith, Hart, Rubow, and Jackson (see Abbreviations), as
well as other scholars mentioned from time to time in the commentary. The annotations to the text record genuine parallels; but the
comparisons that follow (most of them made by the foregoing
writers) reflect, in the opinion of the present editor, some of the more
interesting possibilities or deserve special comment.[3]

i. 179. Cf. *Con.*, I. ii. 33 ('Away I say, and let me heare no more')
with its counterpart in the 'good' quarto of *2H6*, I. ii. 50 ('Away from
me, and let me hear no more!'). Cf., too, *Con.*, III. ii. 178 ('Away, I
say, that I may feele my griefe').

i. 333–57. Rubow compares *Sp.T.*, III. xiv. 135 ff., where the
Duke of Castile enjoins Hieronimo to set 'scandalous reports' aside
and to 'frequent my homely house'.

i. 345. 'Slander's tongue' or 'slanderous tongues' occurs frequently in Shakespeare (so Clark) and elsewhere in Elizabethan drama.

[1] Cf. T. W. Baldwin's reversal of position regarding the parallelisms at
i. 98–100 and at i. 185–6 in *On the Literary Genetics of Shakespere's Plays
1592–1594* (1959), pp. 161–3, and *On the Compositional Genetics of 'The
Comedy of Errors'* (1965), pp. 22–4.

[2] First suggested by the General Editor.

[3] To distinguish the 'interesting' from the 'trivial' has proved difficult at
times. For instance, 'Yet Mistress Arden lives' at viii. 37 could hardly seem
to have a parallel in such commonplace phrasing as 'But *Arthur* lives' in
TRKJ, pt II, ii. 143. What is of possible interest here is that the beginning
of Mosby's soliloquy, in which the former passage occurs, has a more
direct parallel in the same passage of the latter play (see viii. 1, n.); and each
speaker has in mind the elimination of the person who most directly
challenges his power. One sees here at least the possibility of an actor-
reporter familiar with both passages and conflating them. (Cf., too, ll. 5–6
of Mosby's soliloquy with *TRKJ*, pt I, 487: 'This bitter winde must nip
some bodies spring'.) In his Signet edition of *King John* (1966), pp. 153–63,
W. H. Matchett argues for considering *TRKJ* as a 'bad' quarto of Shakespeare's play.

i. 400, 409–13. Rubow compares *S. & P.*, v. i. 34 ff., the passage in which Erastus takes leave of Perseda.

i. 436–7 ('Oaths . . . mutable'). Although proverbial (see annotation to text), the thought and phrasing are especially recurrent in Shakespeare as any concordance will bear out; cf. i. 345 above.

i. 453. Cf. *Con.*, I. i. 75 ('And is all our labours then spent in vaine'); not in *2H6*. Also *Tr.T.*, III. i. 17 ('Your labour is but spent in vaine'); not in *3H6*.

i. 492. Cf. *S. & P.*, v. ii. 58 ('For be it spoke in secret heere, quoth he').

i. 596. A Renaissance critical commonplace, but cf. examples in Shakespeare cited by Onions under 'life (7)'.

ii. 49. The image is commonplace, but the following 'parallels' have been cited: *Con.*, v. i. 53 ('Deepe trenched furrowes in his frowning brow'); *E2*, 94 ('The sworde shall plane the furrowes of thy browes'); *Mas.P.*, 158–9 ('Giue me a look, that when I bend the browes, / Pale death may walke in furrowes of my face'); and *S. & P.*, I. iv. 135 ('Within forst furrowes of her clowding brow').

ii. 91. Taylor compares *Tr.T.*, I. iv. 154 ('Had he bin slaughterman of all my kin'; '. . . to all my kin' in *3H6*, I. iv. 169).

iii. 3–5. Cf. *S. & P.*, II. ii. 4–8 ('After my most hearty commendations, this is to let you vnderstand, that my maister was in good health at the sending hereof. Yours for euer, and euer, and euer, in most humble wise, *Piston.*').

iii. 89. Hart, *S.S.C.*, compares *Tr.T.*, I. ii. 11–12 ('But I would breake an hundred othes to raigne one yeare'; in the 'good' quarto of *3H6*, I. ii. 17: 'I would break a thousand oaths to reign one year').

iii. 104–6. Rubow compares *Sp.T.*, II. v. 52–5:

Seest thou this handkercher besmerd with blood ?
It shall not from me, till I take reuenge.
Seest thou those wounds that yet are bleeding fresh ?
Ile not intombe them, till I haue reueng'd.

iii. 108. Smith compares *2 Tamb.*, 2501 ('To paint in woords, what Ile perfourme in deeds') and *Dido*, 863–4 ('Sister of *Ioue*, if that thy loue be such, / As these thy protestations doe paint forth'). W. Wells, 'The Authorship of *King Leir*', *N. & Q.*, CLXXVII (1939), 438, compares *Leir*, 277 ('I cannot paynt my duty forth in words'). Cf., too, *3H6*, v. vi. 26 ('Ah, kill me with thy weapon, not with words!').

iii. 118. Taylor compares *TRKƷ*, pt I, 890–1 ('Is all the bloud yspilt on either part, / Closing the cranies of the thirstie earth'). But cf., too, *3H6*, II. iii. 23 ('Then let the earth be drunken with our blood') and *R3*, I. ii. 63 ('O earth, which this blood drink'st, revenge his death').

iii. 163. A somewhat commonplace image, but *E2*, 2286–7, is usually cited as a parallel ('My daily diet is heart breaking sobs, / That almost rents the closet of my heart'). But cf. *Sonn.*, XLVI. 5–6 ('My heart doth plead that thou in him dost lie, / A closet never pierced with crystal eyes') and *Sonn.*, XLVIII. 11 ('Within the gentle closure of my breast').

iii. 201–2. Cf. *S. & P.*, v. iii. 43 ('To leade a Lambe vnto the slaughter-house ?').

iii. 208. Cf. the similar idea in *3H6*, II. ii. 9–10 ('this too much lenity / And harmful pity must be laid aside').

iv. 17. Taylor compares *Con.*, v. i. 53 (see above, ii. 49).

iv. 52. Cf. *S. & P.*, I. ii. 52 ('And add fresh courage to my fainting limmes') and *Leir*, 2546 ('And adde fresh vigor to my willing limmes').

iv. 79–80. Cf. *S. & P.*, v. ii. 133–4 ('stab in the marshall, / Least he detect vs vnto the world') and III. 5.10 ('Then stab the slaues, and send their soules to hell').

iv. 81–2. Cf. description of Jack Fitten at ii. 49. Rubow parallels *Sp.T.*, I. ii. 51 ('And gapes to swallow neighbour bounding landes'). But cf. also *R3*, I. ii. 65 ('Or earth, gape open wide and eat him quick'). For the somewhat commonplace association of wrinkles with graves, see *Sonn.*, LXXVII. 5–6. Cf. 'death-threat'ning face' with *3H6*, I. iii. 17 ('cruel threatening look'), and see annotation to text at iv. 75.

iv. 85–6. Cf. *Sp.T.*, II. iv. 62–3 (and note that annotation to text at ll. 87–8 cites parallel that directly follows this quotation):

> *Bel.* Murder, murder: helpe, *Hieronimo*, helpe.
> *Lor.* Come, stop her mouth; away with her.

iv. 92. Taylor compares *Con.*, I. ii. 10 ('But I was troubled with a dream to night'); Clark compares *R3*, v. iii. 212 ('O Ratcliff, I have dream'd a fearful dream!'); and Rubow compares *Corn.*, II. 209 ('The fearefull dreames effects that trouble mee').

iv. 95. Cf. *Tit.*, II. iii. 211–12 ('I am surprised with an uncouth fear; / A chilling sweat o'er-runs my trembling joints'), and also *Leir*, 1501 ('And yet for feare my feeble ioynts do quake').

iv. 98–100. Taylor compares text at v. 34 and *Tr.T.*, IV. vii. 3 ('But soft the gates are shut, I like not this'; in *3H6*, IV. vii. 10: 'The gates made fast! Brother, I like not this').

v. 9. Cf. *S. & P.*, v. ii. 110 ('To send them down to euerlasting night').

vi. 30. Cf. *R3*, I. iv. 63 ('Such terrible impression made the dream') —from Clarence's account of his dream, which Clark compares to Arden's.

vi. 31. Sykes compares *Corn.*, III. 65 ('God graunt these dreames to good effect bee brought') and cites Garnier's French from which

Kyd translated: 'Facent les dieux benins qu'elles soyent sans puissance'.

viii. 24–5. Cf. thought in dedication to *Ven.* ('I shall be sorie it had so noble a god-father: and neuer after eare so barren a land, for fear it yeeld me still so bad a haruest') and in *All's W.*, I. iii. 42–4 ('He that ears my land spares my team, and gives me leave to in [i.e., harvest] the crop').

viii. 39–42. Rubow compares *Brewen*, p. 292, ll. 20–4, which express a similar idea. Cf., too, *Sp.T.*, III. iv. 82 ('But to what end ? I list not trust the Aire').

viii. 45. Cf. *John*, II. i. 544 ('She is sad and passionate').

viii. 58–9. These lines have been thought to have a 'genuine Shakespearean flavour'; cf. *Sonn.*, CXVI, for example, and *R3*, I. ii. 189–90 ('That hand, which, for thy love, did kill thy love, / Shall, for thy love, kill a far truer love'); also *Gent.*, I. ii. 31–2 ('They do not love that do not show their love.' / 'O, they love least that let men know their love') and II. vi. 17–18 ('I cannot leave to love, and yet I do; / But there I leave to love where I should love').

viii. 121. Cf. *Sp.T.*, II. ii. 26 ('But whereon doost thou chiefly meditate ?').

viii. 133. See annotation to text. Headlam and Jackson cite many Shakespearean 'parallels'; and, although the comparison looks commonplace, the frequency in Shakespeare is striking. Cf. *Tit.*, V. ii. 171; *2H6*, III. i. 101 and IV. i. 71–2; *R2*, V. iii. 61–2; *Shr.*, V. ii. 142–3; *Troil.*, III. iii. 303–4; *Wint.*, I. ii. 325; *H8*, I. i. 154; *Lucr.*, 577, 850, 1077–8, and 1707.

ix. 10. Cf. *H5*, II. i. 50–1 ('Pistol's cock is up, / And flashing of fire will follow').

ix. 17–18. Cf. *S. & P.*, I. iv. 74 ('It was worth more then thou and all thy kin are worth').

x. 1–4. Kydians and Shakespearians alike seize on this purple passage (cf. annotation to text at v. 1 ff.). The images are traditional, but Rubow compares *Sp.T.*, I. i. 23–4 ('Ere *Sol* had slept three nights in *Thetis* lap, / And slakte his smoaking charriot in her floud'); Miksch, *S. & P.*, II. i. 9–10 ('when shall the gates of heauen / Stand all wide ope<n>'); Sykes, *Corn.*, V. 156 ('darksome clowde'). Clark compares for style *3H6*, II. i. 21–2 ('See how the morning opes her golden gates, / And takes her farewell of the glorious sun!') and IV. vii. 79–80 ('And when the morning sun shall raise his car / Above the border of this horizon'). Cf., too, *Gent.*, III. i. 154–5 ('Wilt thou aspire to guide the heavenly car, / And with thy daring folly burn the world ?').

x. 17. Crawford cites *S. & P.*, III. i. 101–2 ('The least of these surpasse my best desart, / Vnlesse true loyaltie may seeme desart').

x. 87–90. Sykes compares *S. & P.*, IV. i. 238–40:
> If so your life depend vpon your loue,
> And that her loue depends vpon his life,
> Is it not better that *Erastus* die. . .

Line 223 just preceding these lines contains the same proverb noted at l. 83 in this same scene from *Arden*.

x. 95. Cf. *Leir*, 670 ('Then mountaynes moue by blast of euery wind').

x. 100–1. Cf. *S. & P.*, I. iv. 30–1 ('Leaue protestations now, and let vs hie / To tread lauolto . . .'). The relationship seems slight, but the deranged versification of *Arden* at this point may be due to an actor-reporter's confused recollection.

xi. 27–9. Crawford compares *S. & P.*, I. iv. 83 ('Why then, by this reckoning, . . .') and II. ii. 50–1 ('. . . where you had not best go to him').

xii. 69. Cf. *Con.*, v. i. 71 ('But beard and braue him proudly to his face'; not in *2H6*). Cf., too, *Con.*, IV. x. 14 ('Braue thee and beard thee too'; in *2H6*, IV. x. 36, simply as 'Brave thee!').

xiii. 54. Taylor cites as an 'interesting network' of similar phrasing the following 'Pembroke' plays: *S. & P.*, I. iii. 211 ('the braginst knaue in Christendom'); *Con.*, II. i. 99–100 ('the lyingest knaue in Christendom'); *Tr.T.*, III. ii. 63 ('the bluntest woer in christendome'), and *Mas.P.*, 766–7 ('the proudest Kings/In Christendome'). Cf. also *Arden*, i. 228, and *Leir*, 561 ('the kindest Gyrles in Christendome') and 1225 ('the gainefulst trade in Christendome!').

xiii. 73. Clark compares *Tit.*, v. ii. 205 ('for I'll play the cook') and *Cym.*, III. vi. 29–30 ('Cadwal and I / Will play the cook and servant') and IV. ii. 165 ('You and Fidele play the cooks').

xiii. 75–6. Clark compares, especially for construction, *2H4*, II. i. 143–4 ('Come, an 'twere not for thy humours, there's not a better wench in England').

xiii. 119–21. Clark compares *2H6*, III. i. 201 ('For what's more miserable than discontent?'); Miksch compares 'Impose me penance' to *S. & P.*, I. iv. 28 ('Impose me taske'). Here Clarke's comparison, which involves a similar way of thinking, is the only relevant kind.

xiv. 57–9. Clark compares *R3*, I. iv. 151–2 ('Take him over the costard with the hilts of thy sword').

xiv. 114–15. Sykes compares *Sp.T.*, II. i. 51–2 ('Now to these fauours will I adde reward, / Not with faire words, but store of golden coyne') and *S. & P.*, IV. i. 63–4 ('Which ile not guerdon with large promises, / But straight reward thee with a bounteous largesse'). Miksch, however, compares *James the Fourth*, Induction, 49–50 ('my reward fair words and large promises').

xiv. 146–7. Cf. *Faustus*, 338–9 ('Had I as many soules as there be starres, / Ide giue them al for *Mephastophilis*'). G. Wickham, *Shake-speare's Dramatic Heritage* (1969), pp. 54–6, considers both Alice Arden and Faustus as 'bourgeois heroes': 'Alice Arden shares Faustus' regret for a life wasted by a foolish choice'.

xiv. 235–6. Jackson compares similar phrasing in *3H6*, I. iv. 175–6, and *Tr.T.*, I. iv. 160–1, and observes that 'in every case the two speakers are stabbing a third person'.

xiv. 273. Rubow compares *Sp.T.*, II. v. 34 ('My husbands absence makes my heart to throb') and III. iii. 40 ('Why ? because he walkt abroad so late').

xiv. 328–9, 331. Rubow compares *S. & P.*, v. iv. 3 ff. (Ah, *Brusor*, see where thy *Lucina* lyes . . .') and v. iv. 94 ('Come *Brusor*, helpe to lift her bodie vp'). Taylor compares *Con.*, v. ii. 45–6 ('O! dismall sight, see where he breathlesse lies, / All smeard and weltred in his luke-warme blood').

xiv. 332. Hart, *S.S.C.*, compares *Tr.T.*, I. iv. 132 ('These teares are my sweet *Rutlands* obsequies'; also *3H6*, I. iv. 147). Cf. also *S. & P.*, v. iv. 10–12:

> Go, *Brusor*, beare her to thy priuate tent,
> Where we at leasure will lament her death,
> And with our teares bewaile her obsequies.

xiv. 389 ('But wherefore stay you ?'). Rubow compares *Arden*, xvi. 19, and *Sp.T.*, III. vi. 100 (and elsewhere), and *S. & P.*, I. vi. 37 and III. vi. 19. The phrase seems merely to be actor's fill-in, as well as just a commonplace expression.

xiv. 390. Miksch compares *E2*, 2645 ('My lord, I feare me it will prooue too true'). Like Franklin, the speaker is addressing the sus-pected murderer. The two passages hardly seem 'parallels', but the comparison is interesting in the light of genuine parallels between the two plays.

xiv. 408. Hart, *S.S.C.*, compares *E2*, 372 ('Because he loues me more then all the world'). Sykes, however, compares *Sp.T.*, II. vi. 4–6 ('. . . *Bel-imperia*, / On whom I doted more then all the world . . .') and *S. & P.*, II. i. 284 ('Dearer to me then all the world besides').

xviii. 12. Cf. *E2*, 412 ('Is all my hope turnd to this hell of greefe').

xviii. 35. The phrase is commonplace, but cf. *Con.*, II. iii. 10 ('Euen to my death, for I haue liued too long'; 'corrected' in *2H6*, II. iii. 14, to 'Welcome is banishment; welcome were my death').

xviii. 36. Cf. *Sp.T.*, III. i. 35–7:

> Tis heauen is my hope.
> As for the earth, it is too much infect
> To yield me hope of any of her mould.

xviii. 38. Taylor compares *Tr.T.*, I. iv. 153 ('My soule to heauen, my bloud vpon your heads'; also *3H6*, I. iv. 168).

Q*

The Source of *Arden of Faversham*

in Holinshed's *Chronicles of England, Scotland, and Ireland*

(from the second edition, 1587, Vol. II, pp. 1062–6)

1551

Anno Reg. 5
*Arden
murthered.*

*Arden
described.*

*Loue and
lust.*

*A paire of
siluer dice
worke much
mischiefe.*

About this time there was at Feuersham in Kent a gentleman named Arden, most cruellie murthered and slaine by
the procurement of his owne wife. The which murther,
for the horribleness thereof, although otherwise it may
seeme to be but a priuate matter, and therefore as it were
impertinent to this historie, I haue thought good to set it
foorth somewhat at large, hauing the instructions deliuered to me by them, that haue vsed some diligence to
gather the true vnderstanding of the circumstances. This
Arden was a man of a tall and comelie personage, and
matched in marriage with a gentlewoman, yoong, tall, and
well fauored of shape and countenance,[1] who chancing to
fall in familiaritie with one Mosbie a tailor by occupation,
a blacke swart man, seruant to the lord North, it happened
this Mosbie vpon some misliking to fall out with hir: but
she being desirous to be in fauour with him againe, sent
him a paire of siluer dice by one Adam Foule dwelling at
the Floure de lice in Feuersham.

After which he resorted to hir againe, and oftentimes
laie in Ardens house: in somuch that within two yeares
after, he obteined such fauour at hir hands, that he laie
with hir, or (as they terme it) kept hir, in abusing hir
bodie. And although (as it was said) Arden perceiued right
well their mutuall familiaritie to be much greater than

---

[1] Harley MSS. (see Intro., pp. xli–xliii) add: 'who was the lord northes
wyves dowghtar, and hir husband and she havynge therefore often recowrse
to my lord northes, ther was one mosby . . .'.

their honestie,[1] yet bicause he would not offend hir, and so
loose the benefit which he hoped to gaine at some of hir
freends hands in bearing with hir lewdnesse, which he
might haue lost if he should haue fallen out with hir: he
was contented to winke at hir filthie disorder, and both
permitted, and also inuited Mosbie verie often to lodge in
his house. And thus it continued a good space, before anie
practise was begun by them against maister Arden. She at
length inflamed in loue with Mosbie, and loathing hir
husband, wished and after practised the meanes how to
hasten his end.

*Arden
winketh at
his wiues
lewdnesse,
& why !*

There was a painter dwelling in Feuersham, who had
skill of poisons, as was reported. She therefore demanded
of him, whether it were true that he had such skill in that
feat or not ? And he denied not but that he had indeed. Yea
(said she) but I would haue such a one made, as should
haue most vehement and speedie operation to dispatch the
eater thereof. That can I doo (quoth he) and forthwith
made hir such a one, and willed hir to put it into the bottome of a porrenger, & then after to powre milke on it.
Which circumstance she forgetting, did cleane contrarie,
putting in the milke first, and afterward the poison. Now
maister Arden purposing that daie to ride to Canturburie,
his wife brought him his breakfast, which was woont to
be milke and butter. He hauing receiued a spoonefull or
two of the milke, misliked the tast and colour thereof, and
said to his wife; Mistresse Ales what milke haue you giuen
me here ? Wherewithall she tilted it ouer with hir hand,
saieng, I weene nothing can please you. Then he tooke
horsse and road towards Canturburie, and by the waie fell
into extreme purging vpwards and downewards, and so
escaped for that time.

*Ardens wife
attempteth
means to make
awaie hir
husband.*

*Arden is
poisoned by
his wife but
recouereth.*

After this, his wife fell in acquaintance with one Greene
of Feuersham, seruant to sir Anthonie Ager, from which
Greene maister Arden had wrested a peece of ground on
the backeside of the abbeie of Feuersham, and there had
blowes and great threats passed betwixt them about that
matter. Therefore she knowing that Greene hated hir husband, began to practise with him how to make him awaie;
and concluded, that if he could get anie that would kill

*She deuiseth
another waie
to dispatch
hir husband
Arden.*

[1] Harley MSS.: '. . . was yet so greatly gyven to seek his advauntage, and
caryd so litle how he came by it that in hope of atteynynge some benefits of the
lord northe by meanes of this mosby who could do muche wᵗ hym, he
winked . . .'.

him, he should haue ten pounds for a reward. This
Greene hauing dooings for his maister sir Anthonie Ager,
had occasion to go vp to London, where his maister then
laie, and hauing some charge vp with him, desired one
Bradshaw a goldsmith of Feuersham that was his neigh-
bor, to accompanie him to Grauesend, and he would content him for his pains. This Bradshaw, being a verie honest
man, was content, and road with him. And when they
came to Rainham downe, they chanced to see three or foure
seruingmen that were comming from Leeds: and therewith Bradshaw espied comming vp the hill from Rochester, one blacke Will, a terrible cruell ruffian with a sword
and buckler, and an other with a great staffe on his necke.

Then said Bradshaw to Greene; We are happie that
here commeth some companie from Leeds, for here commeth vp against vs as murthering a knaue as anie is in
England: if it were not for them we might chance hardlie
to escape without losse of our monie and liues. Yea
thought Greene (as he after confessed) such a one is for my
purpose, and therefore asked; Which is he? Yonder is he
quoth Bradshaw, the same that hath the sword and buckler: his name is blacke Will. How know you that, said
Greene? Bradshaw answered, I knew him at Bullongne,
where we both serued, he was a soldier, and I was sir
Richard Cauendishes man, and there he committed manie
robberies and heinous murthers on such as trauelled betwixt Bullongne and France.

By this time the other companie of seruingmen came to
them, and they going all togither, met with blacke Will
and his fellow. The seruingmen knew blacke Will, & salut-
ing him, demanded of him whither he went? He answered;
By his bloud (for his vse was to sweare almost at euerie
word) I know not, nor care not, but set vp my staffe, and
euen as it falleth I go. If thou (quoth they) wilt go backe
againe to Grauesend, we will giue thee thy supper. By his
bloud (said he) I care not, I am content, haue with you:
and so he returned againe with them. Then blacke Will
tooke acquaintance of Bradshaw, saieng; Fellow Bradshaw how doost thou? Bradshaw vnwilling to renew
acqu[a]i[n]tance, or to haue ought to doo with so shameles
a ruffian, said; Why doo ye know me? Yea that I doo
(quoth he) did not we serue in Bullongne togither? But ye
must pardon me (quoth Bradshaw) for I haue forgotten
you.

Then Greene talked with blacke Will, and said; When
ye haue supped, come to mine hosts [*hostesse*—1577] house
at such a signe, and I will giue you the sacke and sugar. By
his bloud (said he) I thanke you, I will come and take it I
warrant you. According to his promise he came, and there
they made good cheare. Then blacke Will & Greene went
and talked apart from Bradshaw, and there concluded togither, that if he would kill master Arden, he should haue
ten pounds for his labor. Then he answered, By his
wounds that I will if I maie know him. Marie to morrow
in Poules I will shew him thee, said Greene. Then they
left their talke, & Greene bad him go home to his hosts
[*hostes*—1577] house. Then Greene wrote a letter to mistresse Arden, & among other things put in these words:
We haue got a man for our purpose, we maie thanke my
brother Bradshaw. Now Bradshaw not knowing anie thing
of this, tooke the letter of him, and in the morning departed home againe, and deliuered the letter to mistresse
Arden, and Greene & blacke Will went vp to London at
the tide.

At the time appointed, Greene shewed blacke Will
maister Arden walking in Poules. Then said blacke Will,
What is he that goeth after him? Marie said Green, one
of his men. By his bloud (said blacke Will) I will kill them
both. Naie (said Greene) doo not so, for he is of counsell
with vs in this matter. By his bloud (said he) I care not for
that, I will kill them both. Naie said Greene in anie wise
doo not so. Then blacke Will thought to haue killed
maister Arden in Poules churchyard, but there were so
manie gentlemen that accompanied him to dinner, that he
missed of his purpose. Greene shewed all this talke to
maister Ardens man, whose name was Michaell, which
euer after stood in doubt of blacke Will, lest he should kill
him. The cause that this Michaell conspired with the rest
against his maister, was: for that it was determined, that he
should marrie a kinswoman of Mosbies.

After this, maister Arden laie at a certeine parsonage
which he held in London, and therefore his man Michaell
and Greene agreed, that blacke Will should come in the
night to the parsonage, where he should find the doores
left open, that he might come in and murther maister
Arden. This Michaell hauing his maister to bed, left open
the doores according to the appointment. His maister then
being in bed, asked him if he had shut fast the doores, and

The match made to murther Arden.

Simplicitie abused.

Blacke Will maketh no conscience of bloudshed and murther.

Why Ardens man con- spired with the rest to kill his maister.

*One murther-
ing mind
mistrusting
another, doo
hinder the
action where-
about they
agreed.*

hee said yea: but yet afterwards, fearing least blacke Will
would kill him as well as his maister, after he was in bed
himselfe, he rose againe and shut the doores, bolting them
fast. So that blacke Will comming thither, and finding the
doores shut, departed, being disappointed at that time.
The next daie blacke Will came to Greene in a great chafe,
swearing and staring bicause he was so deceiued, and with
manie terrible oths threatened to kill maister Ardens man
first, wheresoeuer he met him. No (said Greene) doo not
so, I will first know the cause of shutting the doores.

Then Greene met and talked with Ardens man, and
asked of him, why he did not leaue open the doors, according to his promise? Marie (said Michaell) I will shew you
the cause. My maister yesternight did that he neuer did
before: for after I was in bed, hee rose vp and shut the
doores, and in the morning rated me for leauing them
vnshut. And herewith Greene & blacke Will were pacified.

*The fourth
attempt to
make Arden
awaie dis-
appointed.*

Arden being redie to go homewards, his maid came to
Greene & said; This night will my maister go downe.
Whervpon it was agreed that blacke Will should kill him
on Reinam downe. When maister Arden came to Rochester, his man still fearing that blacke Will would kill him
with his maister, pricked his horsse of purpose, and made
him to halt, to the end he might protract the time, and
tarie behind. His maister asked him whie his horsse
halted, he said, I know not. Well (quoth his maister) when
ye come at the smith here before (betweene Rochester and
the hill foot ouer against Cheetam) remooue his shoo, and
search him, and then come after me. So maister Arden
rode on: and yer [*ere*—1577] he came at the place where
blacke Will laie in wait for him, there ouertooke him
diuerse gentlemen of his acquaintance, who kept him
companie: so that blacke Will mist here also of his purpose.

*Blacke Will
misseth his
purpose.*

After that maister Arden was come home, hee sent (as
he vsuallie did) his man to Shepeie to sir Thomas Cheinie,
then lord warden of the cinque ports, about certeine businesse, and at his comming awaie, he had a letter deliuered
sent by sir Thomas Cheinie to his maister. When he came
home, his mistresse tooke the letter and kept it, willing hir
man to tell his maister, that he had a letter deliuered him
by sir Thomas Cheinie, and that he had lost it; adding that
he thought it best that his maister should go the next
morning to sir Thomas, bicause he knew not the matter:

he said he would, and therefore he willed his man to be stirring betimes. In this meane while, blacke Will, and one George Shakebag his companion, were kept in a store-house of sir Anthonie Agers at Preston, by Greenes appointment: and thither came mistresse Arden to see him, bringing and sending him meat and drinke manie times. He therfore lurking there, and watching some opportunitie for his purpose, was willed in anie wise to be vp earlie in the morning, to lie in wait for maister Arden in a certeine broome close, betwixt Feuersham & the ferrie (which close he must needs passe) there to doo his feat. Now blacke Will stirred in the morning betimes, but mist the waie, & taried in a wrong place.

Ardens wife visiteth, succoureth, emboldneth, and directeth black Will &c: how to accomplish his bloudie purpose.

Maister Arden & his man comming on their waie earlie in the morning towards Shornelan, where sir Thomas Cheinie laie: as they were almost come to the broome close, his man alwaies fearing that blacke Will would kill him with his maister, feined that he had lost his pursse; Why said his maister, thou foolish knaue, couldst thou not looke to thy pursse but loose it? What was in it? Three pounds said he. Why then go thy waies backe againe like a knaue (said his maister) and seeke it, for being so earlie as it is, there is no man stirring, and therefore thou maist be sure to find it, and then come and ouertake me at the ferrie. But neuerthelesse, by reason that blacke Will lost his way, maister Arden escaped yet once againe. At that time, blacke Will yet thought hee should haue beene sure to haue met him homewards: but whether that some of the lord wardens men accompanied him backe to Feuersham, or that being in doubt, for that it was late to go through the broome close, and therfore tooke another waie, blacke Will was disappointed then also.

Note here the force of feare and a troubled conscience.

Blacke Will yet againe disappointed.

But now saint Valentines faire being at hand, the con-spirators thought to dispatch their diuelish intention at that time. Mosbie minded to picke some quarrell to maister Arden at the faire to fight with him; for he said he could not find in his heart to murther a gentleman in that sort as his wife wished:[1] although she had made a solemne promise to him, and he againe to hir, to be in all points as

A prepensed quarel against Arden by the conspirators.

[1] Harley MSS.: '... where as mystris arden egged hym to Kyll hir husbond by some meanse ... but mosbye perceyvynge that he could not by any meanes cawse Arden to fight wᵗ hym (for he had piked a qwarell wᵗ hym rydynge to or from london & callynge hym Knave, vyllane & cokeolde, but arden would not fight, this muche mosby confessed in prison) ...'.

man and wife togither, and therevpon they both receiued
the sacrament on a sundaie at London, openlie in a church
there. But this deuise to fight with him would not serue,
for maister Arden both then and at other times had beene
greatlie prouoked by Mosbie to fight with him, but he
would not. Now Mosbie had a sister that dwelt in a tenement of maister Ardens neere to his house in Feuersham:
and on the faire eeuen, blacke Will was sent for to come
thither, and Greene bringing him thither, met there with
mistresse Arden, accompanied with Michaell hir man, and
one of hir maids. There were also Mosbie and George
Shakebag, and there they deuised to haue killed him in
maner as afterwards he was. But yet Mosbie at the first
would not agree to that cowardlie murthering of him, but
in a furie floong awaie, and went vp the abbeie street toward the flower de lice, the house of the aforenamed Adam
Foule, where he did often host. But before he came thither
now at this time, a messenger ouertooke him, that was sent
from mistres Arden, desiring him of all loues to come
backe againe to helpe to accomplish the mater he knew of.
Herevpon he returned to hir againe, and at his comming
backe, she fell downe vpon hir knees to him, and besought
him to go through with the matter, as if he loued hir he
would be content to doo, sith as shee had diuerse times
told him, he needed not to doubt, for there was not anie
that would care for his death, nor make anie great inquirie
for them that should dispatch him.

Thus she being earnest with him, at length hee was contented to agree vnto that horrible deuise, and therevpon
they conueied blacke Will into maister Ardens house,
putting him into a closet at the end of his parlour. Before
this, they had sent out of the house all the seruants, those
excepted which were priuie to the deuised murther. Then
went Mosbie to the doore, and there stood in a night
gowne of silke girded about him, and this was betwixt six
and seuen of the clocke at night. Master Arden hauing
beene at a neighbors house of his, named Dumpkin, &
hauing cleared certeine reckonings betwixt them, came
home: and finding Mosbie standing at the doore, asked
him if it were supper time ? I thinke not (quoth Mosbie) it
is not yet readie. Then let vs go and plaie a game at the
tables in the meane season, said maister Arden. And so
they went streight into the parlor: and as they came by
through the hall, his wife was walking there, and maister

*Ardens wife,
blacke Will,
& the knot of
vilans meet
and conclude
vpon their
former
prepensed
mischiefe.*

*O importun-
ate & bloudie
minded
strumpet !*

*The practise
to kill Arden
is now set
abroch.*

Arden said; How now mistresse Ales? But she made small answer to him. In the meane time one cheined the wicket doore of the entrie. When they came into the parlor, Mosbie sat downe on the bench, hauing his face toward the place where blacke Will stood. Then Michaell maister Ardens man stood at his masters backe, holding a candle in his hand, to shadow blacke Will, that Arden might by no meanes perceiue him comming foorth. In their plaie Mosbie said thus (which seemed to be the watchword for blacke Wils comming foorth) Now maie I take you sir if I will. Take me (quoth maister Arden) which waie? With that blacke Will stept foorth, and cast a towell about his necke, so to stop his breath and strangle him. Then Mosbie hauing at his girdle a pressing iron of fourteene pounds weight, stroke him on the hed with the same, so that he fell downe, and gaue a great grone, insomuch that they thought he had beene killed.

Here the confederats ioine their practises

The watch-word to the principall murtherer.

Then they bare him awaie, to laie him in the counting house,[1] & as they were about to laie him downe, the pangs of death comming on him, he gaue a great grone, and stretched himselfe, and then blacke Will gaue him a great gash in the face, and so killed him out of hand, laid him along, tooke the monie out of his pursse, and the rings from his fingers, and then comming out of the counting house, said; Now the feat is doone, giue me my monie. So mistres Arden gaue him ten pounds: and he comming to Greene, had a horsse of him, and so rode his waies. After that blacke Will was gone, mistresse Arden came into the counting house, and with a knife gaue him seuen or eight p[r]icks into the brest.[2] Then they made cleene the parlor, tooke a clout, and wiped where it was bloudie, and strewed againe the rushes that were shuffled with strugling, and cast the clout with which they wiped the bloud, and the knife that was bloudie, wherewith she had wounded hir husband, into a tub by the wels side; where afterwards both the same clout and knife were found. Thus this wicked woman, with hir complices, most shamefullie murdered hir owne husband, who most entirelie loued hir all his life time. Then she sent for two Londoners to supper, the one named Prune, and the other Cole, that were gro-sers, which before the murder was committed, were bid-

Arden slaine outright.

Blacke Will receiueth ten pounds for his reward of Ardens wife, for murdering hir husband.

---

[1] Harley MSS.: '. . . and w^t ye beringe of hym downe . . .'. The counting-house was actually in the cellar of Arden's house.

[2] Harley MSS.: '. . . becawse she would make hym sure . . .'.

den to supper. When they came, she said: I maruell where
maister Arden is; we will not tarie for him, come ye and sit
downe, for he will not be long. Then Mosbies sister was
sent for, she came and sat downe, and so they were merie.

Marke what a
countenance
of innocencie
and ignorance
she bore after
the murdering
of hir
husband.

After supper, mistres Arden caused hir daughter to
plaie on the virginals, and they dansed, and she with them,
and so seemed to protract time as it were, till maister
Arden should come, and she said, I maruell where he is so
long; well, he will come anon I am sure, I praie you in the
meane while let vs plaie a game at the tables. But the
Londoners said, they must go to their hosts [*hostes*—1577]
house, or else they should be shut out at doores, and so
taking their leaue, departed. When they were gone, the
seruants that were not priuie to the murder, were sent
abroad into the towne; some to seeke their maister, and
some of other errands, all sauing Michaell and a maid,
Mosbies sister, and one of mistres Ardens owne daughters.
Then they tooke the dead bodie, and caried it out, to
laie it in a field next to the church-yard, and ioining to his
garden wall, through the which he went to the church. In

The workers
of this mis-
chiefe carie
out Arden
slaine into
the field.

the meane time it began to snow, and when they came to
the garden gate,[1] they remembred that they had forgotten
the kaie, and one went in for it, and finding it, at length
brought it, opened the gate, and caried the corps into the
same field, as it were ten pases from the garden gate, and
laid him downe on his backe streight in his night gowne,
with his slippers on: and betweene one of his slippers and
his foot, a long rush or two remained. When they had thus
laid him downe, they returned the same way they came
through the garden into the house.[2]

This she did
to colour hir
wickednesse
which by no
meanes was
excuseable.

They being returned thus backe againe into the house,
the doores were opened, and the seruants returned home
that had beene sent abroad: and being now verie late, she
sent foorth hir folks againe to make inquirie for him in
diuerse places; namelie, among the best in the towne
where he was woont to be, who made answer, that they
could tell nothing of him. Then she began to make an out-

[1] Harley MSS.: '... but they could not find ye keye in halfe an howre ...'.

[2] Harley MSS. are confused at this point but add a little later: 'In ye meane
tyme there fell a great snowe in so muche yt they comynge in a gayne into ye
howse thowght that ye snow woulde have coveryd theyr fotynge (but sodeynly
(by ye good provydence of god, who would not suffar so detestable a murther
longe hydden) it stint snowynge / they not consyderynge ye same, but
thinkynge all had bene sure.'

crie, and said; Neuer woman had such neighbors as I haue, and herewith wept: in somuch that hir neighbors came in, and found hir making great lamentation, pretending to maruell what was become of hir husband. Wherevpon, the maior and others came to make search for him. The faire was woont to be kept partlie in the towne, and partlie in the abbeie; but Arden for his owne priuat lucre & couetous gaine had this present yeare procured it to be wholie kept within the abbeie ground which he had purchased; & so reaping all the gaines to himselfe, and bereauing the towne of that portion which was woont to come to the inhabitants, got manie a bitter cursse. The maior going about the faire in this search, at length came to the ground where Arden laie: and as it happened, Prune the groser getting sight of him, first said; Staie, for me thinke I see one lie here. And so they looking and beholding the bodie, found that it was maister Arden, lieng there throughlie dead, and viewing diligentlie the maner of his bodie & hurts, found the rushes sticking in his slippers, and marking further, espied certeine footsteps, by reason of the snow, betwixt the place where he laie, and the garden doore.

Arden a couetous man and a preferrer of his priuat profit before common gaine.

Ardens dead bodie is descried by one of his acquaintance.

Then the maior commanded euerie man to staie, and herewith appointed some to go about, & to come in at the inner side of the house through the garden as the waie laie, to the place where maister Ardens dead bodie did lie; who all the waie as they came, perceiued footings still before them in the snow: and so it appeared plainlie that he was brought along that waie from the house through the garden, and so into the field where he laie. Then the maior and his companie that were with him went into the house, and knowing hir euill demeanor in times past, examined hir of the matter: but she defied them and said, I would you should know I am no such woman. Then they examined hir seruants, and in the examination, by reason of a peece of his heare and bloud found neere to the house in the waie, by the which they caried him foorth, and likewise by the knife with which she had thrust him into the brest, and the clout wherewith they wiped the bloud awaie which they found in the tub, into the which the same were throwen; they all confessed the matter, and hir selfe beholding hir husbands bloud, said; Oh the bloud of God helpe, for this bloud haue I shed.

Footsteps all alongst from the dead bodie of Arden to his dwelling house.

A peece of Ardens heare and his bloud spilt in the house espied, as also a bloudie knife and a clout found.

Then were they all attached, and committed to prison, and the maior with others went presentlie to the flower de

Some of
Ardens bloud
upon Mosbies
pursse.

lice, where they found Mosbie in bed: and as they came towards him, they espied his hose and pursse stained with some of maister Ardens bloud. And when he asked what they meant by their comming in such sort, they said; See, here ye may vnderstand wherefore, by these tokens, shewing him the bloud on his hose and pursse. Then he confessed the deed, and so he and all the other that had conspired the murder, were apprehended and laid in prison,

The princi-
pals of this
murder fled
awaie.

except Greene, blacke Will, and the painter, which painter and George Shakebag, that was also fled before, were neuer heard of. Shortlie were the sessions kept at Feuersham, where all the prisoners were arreigned and condemned. And therevpon being examined whither they had anie other complices, mistres Arden accused Brad-

Bradshaw as
vniustlie
accused, as
his simplicitie
was shame-
fullie abused.

shaw, vpon occasion of the letter sent by Greene from Grauesend, (as before ye haue heard) which words had none other meaning, but onelie by Bradshaws describing of blacke Wils qualities; Greene iudged him a meete instrument for the execution of their pretended murder. Whereto notwithstanding (as Greene confessed at his death certeine years after) this Bradshaw was neuer made priuie; howbeit, he was vppon this accusation of mistres Arden, immediatlie sent for to the sessions, and indicted, and declaration made against him, as a procurer of blacke Will to kill maister Arden, which proceeded wholie by misvnderstanding of the words conteined in the letter which he brought from Greene.

Then he desired to talke with the persons condemned, and his request was granted. He therefore demanded of them if they knew him, or euer had anie conuersation with him, & they all said no. Then the letter being shewed and

Innocencie
no barre
against
execution.

read, he declared the verie truth of the matter, and vpon what occasion he told Greene of blacke Will: neuerthelesse, he was condemned, and suffered. These condemned persons were diuerslie executed in sundrie places, for

Note how
these malefac-
tors suffered
punishment.

Michaell maister Ardens man was hanged in chaines at Feuersham, and one of the maids was burnt there, pitifullie bewailing hir case, and cried out on hir mistres that had brought hir to this end, for the which she would neuer forgiue hir. Mosbie & his sister were hanged in Smithfield at London; mistres Arden was burned at Canturburie the foure and twentith of March [*the . 14. of March*— 1577].[1] Greene came againe certeine yeares after, was

[1] Harley MSS. and the 1577 Holinshed are in agreement over the dating.

apprehended, condemned, & hanged in chaines in the high waie betwixt Ospring & Boughton against Feuersham; blacke Will was burnt on a scaffold at Flishing in Zeland. Adam Foule that dwelt at the floure de lice in Feuersham was brought into trouble about this matter, and caried vp to London, with his legs bound vnder the horsse bellie, and committed to prison in the Marshalseie: for that Mosbie was heard to saie; Had it not beene for Adam Foule, I had not come to this trouble; meaning that the bringing of the siluer dice for a token to him from mistresse Arden, as ye haue heard, occasioned him to renew familiaritie with hir againe. But when the matter was throughlie ripped vp, & that Mosbie had cleered him, protesting that he was neuer of knowledge in anie behalfe to the murder, the mans innocencie preserued him.

Blacke Will burnt at Flishing.

This one thing seemeth verie strange and notable, touching maister Arden, that in the place where he was laid, being dead, all the proportion of his bodie might be seene two yeares after and more, so plaine as could be, for the grasse did not grow where his bodie had touched: but betweene his legs, betweene his armes, and about the hollownesse of his necke, and round about his bodie, and where his legs, armes, head, or anie other part of his bodie had touched, no grasse growed at all of all that time. So that manie strangers came in that meane time, beside the townesmen, to see the print of his bodie there on the ground in that field. Which field he had (as some haue reported) most cruellie taken from a woman, that had beene a widow to one Cooke, and after maried to one Richard Read a mariner, to the great hinderance of hir and hir husband the said Read: for they had long inioied it by a lease, which they had of it for manie yeares, not then expired: neuerthelesse, he got it from them. For the which, the said Reads wife not onelie exclaimed against him, in sheading manie a salt teere, but also curssed him most bitterlie euen to his face, wishing manie a vengeance[1] to light vpon him, and that all the world might woonder on him. Which was thought then to come to passe, when he was thus murdered, and laie in that field from midnight till the morning: and so all that daie, being the faire daie till night, all the which daie there were manie hundreds of people came woondering about him. And thus far touching this horrible and heinous murder of maister Arden.

A wonder touching the print of Ardens dead bodie two yeares after he was slaine.

God heareth the teares of the oppressed and taketh vengeance: note an example in Arden.

[1] Harley MSS.: 'vengeaunce & plage'.

The Account of Thomas Ardern's Murder
from
The Wardmote Book of Faversham, ff. 59-60[1]

This yere[2] the xv[th] day of Februarij beying Sondaye / one Thomas Ardern of Fau[r]sham foresaid gent / was heynously murdered in his owne plo[r] about / Sevȳ / of the clock in the night / By one Thomas Morsby a tayllo[r] of london / late s[r]uant to s[r] Edward North knight channcello[r] of thawgmentacons / father in Lawe vnto Alyce Ardern wif of thesaid Thomas Ardern / and by one Blackwyll of Calyce a murderer / whyche murderer / was prevely sent for to Calyce / by the Ernest sute / appoyntment / and confederacye / of the aforesaid Alyce Ardern / and Thomas Morsby / one John Grene / Tayllo[r] / and George Bradshawe A goldsmyth / inhitaūnts of Fau[r]sham foresaid / to thintent to murder thesaid Ardern / her housbond / whiche Alyce

The Mannor of Arderns Murder

thesaid Morsby did not onely Carnally kepe / in her owne house here in this towne / Butt also fedd her [*sic*; i.e., him] w[t] dilicate meates / and sumptuous appell / All whiche things / thesaid Thomas Ardern did well knowe and wilfully did pmytt and suffred the same / By reason whereof she pcured her said housbonds death to thintent to haue maryed w[t] thesaid Morsbye / And so first she made of her counsell thesaid Thomas morsby / and one Cislye ponder his Sister / Mighell Saunderson tayllo[r] / & Elsabeth Stafford which Mighell and Elsabeth / were the daylly s[r]uants to thesaid Thomas Ardern / And thabbetto[r]s and councello[r]s / to thesaid murder / were the foresaid John Grene / George Bradshawe / and willm̄ Blackbo[r]ne paynter / whiche Bradshawe fett the foresaid murderer at Calyce foresaid and thesame murderer came ou[r] to Fau[r]sham and brought

[1] In this passage the contemporary custom of indicating contraction by the use of accented letters (*e.g.* plo[r] for parlour) has been retained, but long 's' has been modernized, as have the sums—originally in Roman numerals and in scores of pounds—in the final paragraph.

[2] 1551, new style.

wᵗ hym a coadiutoʳ / named losebagg / who also was made of Counsell
to the foresaid murder / so that he was most shamefully murdred as is
foresaid / as he was playing at Tables frendely wᵗ thesaid morsbye for
sodeynly cam out (of a darke house adioyning to thesaid ploʳ) / the
foresaid Blackwyll whome she and her compleces had bestowed
pʳvely before / and came wᵗ a napkyn in his hand / and sodeynly came[1]
behinde thesaid Arderns back threwe[2] thesaid napkyn ouʳ hes hedd &
face and strangled him / and forthwᵗ / thesaid morsbye stept to him /
and strake him wᵗ a taylloʳs[3] great pressing Iron vppon the hedd to
the Brayne / and iḿediately drewe out his daggʳ which was great
and broad and therwᵗ cutt thesaid Arderns thrott Beyng at the death
of him / thesaid Alyce his wyfe / Mighell Saunderson / and Elsabeth
Stafforde / And after that he was thus murdred he was Caryed out of
thesaid ploʳ / into yᵉ foresaid dark house / and when thesaid Black will
had holpen to laye him there / he Returned forthwᵗ to thesaid Cyslye
pounders house / and there receyved for his thus doying / the Suḿe
of Eight poundes in money whiche was there afore poynted for his
reward And immediatly he depted from Fauʳsham so that he could
not iustly be herd of syns that tyme[4] / And he beying thus depted wᵗ
his reward / thesaid Cisley ponder went to thesaid Arderns / and did
help to beare the deade corps out into a medowe there comonly called
the Amery croft on the backside of thesaid Arderns Garden / and[5] a
Boute Enlevyn of the Clocke thesaid Sonday night / thesaid Arderne
was founde where they hadd laid him / in thesaid medowe / where-
vppon thesaid Arderns house was serched and thervppon his Bludd
was founde / that it was manyfest and well approved that he was
slayne in his owne house / Whervppon thesaid Alyce Ardern Mighell
Saunderson / and Elsabeth Stafford were apprehended & attached of
Felonye / and also thesaid morsbye / and his said Sister thesame
night / And wᵗin ij days next after / were apprehended and attached
the foresaide Bradshawe but[6] the foresaid Iohn Grene / willḿ Blackborne / and George losebagg / eskaped at that tyme And the foresaide Alyce Arderne / Thomas morsbye / Cisley ponder / Mighell
Saunderson George Bradshawe and Elsabeth Stafford were indicted
and[7] arreygned wᵗin thesaid towne and libtyes of Fauʳsham / in the

---

[1] Inserted for *pulled*, which was deleted.

[2] *and* deleted before *threwe*.   [3] Inserted.

[4] Cf. extract from the Privy Council book (MS. Harl. 352, as transcribed
in the notes to *The Diary of Henry Machyn*, pp. 315–16): '1551, 15ᵗʰ June.
A Letter to Sᵗ William Godolphine knighte, of thankes for his dilligence in
the apprehencione of Blacke Will, that killed Mr. Arderne of Feversham,
and to send him in saufe garde, with promise of paymente for the charges of
the bringeres'.

[5] Inserted.   [6] Inserted for *and*, which was deleted.   [7] Inserted.

Abbey Halle wch ye said Ardern pchased[1] and there adiudged for to dye / That is to wytt thesaid Alyce Arderne/ to be Burned at Cantor-burye and thesaid Bradshawe / to be hanged in Chaynes there by the commaundement of the[2] kings ma^yties most honorable counsell, And the foresaide Thomas morsby / and his said Sister / iudged to be hanged in Smythfeld in london / And the foresaide mighell Saunder-son to be drawen and hanged in Chaynes w^tin the liɓties of Fau^rsham foresaid and the foresaid Elsabeth Stafforde to be Burned w^tin the said towne / and liɓties / all whiche was accomplished pformed and fulfylled accordingly[3] / And about the last end of the moneth of Julij thennext folowyng / the forsaid John Greene was apprehended and taken in Corwall [sic] / and brought agayne by men of that Countrye to Fau^rsham where shortly after he was adiudged to be hanged in Chaynes w^tin the liɓties there[4] / And all the appell that belonged to thesaid Alyce Arderne / all the moveable goodes of the foresaide Thomas morsbyes / Cisley pounders / George Bradshawes / and John Grenes / were taken seised and forfeyted to thuse of thesaid Towne All whiche goodes Beyng sold / amounted to the summ of Nyneskore /

[1] 'From "in the" to "pchased" inserted by a later hand' (Jackson).

[2] *commaundement of the* inserted.

[3] Cf. Privy Council book: '1551, 5th Marche. A Lettere to the Justyces of Peace in Kente, advertisinge them the order taken for the punishmente of those that murdered Mr. Ardeyrn; Videliset, Sicely Pounder, widowe, and Thomas Mosbye, to be hanged in Smithfield, in London; Alice Ardeyrn, to be burned at Canterburye, and Bradshawe, to be hanged there in cheanes; Michaell Saunderson, to be hanged, drawne, and quartered, at Feversham, and Elizabeth Stafford to be burned there' (fol. 156^b). Also the same day: 'A Letter to the Sherifes of London, to receave of the Sherife of Kent, Cicelye Poundere, widowe, and Thomas Mosbye, to be hanged in Smithfield, for the Murder of Thomas Ardeine of Fevershame; and a Letter to the Maiore of Canterburye, and Bradshawe, to be hanged there, for the Murder of Mr. Ardeine' (fol. 157).

[4] Cf. Privy Council book: '1551, 28th May. A Lettere to Mr. North, to enlarge one Bate out of the countere, who convayed away one Greene, of Fevershame, after the Murdere of Mr. Ardeine was ther don, and under-taketh to brynge forthe Greene again, yf he may have libertie; providinge that he take sufficient sureties, either to become prisonere againe, or else to bringe forthe the said Greene' (fol. 174). '1551, 20th June. A Lettere to the Lord Chancellor, to directe out a Comission for gaoll delivery unto the Maiore of Feversham and otheres, for the attaynder of Greene, alredie indicted for the Murder of Mr. Ardeine' (fol. 180). 'A Warrante to the receiver of the Wardes, to pay unto them that apprehended Greene of Feversham, xx markes, for their costes in bringing him hether, and convey-ing him to Feversham, to be hanged. ¶A Lettere to the Maiore of Fever-sham, and certain otheres, upon the attainder of Greene, to see him hanged in chaynes' (fol. 180^b).

& foure poundes / ten shillings / foure pense halpeny / ou^r and above
certeyne Iewells of thesaid murderers whiche are conteyned in a
certeyne Boks delyu^{r}ed in to the treasurye house of Fau^{r}sham foresaid as bye the pticlers therof more pleynly appereth / Of whiche
foresaide / £184 10s 4½d [. . .] The Accomptaunts or sellers of the
aforesaid goodes, aske to be allowed vppon two / Bylls of Rekonyng /
bestowed vppon thesaid fellons and their atteynder——£63 15s 7d
And so they haue delyu^{r}ed in Redy money in to the foresaid
Treasurye pcell of the foresaid money after the old rate——£120
wherof ther was lost by the abasing or fall of theseid money
threskore poundes——£60[1]

[1] An added marginal note, earlier in the manuscript, reads: 'Theseid
Black Willm Was afterward app^{r}hendyd in Selland at Flushynge there &
had comytted diu^{r}s murtheris there & so was skorched or half burned to
deth' (transcribed by D. Davidson).

APPENDIX IV

Ballad

[The] complaint and lamentation of Mistresse *Arden* of [*Feu*]*ersham* in *Kent*, who for the loue of one *Mosbie*, hired certaine Ruffians [a]nd Villaines most cruelly to murder her Husband; with the fatall end of her and her Associats.[1]

To the tune of, *Fortune my Foe.*

[woodcut]

Ay me, vile wretch, that euer I was borne,
Making my selfe vnto the world a scorne:
And to my friends and kindred all a shame,
Blotting their blood by my vnhappy name.　　　　4

Vnto a Gentleman of wealth and fame,
(One Master *Arden*, he was call'd by name)
I wedded was with ioy and great content,
Liuing at *Feuersham* in famous *Kent.*　　　　8

[1] Transcribed from the unique copy in the Roxburghe Collection (vol. III, p. 156) in the British Museum. The ballad was part of a collection entered in the Stationers' Register on 8 July 1633; it was printed separately that year as a broadside, in black letter, for Cuthbert Wright. The same woodcut used as the frontispiece to the 1633 third quarto of *Arden of Faversham* also heads the ballad. T. S. R. Boase has observed (in 'Illustrations of Shakespeare's Plays in the Seventeenth and Eighteenth Centuries', *Journal of the Warburg and Courtauld Institutes*, vol. x [1947], p. 85) that the cut is typical of broadside illustrations, 'and that is likely enough its origin'.

Reprints of the ballad are to be found also in: *Old Ballads*, ed. R. H. Evans (1777, 1784, 1810); *Monthly Journal of the Faversham Institute*, CXLVII (1874); *Kentish Garland*, ed. J. H. L. DeVaynes (1882); *The Roxburghe Ballads*, ed. J. W. Ebsworth, vol. VIII (1897, for the Ballad Society), pp. 46–53; and *Six Old Ballads*, ed. A. F. Hopkinson (1906; also appended to his 1907 edition of the play).

In loue we liu'd, and great tranquility,
Vntill I came in *Mosbies* company,
Whose sugred tongue, good shape, and louely looke,
Soone won my heart, and *Ardens* loue forsooke.   12

And liuing thus in foule adultery,
Bred in my husband cause of iealousie,
And lest the world our actions should bewray,
Wee did consent to take his life away.   16

To *London* faire my Husband was to ride,
But ere he went I poyson did prouide,
Got of a Painter which I promised
That *Mosbies* sister *Susan* he should wed.   20

Into his Broth I then did put the same,
He lik't it not when to the boord it came,
Saying, There's something in it is not sound,
At which inrag'd, I flung it on the ground.   24

Yet ere he went, his man I did coniure,
Ere they came home, to make his Master sure,
And murder him, and for his faith and paine,
Susan, and store of gold that he should gaine.   28

Yet I misdoubting *Michaels* constancy,
Knowing a Neighbour that was dwelling by,
Which, to my husband bore no great good will,
Sought to incense him his deare blood to spill.   32

His name was *Greene*; O Master *Green* (quoth I)
My husband to you hath done iniury,
For which I sorry am with all my heart,
And how he wrongeth me I will impart.   36

He keepes abroad most wicked company,
With whores and queanes, and bad society;
When he comes home, he beats me sides and head,
That I doe wish that one of vs were dead.   40

And now to *London* he is rid to roare,
I would that I might neuer see him more:
Greene then incenst, did vow to be my friend,
And of his life he soone would make an end.   44

R

O Master *Greene,* said I, the dangers great,
You must be circumspect to doe this feat;
To act the deed your selfe there is no need,
But hire some villaines, they will doe the deed.   48

Ten pounds Ile giue them to attempt this thing,
And twenty more when certaine newes they bring,
That he is dead, besides Ile be your friend,
In honest courtesie till life doth end.   52

Greene vow'd to doe it; then away he went,
And met two Villaines, that did vse in *K*ent
To rob and murder vpon *Shooters hill,*
The one call'd *Shakebag,* t'other nam'd *Black Will.*   56

Two such like Villaines Hell did neuer hatch,
For twenty Angels they made vp the match,
And forty more when they had done the deed,
Which made them sweare, they'd do it with al speed.   60

Then vp to *London* presently they hye,
Where Master *Arden* in *Pauls* Church they spy,
And waiting for his comming forth that night,
By a strange chance of him they then lost sight.   64

For where these Villaines stood & made their stop
A Prentice he was shutting vp his shop,
The window falling, light on *Blacke-Wills* head,
And broke it soundly, that apace it bled.   68

Where straight he made a brabble and a coyle,
And my sweet *Arden* he past by the while;
They missing him, another plot did lay,
And meeting *Michael,* thus to him they say: 72

Thou knowst that we must packe thy Master hence,
Therefore consent and further our pretence,
At night when as your Master goes to bed,
Leaue ope the doores, he shall be murthered.   76

And so he did, yet *Arden* could not sleepe,
Strange dreames and visions in his senses creepe,
He dreamt the doores were ope, & Villaines came,
To murder him, and 'twas the very same.   80

The second part. To the same tune.

He rose and shut the doore, his man he blames,
Which cunningly he strait this answer frames;
I was so sleepy, that I did forget
To locke the doores, I pray you pardon it.   84

Next day these Ruffians met this man againe,
Who the whole story to them did explaine,
My master will in towne no longer stay,
To morrow you may meet him on the way.   88

Next day his businesse being finished,
He did take horse, and homeward then he rid,
And as he rid, it was his hap as then,
To ouertake Lord *Cheiney* and his men.   92

With salutations they each other greet,
I am full glad your Honour for to meet,
Arden did say; then did the Lord reply,
Sir, I am glad of your good company.   96

And being that we homeward are to ride,
I haue a suite that must not be denide,
That at my house youle sup, and lodge also,
To *Feuersham* this night you must not goe.   100

Then *Arden* answered with this courteous speech,
Your Honours pardon now I doe beseech,
I made a vow, if God did giue me life,
To sup and lodge with *Alice* my louing wife.   104

Well, said my Lord, your oath hath got the day,
To morrow come and dine with me, I pray.
Ile wait vpon your Honour then (said he)
And safe he went amongst this company.   108

On *Raymon-Downe*, as they did passe this way,
Black-will, and *Shakebag* they in ambush lay,
But durst not touch him, cause of the great traine
That my Lord had: thus were they crost againe.   112

With horrid oathes these Ruffians gan to sweare,
They stampe and curst, and tore their locks of haire
Saying, some Angell surely him did keepe.
Yet vow'd to murther him ere they did sleepe.   116

Now all this while my husband was away,
Mosby and I did reuell night and day;
And *Susan*, which my waiting maiden was,
My Loues owne sister, knew how all did passe.   120

But when I saw my *Arden* was not dead,
I welcom'd him, but with a heauy head:
To bed he went, and slept secure from harmes,
For I did wish my *Mosby* in my armes.   124

Yet ere he slept, he told me he must goe
To dinner to my Lords, hee'd haue it so;
And that same night *Blacke-will* did send me word,
What lucke bad fortune did to them offord.   128

I sent him word, that he next day would dine
At the Lord *Cheinies*, and would rise betime,
And on the way their purpose might fulfill,
Well, Ile reward you, when that you him kill.   132

Next morne betimes, before the breake of day,
To take him napping then they tooke their way;
But such a mist and fog there did arise,
They could not see although they had foure eyes.   136

Thus *Arden* scap'd these villaines where [they lay,]
And yet they heard his horse goe by that way[;]
I thinke (said *Will*) some Spirit is his friend,
Come life or death, I vow to see his end.   140

Then to my house they strait did take their way,
Telling me how they missed of their pray;
Then presently, we did together gree,
At night at home that he should murdered be.   144

Mosby and *I*, and all, our plot thus lay,
That he at Tables should with *Arden* play,
Black-will, and *S[h]akebag* they themselues should hide
Vntill that *Mosby* he a watchword cride.   148

The word was this whereon we did agree,
Now (Master *Arden*) *I haue taken ye*:
Woe to that word, and woe vnto vs all,
Which bred confusion and our sudden fall.   152

When he came home, most welcome him I made,
And *Iudas* like I kist whom I betraide,
Mosby and he together went to play,
For I on purpose did the tables lay.   156

And as they plaid, the word was straightway spoke,
Blacke-will and *S[h]akebag* out the corner broke,
And with a Towell backwards pul'd him downe,
Which made me think they now my ioyes did crowne.   160

With swords and kniues they stab'd him to the heart[;]
Mosby and I did likewise act our part,
And then his body straight we did conuey
Behind the Abbey in the field he lay.   164

And then by Justice we were straight condemn'd,
Each of vs came vnto a shamelesse end,
For God our secret dealings soone did spy,
And brought to light our shamefull villany.   168

Thus haue you heard of *Ardens* tragedy,
It rests to shew you how the rest did die:
His wife at *Canterbury* she was burnt,
And all her flesh and bones to ashes turn'd.   172

Mosby and his faire Sister, they were brought
To *London* for the trespasse they had wrought,
In Smithfield on a gibbet they did die.
A iust reward for all their villanie,   176

Michael and *Bradshaw*, which a Goldsmith was,
That knew of letters which from them did passe,
At *Feuersham* were hanged both in chaines,
And well rewarded for their faithfull paines.   180

The painter fled none knowes how he did speed,
S[h]akebag in Southwarke he to death did bleed,
For as he thought to scape and run away,
He suddenly was murdered in a fray.   184

In *Kent* at *Osbridge*, *Greene* did suffer death,
Hang'd on a gibbet he did lose his breath:
Blacke-Will at *Flushing* on a stage did burne,
Thus each one came vnto his end by turne.   188

And thus my story I conclude and end,
Praying the Lord that he his grace will send
Vpon vs all, and keepe vs all from ill.
Amen say all, if't be thy blessed will.   192

FINIS.

Printed at London for C.W.

Index to the Annotations

Words, phrases, and proverbial expressions are indexed in the forms given in the text and only by their first occurrence unless they appear in more than one sense. An asterisk indicates that the annotation supplements the *O.E.D.*

resolve (*vb*), flat, i. 455
rhubarb, i. 631
ribald (*sb.*), i. 37; (*adj.*), xiii. 78
rid . . . away, i. 172
rifle (*vb*), iv. 94
right-down, i. 175
rise (*vb*), i. 59
room, iv. 29
roses . . . thorns, viii. 143
round (*adv.*), xiv. 59
rounded, vi. 14
roundly, iii. 158
ruinated, viii. 52
rushes (*sb.*), xiv. 263

Sack (*sb.*), ii. 110
Salutation (Inn), vii. 25
sanctuary, take, xv. 12
sconce, xiv. 64
seal, Chancery, i. 468
seam rent, ii. 56
season fits, the, x. 5
sect, hold no other, viii. 122
securely, iii. 191
securely, as, i. 50
seeing, i. 276
send, to, iii. 20
sensible, viii. 130
sergeant's, xiv. 21
serve the turn, ii. 94
set up (*vb*), xiv. 12
shall, i. 512
share crowns (with you), ii. 31
sharp-witted, i. 251
sheep, put horns . . . , x. 68–9
sheeting, v. 2
Sheppey, Isle of, ii. 73
Shorlow, ix. 144
shows (*vb*), i. 11
shrieve, i. 167 (*see also* i. 166–7)
sickle in (our) corn, thrust (his), x. 83
sieve, xiv. 122
sighs, deep-fetched, iv. 40
sight, (his), xiv. 84
sight, supper with (his), xiv. 176
sighted, viii. 126
sign pulled down, xiv. 26
silly, i. 389; xiv. 152

silver noses, xiv. 7
sirrah, i. 310
sith, iii. 154
Sittingburgh, ii. 61
'size, ii. 40
slip (*vb*), v. 24, ix. 36
slipshoe, xiv. 398
sluttish, xiii. 111
Smithfield, xviii. 29
smoothly, i. 509
smother . . . wax, viii. 27
snatch (*sb.*), ii. 23
so, i. 477
so as, i. 481
softly, ix. 68
softly as, i. 632
Sol, x. 3
solicit, iii. 122
solus, xv. 0.1
Somerset, Duke of, i. 2
song, mermaid's, i. 213
sound (*sb.*), xii. 5; (*vb*), xviii. 17
sounded, ix. 27
Southwark, xiv. 243
Spanish needle, i. 313
speak still, xii. 4
speed (*sb.*), v. 13; (*vb*), iii. 40
spirit, airy, i. 94
spirits, i. 1
spleen, x. 59
spoke, viii. 128
spurned, xv. 8
stage, *Epil.* 6
(*Stage business*, i. 242.1; i. 359.1; iii. 51.1–2; iv. 101; ix. 50.3; ix. 56; xiv. 141.1)
stall (*sb.*), iii. 50
stand close, iii. 39
stand so nicely at, viii. 81
stand to it, (I'll), xiv. 63
standing, iii. 39
starry gale, gentle, viii. 17
starven, iii. 110
state (*sb.*), ix. 93
state, in, i. 465
stated . . . state, viii. 84
statute (against artificers), i. 311
stay, . . . , stay, i. 121, xiv. 326
steward, i. 29

DATE DUE	BORROWER'S NAME

Harnsey · Walthamstowe · Wansted · Raynford
Higate · X · Newigton · Layton · Hornchurch · Wareley · Buluane · Hor
Ilford pna · Ilford magna · Cranehm · Vpminster · S. Okingham
bone LONDŌ · Paewick · Hackney · Stretford · Langthorn · Dagenhm · Ranehm · Orset · M. uc
Shordich · W. hm · E. Cam · Wenyngton · Stifford · W. Tilburye
Berkinge · Aueley · Thurroks · Chaduell · E. Tilburye

Lambeth · Redreth · Charleton · Plumsted · Erith · Groue · hith · N. fleto · Stanstonch · Milton
Newinton · Sinework · Deptford · Wolwich · breache · Crayford · Stone · Southflett · Graueslend · Dent
Camewel · Grenwich · Sheereshull · Wickhm · Cray Mill · Bexley · Dertford · Darenhche · Chalke
Peckham · Keebrok · Wellingstreet · Windingeon · Ste. Mergrets · Iselde
Streethm · Leysham · Lye · Elthm · N. Cray · Sutton · Horton · Cobhm · Nutsted · Colkesto
Towingbed · Michm · K · Chiselherst · Fotescrey · Peukscrey · Mayeye · Orpingeon · Longesfele · Hartley · Hawlne
Beckenhm · Brumley · Ferneborough · Chellsfelde · E · Farmingthm · Ashe
Croydon · Addescombe · Hayse · Bovent · Stoerchm · Wodlande · Kingesdowne
Addingeon · Wickhm · Cowdhm · Halsted · Stansted · Trosley · Addingm
Sandersted · Ferley · Neckhold · Otford · Kemsing · Wrothm · Ofthm · Ferstam
Chyrsted · Warlingthm · Chellsm · Cheuening · Sole · Ightm · Mereworth
Chaldon · Cullesden · Waldinghm · Tateshelde · Seuenak · G · Mote · W. Pekhm · Neelestoch
Caterhm · Tyshe · Sundridge · Knole · Sheborn · E. Pekhm · Hadlon
Moshm · Oxted · Derent flu · Riuersted · W. Peerehm · Lighe · Tumbrydge · Hu
Bleechinghygh · Lymsfelde · Wolstree · Bereplace · Midney · Tudeley
Nutfeld · Gediton · Tanridge · Denshers · Bidberow · St. Fruh · Wood · Capell · Brenchy
Y · Crawherst · Hever · Chidingsted · Spelherst · Peuenburye · ah Pembaye · Hor
Herly · Burstow · Edinbridge · Cowden · Ashherst · Groue · Lamberh
fleerne · Staerborow castle · Lingsfelde · Sherfield · Gate
E. Grinsted · Worde · Harefeld · Wickhm · Eruge · Frant
Worde forest · Buckherst · Birchile · Waterdowne forest
Balebr · Hothholt · Ashdowne forest · Wadeherst
Leonerds · Slaughm · Ardinghgh · Rocherfild